POETRY

INTERNATIONAL

17

2011

THE SAN DIEGO STATE UNIVERSITY PRESS

Poetry International

is published annually at

San Diego State University
The Department of English
and Comparative Literature
5500 Campanile Drive
San Diego, CA 92182-6020

THE PUBLICATION OF THIS JOURNAL IS MADE POSSIBLE BY A GENEROUS GRANT FROM THE

Edwin Watkins Foundation

phone: 619.594.1522
fax: 619.594.4998
e-mail: poetry.international@yahoo.com
web site: http://poetryinternational.sdsu.edu

Single issues of Poetry International are
$15 for individuals and $20 for institutions.
Individual subscriptions: 2 years, $30; 3 years, $45
Institutional subscriptions: 2 years, $40; 3 years, $60

Cover photograph: Patricia Cué
Design: Patricia Cué with Lindsey Messner

ISSN: 1093-054-X
ISBN: 1-879691-97-3

SAN DIEGO STATE UNIVERSITY PRESS
PRINTED IN CANADA

Follow, poet, follow right
To the bottom of the night,
With your unconstraining voice
Still persuade us to rejoice.

With the farming of a verse
Make a vineyard of the curse,
Sing of human unsuccess
In a rapture of distress.

In the deserts of the heart
Let the healing fountain start,
In the prison of his days
Teach the free man how to praise.

—W. H. Auden

Poetry International Notable Books, 2010–2011

A Village Life: Poems, **Louise Glück**, Farrar, Straus, and Giroux

Adonis: Selected Poems (The Margellos World Republic of Letters), **Adonis**, tr. Khaled Mattawa, Yale University Press

American Husband, **Kary Wayson**, Ohio State University Press

Book of the Edge, **Ece Temelkuran**, tr. Deniz Perin, BOA Editions

Break the Glass, **Jean Valentine**, Copper Canyon Press

Building the Barricade and Other Poems of Anna Swir, **Anna Swir,** tr. Piotr Florczyk, Calypso Editions

Cold Spring in Winter, **Valérie Rouzeau**, tr. Susan Wicks, Arc Publications

Collected Body, **Valzhyna Mort**, Copper Canyon Press

Come On All You Ghosts, **Matthew Zapruder**, Copper Canyon Press

Core Samples from the World, **Forrest Gander**, New Directions

Corinthian Copper, **Regina Derieva**, tr. J. Kates, Marick Press

Culture of One, **Alice Notley**, Penguin

Days of Unwillings, **Cal Bedient**, Saturnalia Books

Dear Darkness: Poems, **Kevin Young**, Knopf

Demos Oneiron, **Harry Polkinhorn**, Junction Press

Entrepôt, **Mark McMorris**, Coffee House Press

Every Riven Thing, **Christian Wiman**, Farrar, Straus, and Giroux

Far District: Poems, **Ishion Hutchinson**, Peepal Tree Press

From a Terrace in Prague: Anthology of Poems about Prague, ed. **Stephan Delbos**, Litteraria Pragensia

From The Box Marked Some Are Missing: New and Selected Poems, **Charles W. Pratt**, Hobblebush Books

From Threshold to Threshold, **Paul Celan**, tr. David Young, Marick Press

Ghost in a Red Hat, **Rosanna Warren**, W.W. Norton

Gospel Night, **Michael Waters**, BOA Editions

Grain, **John Glenday**, Macmillan UK

Heavenly Questions: Poems, **Gjertrud Schnakenberg**, Farrar, Straus, and Giroux

Honeycomb: Poems, **Carol Frost**, Triquarterly

Horse, Flower, Bird, **Kate Bernheimer**, Coffee House Press

How Long, **Ron Padgett**, Coffee House Press

Human Chain, **Seamus Heaney,** Farrar, Straus, and Giroux

Island Light, **Katherine Towler**, MacAdam/Cage

Lend Me Your Voice, **Kjell Espmark**, tr. Robin Fulton, Marick Press

Contents

Poems

Feature: Caribbean Poetry
Edited with an introduction by Ishion Hutchinson

M.A. Vizsolyi Portfolio

Shaking the Pumpkin Revisited: Some Poems & Ritual Events from the Indian Americas
Edited with Commentaries by Jerome Rothenberg

Symposium on Translation

Feature: Poetry and the Natural World

Edited with an introduction by Sandra Alcosser

Book Reviews

POEMS

NAVAJO

From **The Night Chant**
(after Bitahatini)

In Tsegihi
In the house made of the dawn
In the house made of evening twilight
In the house made of dark cloud
In the house made of rain & mist, of pollen, of grasshoppers
Where the dark mist curtains the doorway
The path to which is on the rainbow
Where the zigzag lightning stands high on top
Where the he-rain stands high on top

O male divinity
With your moccasins of dark cloud, come to us
with your mind enveloped in dark cloud, come to us
With the dark thunder above you, come to us soaring
With the shapen cloud at your feet, come to us soaring
With the far darkness made of the dark cloud over your head, come to us
      soaring
With the far darkness made of the rain & mist over your head, come to us
      soaring
With the zigzag lightning flung out high over your head
With the rainbow hanging high over your head, come to us soaring
With the far darkness made of the rain & the mist on the ends of your wings,
      come to us soaring
With the far darkness of the dark cloud on the ends of your wings, come to
      us soaring
With the zigzag lightning, with the rainbow high on the ends of your wings,
      come to us soaring
With the near darkness made of the dark cloud of the rain & the mist, come
      to us
With the darkness on the earth, come to us

With these I wish the foam floating on the flowing water over the roots of
      the great corn
I have made your sacrifice
I have prepared a smoke for you

My feet restore for me
My limbs restore, my body restore, my mind restore, my voice restore for me
Today, take out your spell for me

Today take away your spell for me
Away from me you have taken it
Far off from me it is taken
Far off you have done it

Happily I recover
Happily I become cool

My eyes regain their power, my head cools, my limbs regain their strength, I
        hear again

Happily the spell is taken off for me
Happily I walk, impervious to pain I walk, light within I walk joyous I walk

Abundant dark clouds I desire
An abundance of vegetation I desire
An abundance of pollen, abundant dew, I desire

Happily may fair white corn come with you to the ends of the earth
Happily may fair yellow corn, fair blue corn, fair corn of all kinds, plants of
        all kinds, goods of all kinds, jewels of all kinds, come with you to the
        ends of the earth

With these before you, happily may they come with you
With these behind you, below, above, around you, happily may they come
        with you
Thus you accomplish your tasks

Happily the old men will regard you
Happily the old women will regard you
The young men & the young women will regard you

The children will regard you
The chiefs will regard you

Happily as they scatter in different directions they will regard you
Happily as they approach their homes they will regard you

May their roads home be on the trail of peace
Happily may they all return
In beauty I walk
With beauty before me I walk
With beauty behind me I walk
With beauty above me I walk
With beauty above & about me I walk
It is finished in beauty
It is finished in beauty

Translated from the Diné by Jerome Rothenberg

In the Garden

This is how it went after the war:
those left dropped their whistles, torches,
guns, their implements of trade, their sweethearts,
and began to dig

towards the center of the earth where
they laid the maculate bulbs of each brother
swaddled them in damp shadow in dark
soil and for a while

waited. No one knows who lost patience first.
Who scattered a white confetti of crosses
to mark that place, that would-be harvest
where they feared

only grass would grow. Where the old burnt horse
of victory grazes. Where children play, and a few
sit cock-eared to the grass, saying, "So quiet I can almost
hear it."

ANNA ŚWIRSZCZYŃSKA (SWIR)

PORTFOLIO

Introduction

Anna Świrszczyńska [Swir] (1909-1984), who lived and died in Warsaw, was a severe poet. She famously compared the poet's experience with that of an "aching tooth." Nowhere is her severity more evident than in the cycle *Building the Barricade* (1974), commemorating the sixty-three day Warsaw Uprising of August–September, 1944.

Building the Barricade resonates with the percussive echoes of machine guns and bursting shells, but it is also marked by silence and wordless tremors. These silences are often broken, as in "He Had No Coat" and "A Conversation Through the Door," by a single woman's sobs. But that weeping woman is not our speaker. Swir, who built barricades alongside "the streetsweeper, the stallholder, the pensioner" and the rest of Warsaw's beleaguered citizenry, was an active member of the resistance. She was a nurse. She saw many soldiers die prolonged deaths, heard many mothers "[begin] to cry / as if in labor" through double-locked doors. "A Conversation Through the Door" is only *a* conversation, one of many, but it strikes the reader with the skeletal starkness of an insistent, irrepressible memory. Swir, the nurse, who is entirely absent from many of these poems, who generally merely "look[s] on in silence," is one of this conversation's interlocutors—but she might as well be gone. What good has she done? The soldier will die alone, with or without the wine, and "his mother will not come." No wonder our speaker adopts the dissociative, affectless monotone so unmistakably suggestive of post-traumatic stress. No wonder it took a full thirty years for Swir to set the *Barricade* experience to paper.

The cycle's form, with its jagged and metrically free but consistently rhythmic lines, is particularly well-suited for rendering remembered trauma. The poems' *mise-en-page* mimics "the rubble, the mud, the corpses" littering a war-torn cityscape. But as prosodically free as they seem, the poems are as profoundly formal as the madrigals which inspired Swir in her youth, and to which she returns in the erotic verse of her later years. Here, however, the madrigal's devices gain pathological significance. Anaphora, polyphony, and all manner of repetition—structures meant to evoke harmony and balance—are here deflated, defeated, and turned on their heads; Swir's steady music accompanies "soldiers [...] into captivity." Her counterpoint conversations cease with two turns of a key and a women's cry, her duetting, humpbacked sisters collapse into each other, each dying "of her sister's wound / the death of her humpbacked sister."

Medieval and Baroque designs have turned grotesque. Rhythm and alliteration, too, make an essential contribution.

In translating this selection, I sought to improve on the rhythms, sound patterning, and colloquial constructions of Magnus Jan Kryński and Robert A. Maguire's otherwise stellar renditions in *Building the Barricade* (Kraków: Wydawnictwo Literackie, 1979). Those interested in Swir's remarkable erotic and feminist verse should consult Czesław Miłosz's and Leonard Nathan's translations in *Talking to My Body* (Port Townsend, WA: Copper Canyon Press, 1996). Miłosz was Swir's friend and greatest advocate.

Boris Dralyuk

Building the Barricade

We were afraid, building the barricade
under fire.

The barkeeper, the jeweler's lover, the barber,
all of us cowards.
The servant-girl fell to the ground
hauling a pavement stone, and we were very afraid,
all of us cowards—
the streetsweeper, the stallholder, the pensioner.

The pharmacist fell to the ground,
dragging the toilet door,
and we were even more afraid, the smuggler-woman,
the dressmaker, the streetcar driver,
all of us cowards.

The boy from the reform school fell
dragging a sandbag,
so we were really afraid.

Although no one forced us,
we did build the barricade
under fire.

Translated from the Polish by Boris Dralyuk

He Steals Furs

A shell tears apart the doors
of a fur shop.

A man jumps in,
grabs an armful of furs,
runs, hoisting them, toward the doorway.

At the doorway another shell
tears apart the man.

Translated from the Polish by Boris Dralyuk

A Conversation Through the Door

At five o'clock in the morning
I knock on his door.
I say through the door:
in the hospital on Śliska Street,
your son, the soldier, is dying.

He opens the door,
without removing the chain.
Behind him his wife
trembles.

I say: your son asks for his mother,
that she come.
He says: his mother will not come.
Behind him his wife
trembles.

I say: the doctor will let
him have some wine.
He says: please wait.

He passes a bottle through the door,
locks the door with a key,
locks it with another key.

Behind the door his wife
begins to cry
as if in labor.

Translated from the Polish by Boris Dralyuk

I'm Afraid of Fire

Why am I so afraid
running down this burning street.

There's no one here
except flames roaring skyhigh;
and that bang was not a bomb
only three floors collapsing.

Naked they dance, liberated,
waving their hands
from the window caves.
What a sin to spy
on naked flames,
what a sin to eavesdrop
on breathing fire.

I flee this speech,
which sounded
on earth before the speech of man.

Translated from the Polish by Piotr Florczyk

To Shoot into the Eyes of a Man

in memory of Wiesiek Rosiński

He was fifteen years old,
the best student of Polish.
He ran at the enemy
with a pistol.

He saw the eyes of a man,
and should have shot into those eyes.
He hesitated.
He lies on the pavement.

They hadn't taught him
in Polish class
to shoot into the eyes of a man.

Translated from the Polish by Boris Dralyuk

Two Humpbacks

—I cannot die, ma'am,
what will my sister do without me.
She has a hump, lies beneath the window.

—I cannot die, ma'am,
what will my sister do without me.
She has a hump, lies by the door.

Each died
of her sister's wound
the death of her humpbacked sister.

Translated from the Polish by Boris Dralyuk

A Woman Said to Her Neighbor

A woman said to her neighbor:
"Since my husband's death, I can't sleep,
when they shoot, I put a blanket over my head,
all night I tremble under the blanket.
I'll go crazy if I'm alone tonight,
I have my husband's cigarettes, sir,
do drop in tonight."

Translated from the Polish by Piotr Florczyk

He Made It

for Professor Władysław Tatarkiewicz

An old man
leaves the house, carrying books.
A German soldier grabs the books
and throws them in the mud.

The old man picks them up,
the soldier hits him in the face.
The old man falls,
the soldier kicks him and walks off.

The old man
lies in mud and blood.
Beneath him, he feels
books.

Translated from the Polish by Boris Dralyuk

Said the Major

i.m. Anna Ratyńska

"This order must be delivered within an hour,"
said the major.
"That's not possible, it's an inferno out there,"
said the second lieutenant.
Five messenger girls went out,
one made it.

The order was delivered within one hour.

Translated from the Polish by Piotr Florczyk

It Lives an Hour Longer

in memory of Stanisław Świerczyński

The child was two months old.
The doctor says:
it'll die without milk.

The mother walks all day through cellars
to the other end of town.
The baker on Czerniaków
has a cow.
She crawls on her belly
amid the rubble, the mud, the corpses.

She brings three tablespoons of milk.
The child lives
an hour longer.

Translated from the Polish by Boris Dralyuk

He Had No Coat

The soldiers were walking off into captivity,
the people looked on in silence,
the people stood by in silence
on both sides of the street.

The youngest soldier had no coat,
a woman ran up with a coat,
a gendarme blocked her way,
she was running, weeping.

The people looked on in silence,
the soldiers were walking off into captivity,
the youngest soldier was ten.

Translated from the Polish by Boris Dralyuk

Waiting Thirty Years

He must've been 6'5," that young beanpole,
cheerful laborer from Powiśle,
who fought
in a hell at Zielna Street, in the telephone company headquarters.
When I was re-bandaging
his torn-up leg,
he winced and smiled.

"When the war ends
we'll go dancing, little miss.
I'm buying."

I've been waiting for him
for thirty years.

Translated from the Polish by Piotr Florczyk

First Madrigal

That first night of love
was pure
like an old musical instrument
and the air
that surrounded it.

It was rich
like a coronation ceremony.
It was fleshy
like a stomach of a woman in labor
and spiritual
like a number.

It was only a moment of life,
though it wanted to be a conclusion.
By dying
it wanted to understand the mystery of the world.

That night of love
had ambitions.

Translated from the Polish by Piotr Florczyk

Second Madrigal

A night of love
exquisite
like a concert in Old Venice
played on exquisite instruments.
Healthy
like the buttock of a little angel.
Wise
like an anthill.
Glaring
like air in a trumpet.
Abundant
like the reign of a Negro couple
seated on two thrones
made of gold.

A night of love with you—
a big baroque battle
and two victories.

Translated from the Polish by Piotr Florczyk

ANNA SWIR

I Banged My Head Against the Wall

As a child
I stuck my finger in the fire
to be a saint.

As a teenager
I banged my head against a wall every day.

As a girl
I climbed from the attic window
onto the roof
in order to jump.

As a woman
I had lice.
They cracked
when I was ironing my sweater.

I waited an hour
before a firing squad.
I went hungry
for six years.

Then, when I gave birth to a child,
they cut me open
without anesthesia.

Then I was killed
by lightning three times,
and I had to be resurrected three times
without anybody's help.

Now I am resting
after three resurrections.

Translated from the Polish by Piotr Florczyk

Poetry Reading

I'm lying curled up
like a dog
that's cold.

Who will tell me
why I was born,
why exists this monstrosity
called life.

Suddenly, the phone rings.
I'm to give a poetry reading.

I'm to tell them
why they were born,
why this monstrosity called
life exists.

I show up.
A hundred people, two hundred eyes.
They watch. Wait.
I know what for.

Translated from the Polish by Piotr Florczyk

JESSE NATHAN

I Froth, I Am Froth: On Anna Swir

Anna Swir's poems are often sparse and short, contained moments that remind me of dioramas. With each one, it's as if she leads me to an eyehole through which I see the world compressed into some startling and miniature configuration. As if entrusted with a secret, I am allowed the intensity of intimacy. "After all, one needs / someone who is close," writes the poet in "The Same Inside."[1]

Eroticism arises in anything heightened. Erato—the muse of lyric poetry—is well known as an ambassador in the office of Eros. The first verse I wrote was a crappy love poem to a woman leaving me for Pennsylvania. The metaphor was a line of telephone wire, because it would carry our voices. Anyway, the poem was neither marble nor the gilded monuments, and fine lyrics are written in rage. Whatever the mood, lyric poetry brings into being a charged space between dynamic poles: between two lovers, two friends, two enemies, daughter and father, between person and animal or force or deity, or just as often between the disparate selves within the self.

Between, one to another—this is key. Frank O'Hara riffs on the matter when he describes "Personism," which was founded

> by me after lunch with LeRoi Jones on August 27, 1959, a
> day in which I was in love with someone (not Roi, by the
> way, a blond). I went back to work and wrote a poem for
> this person. While I was writing I realized that if I wanted
> to I could use the telephone instead of writing the poem,
> and so Personism was born.

Anna Swir does not phone, but she leads us to her dioramas, and had been well before O'Hara's articulation. She was born in Warsaw in 1909 and died of cancer in 1984. World War II cast a shadow across her life. She was a fighter and a nurse during the horrific intensity of the fall 1944 Warsaw Uprising. She once described herself as "terribly shy, ugly, and crushed by a mountain of complexes." "She is fierce, lucid, ecstatic, terrifying," her friend and English translator, Czesław Miłosz, counters. "Though recognized as an eminent poet, she

---

[1] All Swir poems herein are from *Talking to My Body*, translated by Czesław Miłosz and Leonard Nathan, and published in 1996 by Copper Canyon. The one exception is "He Made It," translated by Boris Drayluk.

occupies a place somehow apart, perhaps because she often disconcerts critics." Happily disconcerted, I want to try nonetheless to set forth the characteristics of the electrifying lyric place Swir creates with words.

—

Words characterize the lyric, which seems obvious, but it's where I start. "I say to my body / – You carcass," writes Swir. "As soon as / I speak, I / speaks," is how Creeley puts it. Words separate the "I" from the speaker of the "I," externalizing the self. This is unnatural. Our primary sense is sight. We understand the world as a series of images before we understand it as language. In the moment of birth, we fall into images, eyes open. You can glance at an abstract painting and in an instant get something from it, even if just emotional responses to color patterns. Learning to read even rudimentary sentences, on the other hand, is an ordeal. A block of text intimidates. Whereas, say, a television allows us to passively input input, reading is labor.

Marshall McLuhan distinguished between "hot" and "cool" media. "Hot" invites participation, "cool" less so. Movies are hotter than still images. Still images are hotter than words.[2] Within the realm of words, though, lyricism turns words hottest.[3] Here is a sentence: When the window opens a breeze comes off the fog and fills the room with wet cold air and the sound of a stroller and two young parents and also the ornery groan of a mailbox squawking open, thunking closed, and a car horn, beep, beeeeep, beep, and the swish of cars winding around over the hill, swish, swish, swish, tires on pavement and the faint scream of sirens, the smell of dirt, the reeeeeeee of a chainsaw, the salty air and the half lost gulls calling out overhead, raw raw raw raw. It's a primitive demonstration, I know, but I'm trying to say that it's more than telling *about* something. You go with me on the words and, as nearly as the laws of physics allow, are here in the room with me now, as that window opens and the sounds and the smells tumble in.

Swir makes words hot, experiential, when she conjures fire during a WWII bombing in "I Am Afraid of Fire":

Naked liberated flames dance,
they wave their arms
through the holes of windows.

---

[2] Scott McCloud makes a variation on this point in Chapter 2 of his seminal *Under-standing Comics*. Words, he explains, are the ultimate symbol. They mark the end of a spectrum that includes images. McCloud says the difference between a depiction of a face and the word "face" is only in degree.
[3] Robert Frost pronounced in "Poetry and School" (1951) that "poetry and prose too regarded as poetry is the renewal of words."

It's sinful
to spy on
naked flames,
it's sinful to eavesdrop
on the speech of free fire.
I run away from that speech
which resounded on the earth
earlier than the speech of man.

And she goes further in "My Body Effervesces," in which she elides her self with her words, disappearing into the intensity of metaphor, as in this fragment from the poem:

I am born for the second time.
I am light
as the eyelash of the wind.
I froth, I am froth.

The preposition ushering in the simile dissolves into the assertion of metaphor. To read these words is not to think about froth, it is to seek to *be* froth, to feel as froth feels if froth can be said to.[4] The lyric place is characterized by words enacting an experience vividly enough for it to lodge in the mind like a memory of something actually lived—as real as having once been kissed or punched. Ten years after the kiss, do I remember it? Memory is a kind of tracer, like PH paper you dip in the art to read its strength. Or to keep to McLuhan's metaphor, a thermometer registering an experience of heat. A poet who wrote about painting, James Schuyler, nails what I think lyricism does, in a blurb in *ARTnews*, January 1959, on Alex Katz: "the colors feed each other so the red of the lips not only makes its necessary effect but the lips have the sharpness lipstick actually gives." You don't forget those lips.

—

To heat up words, the lyric uses them as sound, and only secondarily as vehicles for information. I can't read Polish, so I can't hear Swir's original music, but I

---

[4] In Miłosz's poem, "Translating Anna Swir on an Island of the Caribbean," he praises her ability to "delight" in sensations "of touch in lovemaking, the delight of running on a beach, / of wandering in the mountains, even of raking hay…"

can hear how the words land in English in the masterful translations by Miłosz and Nathan. Here is the last half of "An Artist Moves," a poem about Swir's father, a painter:

> We load it all on a cart, quickly,
> so the janitor does not see.
> My father
> is pulling the cart, quickly,
> my mother pushes at the rear, quickly,
> I push also, quickly, quickly, quickly,
> so that the janitor does not see.
>
> We owe
> a half-year's rent.

That adverb makes a marionette of my tongue with its repetitions (quickly, quickly, quickly). Repetition itself can be a trait of fear or neurosis—a verbal hand wringing, a pacing back and forth. The word is present several times not to give me its information—I get, from the first use, that things are being done hastily—but rather to offer *quickly, quickly, quickly* as a portion of sound with a particular tonal flavor. It is the mixing of these sounds with others that generates the poem. Sound is the engine of a lyric's meaning, any information growing out of sound, less often the other way around.

I feel stuffed, by the way, with information. Fed it constantly, often by the internet or email or this or that application, but just as often by the books on the apartment walls, by the newspaper at the door, by the fridge plastered with notices and postcards, by the magazines in the john, the scribblings and lists I leave everywhere. "Information comes to seem like an environment," writes Sven Birkerts in an essay on reading in a digital age. Words traffic this information. The computer I'm using now bristles with information. So does my daily planner. So does the newspaper half unfolded on the couch, and the guide to the trees of Kansas on my desk, and the phone book in the kitchen, and the pamphlet of Giants stats someone at work gave me...

The lyric place that a poem carves out, by contrast, employs words primarily for non-informational purposes. Walter Benjamin connects this notion to storytelling, and it is true that great fiction writers (think of Faulkner or Proust) have a powerful lyric element undergirding their language. "It is not the object of the story to convey a happening *per se*, which is the purpose of information; rather," says Benjamin in his essay on Baudelaire, "it embeds it in the life of the storyteller in order to pass it on as experience to those listening." This is why average material—a few scant facts, a setting—comes alive in the hands of a great storyteller, because the experience is not about the information conveyed, it's about the conveying. Benjamin speaks, too, of the lyric as extracted from the hoard of information we suffocate under. "It is the phantom crowd of words, the fragments, the beginnings of lines from which the poet, in the deserted streets, wrests the poetic booty."

I think this is why, incidentally, poetry sometimes gets deemed "difficult." One meets words used everywhere in the world for informational purposes. A lyric poem often asks something else. It would be annoying to be trying, with an abstract poem for instance, to pull information from words—to "get it"—when the purpose of those words might mainly be to generate an intangible emotional effect. This demand on the reader, and the surprise of it, is not always received well. This confusion is one reason people don't read poems when they don't read poems.

Consider Gertrude Stein. "Stick stick call then, stick stick sticking, sticking with a chicken" or "Sweet sweet sweet sweet sweet tea" is Stein calling our attention to the words themselves, as tactile sound-objects. Think of words, for the moment, as archways, things we go through en route to something else. Certainly this is the informational mode—a word as a means to an end. Stein does not go through the archway. She stops to admire the brickwork, the line of ants crawling up the side, the strange flowers growing at the archway's base. She points these things out to us—a word is no longer a means, it is itself the end.

While Stein radically highlighted the sound-object aspect of language, music has always been the ancient core of poetry. Music—remember that the word 'lyric' comes from lyre, and that Orpheus did not speak, he sang—thrives or dies in time. Time, as gauged by metronomes or key signatures. In this sense, the poet's medium is not words, it is time. In the anonymous introduction to a 1945 vinyl recording of Langston Hughes reading his work, someone at Asch Records notes that the poet composes (it's the appropriate verb here) "poetry as some piano players play music—by ear. Without conscious thought of form, he puts his poems down as they come to him. Then he listens to them over and over in his head until they 'sound right.'" Music exists within time, and it is music the lyricist seeks.

Time permeates Swir's poems. She declares it her medium in "Happiness": "I sink / I sink into time." Or it is her opponent, to be resisted, as lamented in the music of "Woman Unborn": "I go back, / I run / into my minus life," which in the English catches the alliteration and rhyme of "my" with the "mi-" of "minus" and the "li-" of "life." Often, time disappoints Swir like a lover, as in "In Railway Stations" ("I lost so much time / with you"). Time is ultimately death's keeper, as in the short poem "I Am Filled with Love":

> I am filled with love
> as a great tree with the wind,
> as a sponge with the ocean,
> as a great life with suffering,
> as time with death.

It is because of the way the machinery of the poem unfolds, because of those sounds (as a, as a, as a) breaking on me, that the shock of the final line registers so directly. These handholds within time lead me into the poem's forceful presence. In ecstasy I suffer the end.

It's a poem I can't get out of my head, and the notion of "memorizable" poetry, not to be confused with what's called "formal" poetry (sonnets, etcetera), is relevant here. A good lyric is memorizable largely because of its music, formal or otherwise. Formal poetry more blatantly—and this is an observation, not a point of judgment—crafts a structure within time for our minds to glom onto. But any music has the capacity to groove the brain. We make up ditties to remember things. Memory, again a kind of tracer. In sixth grade, Mr. Preheim made us each memorize a poem, and I will never forget "Stopping By Woods on a Snowy Evening" even when everything else about sixth grade has faded. I stood in front of the brown chalkboard facing the class, and behind the class my teacher, and behind and above him on the wall the large and indifferent clock face. I stumbled a few times, but it was okay, everyone did. Frost's poem continues to work on me, a structure slowly covering over in moss in my memory like an old stone building. Lines and images from the poem float back to me at random. There is great power in a device—in this case constructed of words—that leaves so impressive a mark.

But the lyric slips away from us like time, because like time, it never tangibly exists. A lyric comes so close to making an object out of thought and sound. This delights and frustrates and drives me from poem to poem. "You, who forever eludes" whispers Rilke to his Erato in an uncollected fragment jotted down in the winter of 1913 as he hammered away on his famous elegies. Swir on this matter is more cynical and more radically idealistic. "Nonexistent, / come to me," writes the poet, after despairing in the previous stanza that there is "no space /

waiting for the shadow / of your moving hand." The elusive, it seems, may be had, but rarely, and barely. One is left only with Swir's unblinking plea: "come to me."

It is unemotional, stripped down language about something deeply, almost desperately, emotional. A friend wrote recently to me of Swir's "piercing straightforwardness and stripped-down voice" that never allows "an unnecessary flourish. She seems," Katie said, "to forbid herself such things, almost as if it's unethical." I think it was in the air in Eastern Europe, especially as the century progressed: Polish poetry was leaning toward a music of fewer and fewer words. For Poland, the twentieth-century was abandonment and destruction. In *The Captive Mind*, Miłosz elaborates, and the emphasis is his: "In the intellectuals who lived through the atrocities of war in Eastern Europe there took place what one might call the *elimination of emotional luxuries*." Surviving shuns all but the necessary. It isn't really surprising that twentieth-century Polish poetry, as Miłosz writes elsewhere, "is the result of a distillation of themes and forms, conducted by successive vanguards. Great conciseness is often achieved, and very short poems contain intricate meanings." Swir is filled with short lines, terse phrases, minimalist scenes, and adjective-less nouns.

Still, the lyric place comprises something approaching substance. To Kierkegaard that almost-substance can be positioned between two other art forms. From *Either/Or*: "Poetry is the art that best knows how to affirm the meaning of time. It does not need to limit itself to the moment in the sense that painting does; neither does it disappear without a trace in the sense that music does." Nonetheless, to get at the mechanics of the lyric it is a painting I look to next.[5]

—

In the months I've been writing this, a buddy experienced in person his favorite painting—"The Polish Rider," a disputed[6] Rembrandt hanging at the Frick. It was done around 1655, oil on canvas, 46 inches by $53^{1/8}$. A young man with a shy, impish naïveté about his face sits—hand on hip, axe in hand, bow and quiver at his belt—on a white horse. He has a fistful of reins in the other hand. His garb is garish, medieval, and his hair is long. The horse is stamping, "veering left on its own accord, out of the sun and into the shade—the man seems entirely unaware

---

[5] The goal in this essay is to illustrate the specific combination of effects and imperatives that define a lyricism of words, as exemplified in Swir. I admit, trying to do this via comparisons to music and painting is mildly paradoxical, but the language of other art forms can sometimes be the most illuminating.

[6] Some scholars think it was mainly completed by one of Rembrandt's students.

of his (grim?) fate, engrossed in this little moment of God-given spotlight," Michael wrote in an email after looking at the painting in New York. The background is mottled and dark, scratchy in places, completely and consciously underemphasized. The man's leggings and the top of his hat are red, otherwise the whites are murky, mixed with blue and yellow and behind horse and rider a deeper red is contaminated by blackish earthy hues. You can see the teeth of the horse, and if you got close enough, you could count them.

Miłosz thought Anna Swir to be a vastly different type of artist than Rembrandt. Swir, he argued, made miniatures, beautiful "little drawings," whereas Rembrandt did epic canvases. Milosz's point is scale. And though he is not wrong, I think a comparison between Swir's work and "The Polish Rider" throws light on the lyric place. Swir's father, as mentioned, was a painter—"I hate father's paintings" and "I love father's paintings" she confesses in "I Am Eleven." In "He Sang All His Life" she conflates singing with painting: "all winter, in the unheated workshop / he sang, his brush / gripped with fingers blue with cold."

My point is that Swir would have been aware, probably from a young age, of the logic, if it can be called that, underlying a piece of great visual art. Logic, though, seems too confining a word for what's at work in "The Polish Rider," with its instinctually composed visual shiftiness. Not that there aren't calculations made and measurements taken—we are not speaking of guesswork, forms are as ordered as millipedes and flowers. The principles at work, though, are the principles of beauty in nature or in art, and these principles simultaneously draw on logic and resist it. Better maybe to say there is "unity within variety," as Robert Henri has written of Rembrandt's work, combined with, to quote Robert Hughes in *The Guardian*, an "ambiguity, so to put it, that hangs over all beauty, all desire." In painting, this unity and ambiguity are a function of the painter's use of an image or a color or a line set against the viewer's conscious expectations of the use of that image or color or line.

In any case, "your animal body / understands more than you do" writes Swir in "A Bitch," and what congeals in a great work of visual art is an order determined by instinct more than anything. In terms of the lyric, this can translate into, for instance, jagged lines or sentence fragments, corresponding perhaps to the choppiness and unpredictability of the mind. Here's a line from Swir's "Seventy Years" that's compressed, spastic, and unspools instinctually: "He collected old cans, newspapers, bolts / his room full, read mystics." Or there's the circumstance described by Jane Hirshfield, in which the order created by a lyric poem asks for a particular rhyme scheme, and that rhyme scheme translates into the discovery of unexpected truths uncovered as the poet "hunts for a rhyme."

By conforming to a chosen constraint, as a painter does in choosing a canvas size or paint type or brushstroke, the poet allows her words to be shaped into something the conscious mind might never have found. The lyric place, then, grows partly out of the unconscious, the emotional, the messily human.

Here, for example, is all of Swir's "A Cardboard Suitcase":

My father was sixteen,
under his bed he kept a cardboard suitcase
with a hole in it.
In the suitcase there were a dirty shirt
and political tracts.

He passed these out where he was told to,
after quitting time.
His crew was then painting the ceiling in a theater.
He would leap
through scaffoldings, floors
down,
headlong.
He was sixteen.

Begin with the shape, the figure increasingly foregrounded (four lines in the second stanza begin with him) until he is standing before you, youthful and impish as the Polish Rider. The implied colors—suitcase brown, flushed-face red—and the colors not given—of the ceiling, the floor—mesh in an ominous confusion like the background of the Rembrandt. That dive down floors in the last stanza, after unfurling lines two and eight, exhilarates and dizzies. Mystery permeates the reportorial voice offering in the end only the boy's age. And what is it to be sixteen? In the youthful recklessness that emanates from the word "headlong," I see the image of the Polish Rider's horse, turning towards something dangerous.

What is most striking, though, is the way Swir's poem and "The Polish Rider"—or any great verse or painting—are inexhaustible. Valéry spells this out further:

We recognize a work of art by the fact that no idea it
inspires in us, no mode of behavior that it suggests we
adopt could exhaust it or dispose of it. We may inhale the

smell of a flower whose fragrance is agreeable to us for as
long as we like; it is impossible for us to rid ourselves of
the fragrance by which our senses have been aroused, and
no recollection, no thought, no mode of behavior can
obliterate its effect or release us from the hold it has on us.

Frost agrees, almost impatiently: "Almost everyone should almost have
experienced the fact that a poem is an idea caught fresh in the act of dawning."
That dawning does not cease—it is frozen. In this way, an ekphrasis by Derek
Walcott called "The Polish Rider" is instructive. In the final couplet of the
sonnet, Walcott freezes things: "The immortal image holds its murderer / In a
clear gaze for the next age to read." Walcott's asking us to read the image like
words in a lyric, and to do so illuminates the way the painting, in Kierkegaard's
words, becomes "continually present," happening in space the way a lyric poem
happens in time.

—

If I say "Death, be not proud," these seventeenth-century words become alive
and present, telling death to step off. My brain retraces *exactly* Donne's thought.
He encoded that thought in these words, and so there arises a terrific intimacy
that obviates centuries and miles when I recite them. "We breathe as the
author breathed," writes Hirshfield, "we move our tongue and teeth and throat
in the ways they moved in the poem's first making." This intimacy is the last
characteristic of the lyric place I want to mention, and it returns me to the realm
of O'Hara and dioramas.

There is something electrifying about the intimacy O'Hara, like Swir,
permits us. O'Hara brims with a wild-eyed familiarity, like a talkative stranger
on a quiet train, pulling everyone close as he speaks, even as they pull away,
pretending not to hear this stentorian eccentricity in their midst. Think of his
poem "Steps," which ends

oh god it's wonderful
to get out of bed
and drink too much coffee
and smoke too many cigarettes
and love you so much.

Love and lust are difficult to separate in Swir, and so the feeling of intimacy achieves an erotic, though never exactly confessional, air. That is, if it were not so well crafted, passages in, say, Swir's "A Woman Talks to Her Thigh" would drill us with straight voyeurism. There is this burning moment about fucking, for instance, in the fourth stanza:

> I look as does a sculptor
> on his work
> at their faces snapped shut with eyelids,
> martyred by ecstasy,
> made dense by happiness.

My mind leaps to a passage in a short story, "Offertory," by Amy Hempel. A couple is watching a porno and the guy says, "The thing about these films is that this really happened. We're seeing something that actually really happened."

But unlike O'Hara's, Swir's lyric intimacy (and the accompanying feeling of honesty it fosters) is infused with a darkness that lingers in all post-WWII Polish poetry. "A historical steamroller has gone several times through a country whose geographical location, between Germany and Russia, is not particularly enviable," writes Miłosz. In his history of Poland (titled *God's Playground*), Norman Davies acknowledges that many consider the country's geography to be the "villain of her history." In *Building the Barricade*, written thirty years after Warsaw, Swir's intimacy is the intimacy of the eyewitness.[7] Listen to the three stanzas of "He Made It":

> An old man
> leaves the house, carrying books.
> A German soldier grabs the books
> and throws them in the mud.
>
> The old man picks them up,
> the soldier hits him in the face,
> The old man falls,

---

[7] The work of another Polish poet, Tadeusz Różewicz, born in 1921, is one of the few analogues to Swir's verse. "I guess she may have been influenced by him," writes Miłosz in remarks published in *Talking to My Body*. "His poetry has been defined by a critic as 'casket-oriented somatism.' And it has been said of him that he was marked by his wartime experiences when he was in the Resistance, and since that time a permanent feature of his poetry is a completely desperate view of human beings as flesh that is condemned to die. So she's not alone in this respect."

the soldier kicks him and walks off.
The old man
lies in mud and blood.
Beneath him, he feels
books.

What is seen is recorded, framed, and that's it. It is hard to fathom the leveling of life wrought on Eastern Europe in the first half of the twentieth century. "Yet the [Polish] poet emerges perhaps more energetic," writes Miłosz spryly, "better prepared to assume tasks assigned him by the human condition, than is his Western colleague."

Swir's witness ultimately fulfills what Auden described as one of poetry's great tasks: to bring comfort to the ailing. In "When a Soldier is Dying," from

Building the Barricade, I see all the elements of the lyric place in Swir's graceful prayer: an experience of words, music, instinctual order and the inexhaustibility of a painting, conveyed with the intimacy of a whisper.

By the stretcher, on the floor
I knelt close to him,
I kissed his tunic,
I was saying: you are beautiful,
you can give so much happiness,
you don't know yourself how much happiness,
you will live, my beautiful,
my brave boy.
He smiled and he listened,
his eyelids heavier and heavier,
he did not know that such words
are said to a soldier
only when he is dying.

Edward Hirsch

God's Insomniacs

Those sleepless blurry-eyed mystics—
Cioran called them "God's Insomniacs"—
mortified themselves
in the arid and obscure night.

They were spirituels, contemplatifs,
voluptuous sufferers
who could scarcely see the stars
through the bitter light of their tears.

One of the saints never slept
more than two hours per night.
She stood up to pray
and nailed her hair to the wall.

One of the saints dipped her forehead
into a candle, another tasted the flame.
She said it would start raining roses
after her death, though it never did.

Their austerities enthralled you,
one of the lonely agnostics
lying awake at night and brooding
about the hole in your chest.

James Arthur

Fatherhood

Someday I'd like to have a daughter
      and give her a stuffy name that she'd hate.
She and I could go galumphing out to a pond
and net minnows she'd briefly keep alive. A serious, small person,
      a lover of ribbons and toboggans.
Of talking, waistcoat-wearing otters.
        She and I would rake up every leaf in November.
          Am I such a sap? Forgive me—

maybe I know more about sons. If I had one, I'd expect him
      to fling any tenderness back on my plate, to say
"you're nudging me into the grave"
      when I'm telling him to live, to not forgive,
forget all but the worst of what I say, and magnify
      his victories to win my love.

At Mount St. Helens

An eye of the earth,
open and shut. Smoke winding out
through the sky. The loggers' road
swept away, and camps,
trees, trains … Midday burning
the tarmac dry.
              Anyone here
to hear? I'm several miles
above the rain. I came by car. I'm
no one. I'm thirty-three.

Daylight Savings

Give me some light
in the maplefire, in the sudden fierce embranglement

      and rapid setting on
of this wind, its sweep that bends the saplings
and deforms the standing leaves.
I rewind the hour hand… evening takes over
the road. A bus making headway
on a splashing lane; its taillights

smear and bend. I drank all I could, couldn't die,
now I'm here alive.
I'll take all the day I can find, and dig,
and break stone till it gives ore.

AMY GERSTLER

PORTFOLIO

Ember Days

Dear Maker, I've failed.
Lost my tongue. Put words
back in my mouth again,
or blackberries maybe,
and concepts back in my
head. Lead me down
into your backyard
which never ceases,
with its apricots
and onyx, its green breath
and feces, being Eden.

Christmas

Brother and sister kiss, then lie
flat on their backs, while
clouds change shape overhead.
They wonder why they have been
kissing like this. Years go by.
They lose track of each other.
The girl takes a job in a hospital
cafeteria, serving meals to night
nurses. She stares out the steamed-
up kitchen window. It's midnight.
Tomorrow's Christmas. The city
lights outshine the stars.
Lately she's afraid to go home.
She thinks her brother will be
sitting on the bottom step
of the stairs leading to her apartment,
eating something, looking up at her
like he knows just what she wants him
to do.

Direct Address

Malign my character, but do it under a willow,
with my ready-made mourner already bent at the waist.

Listen, peabrain, you have influence. Use it.
Do as I say. Start by kneeling. Tell him you're sorry
and you'll never do it again. Get him to spit out his gum and pay attention.
It's easy. Kiss him as if you're a little bit thirsty.

I was patiently waiting for you to explain these flowering phenomena.
Now I might as well be a prehistoric ear of corn, so ancient its kernels
are working loose, like some old geezer's teeth.

Birds nest on the shores of a secluded lake.
Reptiles and waterfowl that populate the swamp watched
the skiff drift downriver, guided by the current.

The pastor receives letters from parishioners that pose
questions about heaven: 1. Will we be conscious
of the world's continuance? 2. Will we be cognizant
of those loved ones left behind?

"You go on ahead. I'll be out in a minute,"
she had said at the back door. She hated to think
they'd come all this way for nothing, so she went
upstairs, to have herself one last look.

Sexual Monotony

He touches her right breast.
She turns fierce. If he fondles
the left, she grows melancholy
for years. Slowly she becomes
just one more pale criminal.
How tiresome. Nothing's less
erotic than what he's sure of.
Still, he craves a little certainty
to offset the threat of the lesions
he reads about lately:
those puckered flowers—
the first signal the nervous system
is turning to quicksand.
Men once believed plagues
were inflicted by blasts
of hot air, not unlike the gasps
of her complaint-tainted breath.
If only it were that simple.

Sublime Moments on Hold

Press one if you'd like to speak to Atilla the Hun.
Press two if your jacuzzi is filled with eels.
Press three if bitten by an animal you teased while it was eating.
Press four if being heartsore dulls you to the delights of this world.
Press five to put continents between you and a thriving former love.
Press six if your whiskey "fix" (that floaty limbo following on the heels of
      your initial sip) is the high point of your day.
Press seven to hear actor Kevin Bacon explain the limbic system.
Press eight to be connected to an invertebrate.
Press nine to explore origins of the phrase "time out of mind."
Press ten to listen to Neandertal bone-flute music (again).

Dear Boy George

Only three things on earth seem useful or soothing to me.
One: wearing stolen clothes. Two: photos of exquisitely
dressed redheads. Three: your voice on the radio. Those songs
fall smack-dab into my range! Not to embarrass you with my
raw American awe, or let you think I'm the kinda girl who
bends over for any guy who plucks his eyebrows and can make
tight braids—but you're the plump bisexual cherub of the
eighties: clusters of Rubens' painted angels, plus a dollop of the
Pillsbury dough boy, all rolled into one! We could go skating,
or just lie around my house eating pineapple. I could pierce
your ears: I know how to freeze the lobes with ice so it doesn't
hurt. When I misunderstand your lyrics, they get even better.
I thought the line I'M YOUR LOVER, NOT YOUR RIVAL, was I'M
ANOTHER, NOT THE BIBLE, or PRIME YOUR MOTHER, NOT A
LIBEL, or UNDERCOVER BOUGHT ARRIVAL. Great, huh? See, we're of
like minds. I almost died when I read in the *Times* how you saved
that girl from drowning…dived down and pulled the blub-
bering sissy up. I'd give anything to be the limp, dripping
form you stumbled from the lake with, draped over your pale,
motherly arms, in a grateful faint, as your mascara ran and ran.

AMY GERSTLER

The Unforseen

In Bible times heavenly messengers disguised as beggars were everywhere. Divine communiqués arrive nowadays via strange mediums. Meanings profuse and profound are inscribed in everyday life's most minor designs: the way glasses and plates rearranged themselves when our backs were turned, how my sisters and I seemed to read each other's minds, and times when something in the attic groaned at such appropriate moments. These were glimmers, little inklings, of what we longed for. At times, from our window, we'd watch homeless men sulk around our yard, exhibiting big discrepancies between their teeth. Father would send them away. But those poor prevented messengers! How could father have known the effects his protections would have on four daughters, stuck in this small town few people ever leave? High hopes deteriorate here like houseboats sunk into mud at the bottom of an ancient Chinese waterway. We offer God strict, intimate prayers, but perhaps it would be better to simply admit our helplessness and send up waves of that agony instead. The homeless men paced under our windows at dusk, sometimes singing a little—"River Jordan is deep and wide / Milk and honey on the other side." Those lyrics, in earthy baritones, sung by shirtless sweating men, seemed to beckon us toward unchristian vistas. Something in the thirsty way they mouthed the word "Milk" made me want to jump down from our window, into their midst, though it was some distance. These were sooty, threatening men, wearing huge weathered boots. Men with cabbage or worse on their breaths. Men on whom all clothing looked baggy and unnatural. Men who washed by sloshing trough-water on their chests and upper arms. We girls pined to be pinned down by something heavy and gruff. One of us would sometimes rub her cheek against a tree trunk, scraping her skin on its bark. There was one man in particular, less well built than the others. At noon I caught sight of him bending down, across the meadow. When he lifted his head, sunlight shone through his ears, giving them a red glow, and I remembered the blood in him. I could almost see his delicate, hairlike capillaries, and I thought about my downfall.

Alps

Until recently there was no map of our minglement.
Reproachful minarets protected frigid snowmelt,
shading lakes of pain. Sweet voiced mules conveyed
baggage past rugged cliffs and savage valleys. Rest
was never obtained in our beds. One boy, a ragged
fellow, mixed hot wine with salt and rubbed it
into the other's
cuts.

At last the pinnacle of Devil's Chimney rose into view.
Schoolboys all, we climbers likened dense clouds
swathing the peak to the cottony tongue of a young
governess we knew. We passed that night in a hay loft,
a repose, that come morning, gave fresh vigor to our
limbs. They sleep without undressing in his country,
or so he
said.

Housebound

When we fuck, stars don't peer down: they can't.
We fornicate indoors, under roofs, under wraps;
far from nature's prying eyes—from the trees'
slight green choreography, wrung from rigid trunks,
that leaves us unmoved. In full view of the shower
head and bookcases, we lick and tickle each other.
Every stick of furniture's a witness. We'd like
to believe our love's a private sentiment, yet
how many couches, cots, and benches have soaked up
some? Lust adheres to objects, becomes a prejudice
instilled in utensils by human use. How can I blind
these Peeping Toms—silence the libidinous whining
of these sipped-from paper cups and used toothbrushes?
I can't. I wait for the outspoken adolescent spoons
to rust and hold their tongues so we can be alone.

Clairvoyance

I've an uncommon calling.
I was born without immunity
to this din in the air:
the sad humming of the long lost.
Imagine not being able
to help hearing every word
that's been moaned in this kitchen
for the last thousand years,
and random sounds too, from snorting
in the stable that stood here
before your house was built,
to the croakers' whisperings
at the bottom of the pond
which filled this hollow before that,
when this county was all swamp. The song
of every being that passed through here
still echoes and is amplified in me.
The sour spirits of the drowned
who imbibed brackish water
remain huddled here, dripping,
in your kitchen. Mouth to mouth
they resuscitate themselves
and speak, lip-syncing twice-baptized cries
an ironclad silence now surrounds.
They're hemmed in, like we are, on all sides…
Chastity and impatience keep us from each other;
the barbed wire of gossip, Catholicism
and obstinacy all come between us.
But we can still do something about it.
Think of the poor ghosts,
with no pleasures left, except watching us.
Let's keep them amused. It's all we can offer.
I'm begging now, like those ghosts
who no longer know any better,
who often entreat me to trespass

outside the confines of my slight
power. I don't know how else to ask:
I want to have you to ponder
when I join their damp precincts.

Shrine

The house of her birth was pulled down,
having stood many years waiting
in patience for her return, which took
place not long afterwards. *Kiss the dust*
of the vacant lot. Reunite with it.
Preserve your solitude, the only holy
thing about you! She labored under
a false notion of the heroic.
She revered her teachers,
beside whose brilliance she felt
stumbling and stupid. Now that's my kind
of saint. The more neurotic, unattractive
and accident prone, the better.
The more easily redeemed. *When you*
finally recognize me, please kneel.

In Place of a Heart,

          (that trembling wet beefsteak
tomato) he hoarded black market vodka.
In place of that blood-pump, snapshots
plastered his chest walls: Betty Page naked
with cheetahs, home run sluggers, a 15
year old gymnast from Kazakhstan mid-flip.
In his heart's scarlet apartment, a shy wife
did quietly reside. A dog barked herself hoarse
in the rustic hut where his heart once stuttered.
Let thousands of bats streaming from a cave at twilight
symbolize decades gone by. Now the stockpiled vodka
emits a muted glow. The dry-witted wife
multiplied, then died. The faithful dog yawns.
These days, will shrubs that thrive after wildfires
(bluestem and wild lilac) germinate and spread
in his ticker's stead?

Saints

Miracle mongers. Bedwetters. Hair–shirted wonder workers. Shirkers of the soggy soggy earth. A bit touched, or wholly untouched living among us? They shrug their bodies off and waft with clouds of celestial perfume. No smooching for this crew, except for hems, and pictures of their mothers… Their lips trespass only the very edges of succor. *Swarms of pious bees precede her.* One young girl wakes up with a ring on her finger and hole in her throat. Another bled milk when her white thigh was punctured. All over the world, a few humans are born each decade with a great talent for suffering. They have gifts that enable them to sleep through their mistreatment: the sleep of the uncomplaining just, the sleep of the incomplete. Our relationship to them is the same as our relationship to trees: what they exhale, we breathe.

KIMBERLY JOHNSON

Orb-weaver

Fie I say to the knitting needles, fie
On their knotted purls, on the pliant loops

Of the crochet hook. Fie on macramé,
The embroiderer's gaudy floss, and fie

On all those green Minervas, each one shuttling
The warp of her tragedy line by line

Until the last picturesque thread pulls tight.
That's the trouble with art, how it aspires

To have been made: the throw-pillow's
Cross-stitched *price above rubies* never frays

Into subclauses; on the tapestry
The woman forever waits at the seaward window,

Her lachrymal faith never unraveling
To resignation, to rage, to the day

She shucks the sackcloth, unpins her hair,
And bulldozes the porticoes down.

My spinnerets are honest: when I dragline
My aminos across the loom of sky,

The pattern grows more perfect in its *unmaking*—
The websilver franticked in tangles,

The spokes thrashed to snips. I would scorn
A thousand squares of finest linen

For one rag with a bulb of blood at its heart.
How lifelike the design that starts in assurance

And ends with a corpse——. How providential.

GÜNTER EICH

Inventory

This is my cap,
this is my coat,
here's my shaving kit
in a linen bag.

A can of rations:
my plate, my cup,
I've scratched the name
in the tin.

Scratched it with this
valuable nail,
which I hide
from desirous eyes.

In the haversack is
a pair of wool socks
and a few things that I
disclose to no one.

It all forms a pillow
nightly for my head.
A cardboard here lies
between me and the earth.

The lead in my pencil
I love most:
By day it writes the verses
I make up at night.

This is my notebook,
this my tarpaulin,
this is my towel,
this is my thread.

Translated from the German by Monika Zobel

Valzhyna Mort

Aunt Anna

I

To see Aunt Anna you have to step back; you have to glimpse a ghost slipping through the long narrow corridor of her body – her face vanishes as abruptly as it appears. "Today, as hours flew by, I sat looking at Aunt Anna and suddenly recognized her," would be the right answer to whether you have seen Aunt Anna. Her speech has also abstracted itself to the apparitions of interjections: oh – ah – no. Even to the happiest of news, she shakes her head and weeps. Her lips, pursed into a crescent, grow in perfect accordance with the lunar calendar into a full moon, a white moon of an open mouth filled with oversized false teeth. In the darkness of her face, the moon-mouth shines, heavy with breath, breath that suddenly seems too complicated of a mechanism to operate, and Aunt Anna, convinced that there has to be an old-fashioned way of breathing, a manual way of breathing, an easy way, tried and true, without the extravagances of holding breath, or breathing hard, turns her body inside out in attempts to bring that old breathing mechanism back. Aunt Anna rediscovers the technique of breathing through a prayer, when her breath sneaks in unnoticed, disguised among Catholic rhythms, and so she patters them, one after another, believing a pause would cost her a life.

As a young girl, Aunt Anna married into the village of M., three miles from P., where later my family bought a summerhouse. The land there was so plain that playing dominoes on our veranda I could always keep focus on M. without failing at the playing board. Since early morning I stayed out in the pasture catching tadpoles and tidying up mole casts pretending they were graves. With the approach of the dark green hours I headed back to the house, shuffling my feet over the gravel. Balancing milk and blood, cows followed me into the village with all the melancholy of a funeral procession. Maple and linden trees robed themselves into their warm shadows, and stars sucked the moist belly of the sky. The lock on our metal gate thundered between my fingers announcing my return to the whole village. If the front door was already locked, I was going to get a whipping. If it was open, the night was only beginning.

Our veranda of purple jam that burned on the reheated for supper pancakes; a veranda of a subtle yellow crack marking the damned double-six tile; a veranda of a thin-legged mosquito balancing on a drop of blood like Picasso's acrobat. In the distance, highway lights, softened by fog and nightfall, beaded themselves on the string of the horizon. The sunset tried to take the village into its red parenthesis. And there, on the west, seemingly almost at arm's length, the flock of M.'s gardens shrunken by perspective into a single bush, as if it were the pubis of a woman, lying flat on her back, naked.

Among all of its gardens, the most beautiful garden in M. was undoubtedly M.'s cemetery. Its fence had fallen down in several places under the pulsation of sickly sweet rose shrubs and swelling buds of peonies that, extending and retracting in tune with chameleons' dewlaps, had overgrown even the freshest graves. The roses and peonies shedded their seeds across the fence, often getting all the way to the village road, from where girls, playing at their future weddings, took the flowers into their backyards and onto dinner tables, spreading the oversized cemetery bloom all over the village. Girls ripped the saccharine mastic that held a bud together, and, while the premature petals unfolded, they put the mastic into their mouths and tried chewing on it when they thought no one was watching.

Every summer, in exchange for a bottle of sweet currant wine, you got us a horse carriage and took me to M. to visit your mother's grave. Your mother Yusefa, Aunt Anna's sister-in-law, was, the other way around, born in M. and married into P. several years before Aunt Anna married Yusefa's brother Adolf.

Yusefa's feet would launch thousands of miles of walking in our family. In her short life she walked from P. to M. to visit her own mother so many times, that the only thing left for her daughter was to become a limping invalid. Clouds of bumble bees thundered over the bell-flowers, nipples of corn were getting harder and darker, while Yusefa walked barefoot, carrying her body, that had already erupted with five children, on those two peapods of her toes, through the smell of dead-water blanketed with vegetation stronger than ice, all the way across a marshland coated with last year's hoarfrost. Eventually she got unwell, and later came down with tuberculosis, the same year when the water took root in her husband's body. Drafted into a short territorial war, he was crossing the Nioman River when his horse must have stumbled, jerking itself up, a hungry pitiful horse, in that upward movement followed by a horselaugh it became a mere squalling rooster, hushed by the aggressive clapping of water. The musculature of the river held my great-grandfather forever down, his wife, coughing out our family's blood into a pillow, sent their children to an orphanage. She died and was buried in M. just before World War II.

In the cemetery, birds and flowers merged into one species. Birds sang as if a pistil were growing out of their pricks, its pollen tickling their throats; and flowers, on their part, opened up their mouths dying to produce a sound. They stretched and strained their long necks able to force out only a smell that, even though couldn't speak, made you lose your speech for a moment.

What grabs me most about those cemetery visits is how brightly lit these summers in M. were. I hold onto the conviction that it is not the light of my memory, but the sun beating so hard that it is impossible to raise my eyes to check how tall the trees are in M. The unseeable in M. starts below the tree level. This proximity gives the small cemetery the air of a convenient advantage. Once you get through the gate stalled in the hard bindweed, the unseeable is just one step up, one simultaneous eight-arms lift up in a wooden coffin. The bees suck the breath out of flowers, pulling them taller and looser, wearing them out, until, swept by a single passing shadow, they fall apart. My dead keep quiet as if they had been buried facedown, and decompose with grace and decency.

After the cemetery you took me to a blue house, its door thrust wide open by a woman — her breasts like the Ural Mountains separating her face from her body. She moved with brisk loudness, dressed in so many layers flaring one under another, sweaters and shirts opening like the doors into new rooms and floors, that it seemed the blue house itself lived inside her, not the other way around. She invited us in — the mudroom revealed rows of milk cans filled up to the brim and covered with carefully cut squares of yellowish gauze. The smell of motherhood around that woman — the mudroom was its source. Daily milking with her forehead pressed against the cow's side like a child hunched over a piano. Milking the white piano keys into a can, giving each tit a drowning man's grip. The steam rising over the milk warmed up by the cow's blood — the same steam that raises over its manure, like a halo which crowns indiscriminately the saint and the disturbed. To which does motherhood in M. belong? Sanctity or disturbance; milk or manure? Mothering a child into a country unfit for history, as if history were the kind of a fruit which required a warmer climate, a richer soil, abler cultivation. A child who, before learning her own name, would learn that history, like happiness, was something that happened only to other people, that the mere want of it would be a sin of luxury against the local absence of religion.

Mothering a child into the land one can neither walk to, nor fly to, nor swim; the land reachable only through a mother's womb, which is a dangerous road and many die trying. Mothering a child into the land where the grains of sand are still being separated into those that would become stones and those that would grow into mountains; where birds are so huge, their crest is a herd of galloping horses, and their eyes take a day to close and another day to open; where grass is so tall, it is deemed as the underworld; and, underneath the grass

— the lighting of roots, the cable where electricity lives like a mammal that knows its way into the quietest house, where it steals the dark and eats the cold. This is where you were mothered into, in the kitchen, where bread was being baked, and the mothering Yusefa, steaming with blood and sweat, raced against the kindled baking oven. The moment your head showed, a sudden the kindled baking oven. The moment your head showed, a sudden spasm of smoke from the oven erased the room, and your blinded mother couldn't decide what to deliver first: a loaf of bread or a baby. Somebody must have thought there still was a chance to erase that moment from the face of the earth, to start blank, to redraft, to replace a kitchen with a hospital in Paris and call you Serge Gainsbourg, or in Chicago – James Dewey Watson; you could have been the King of Malaysia, or several weeks old in Italy, you could have become a casualty of a bomb attack against Mussolini, you could have been swept by three earthquakes, but your grandmother whiffed "a girl!" and that word began your world of low log houses ingrained in the black soil, where you learned the meaning of pink from a cow's nipple, the meaning of maroon from a boiled beet, and the meaning of blue from a dead man's body. Born in a caul, you were promised wealth, health, fool's luck, and bird's milk. In truth, you had dragged the caul with you because you knew what misery and need awaited you outside. The caul was your only chance at having something of your own. You smuggled it out of a womb. You were born already a suitcase-trader. On your exit from the vagina, you were caught, undressed, and rinsed with a stream of smoke.

Your mother keened with her squirrel hands at her face. Or maybe I'm retelling it wrong. Maybe those were not the squirrel hands that she had, but two front squirrel teeth: the tooth of good and the tooth of evil. She bit them through you, threaded a needle through the bites, and sewed you to that soil like a button. And so that you didn't have any doubts, she threw over your neck – a noose.

First thing, the woman seats us in the kitchen of the blue house. Clusters of grapes stare into the windows like blistered lepers. The smell of bittersweet geranium from the windowsills saturates all of the food. Most of it – sausage, eggs, fresh bacon, smoked chicken – come out wrapped in newspaper pages dated back from five to ten years ago. A wind-swept farmer extending cupped hands full of the year's first harvest as if he were about to wash his face with it; a driver trying out a new crop-collecting machine; a midwife pressing two loafs of newborn twins to her breasts. Faces of missing persons, deformed faces of unidentified victims, even among the dead there's rarely a mouth without a smile, even rarer – a mouth with regular teeth. All of these people are mummified according to the unique method of stuffing their paper-thin skin with home-made meats, eggs and pinkies of pickled cucumbers, immortalizing their twenty-four hours of daily-paper glory with the flesh of the animals fed with the crops these people have harvested with their bare hands and their new shining machines. Stains of grease show through the yellowed paper as if the stuffed bodies were already breathing on the hoarfrost of print. The woman skins them again, cuts them up, their meat still thinking in provincial journalistic clichés as it approaches our three willing to listen mouths.

You have to always sit at the very corner of the kitchen table, its arrow pointing onto your belly – your belly, on which nobody would ever place high stakes, wins every time. You sit fidgeting in that corner – your idea of showing respect to the house; on the edge of the chair, your right leg unbendable. If you had an arm that didn't bend in the elbow, it would have made it easy to simply choose begging, but it was your leg that was always thrust ahead of you like the stick ahead of the blind. You tricked it only once, when, on the way to the surgery, you asked the driver to stop the ambulance car at the registry office, borrowed the whites from the nurse, and got married. Pashka had fallen in love while reading your letters over your brother's shoulder in the aviation college somewhere in Russia, and arrived a day before the surgery, with three kopeks and a toothbrush. "What an ugly man, what a beautiful girl," the doctor said when he opened your knee like an oyster.

The surgery was initially scheduled for the first week of July – the July you were fourteen. In March, the dying Yusefa sent two of your brothers and you to an orphanage. The youngest had to be placed in a separate institution for the children under five. The oldest, Vaclav, had been staying with relatives in Poland since Anton's death. He was later evacuated to Mordavia, from where, once the war was over, he walked by himself to Moscow to enroll in the aviation college.

On June 21st you dreamed of entering a crowded house, Yusefa walking towards you across the room with two buckets filled with water to the brim, and woke up torn among the pain of seeing your mother alive, the fear that she wanted to soak you, and the two-full-buckets' promise of good fortune. The night of June 22nd, hurling back sleep, you got out of bed, dressed, woke up your brothers Yanak and Kazik, marched with them straight into the headmistress' bedroom, and announced that you wanted to leave for P., to stay with Aunt Anna's sister Viktsya. The headmistress, through sleep, moved her head just slightly, but nevertheless enough to be read as permission. Hastily, without looking at each other, the three of you took off your shoulders the long sleeves of the orphanage corridors, the pleated skirts of its silent staircases, the worn-out collars of its windowsills – left all of this to the sleep of the children whose chests moved up and down in breathing meant not for living, but only to fan away hunger. Death, like a spoiled child to whom nobody ever said "no," was already licking the cream off their sleeping lives, leaving behind the bland crust of their bodies.

You took the first bus reaching the village two hours later. Chasing the bus, pages of paper flew framed into fire; books, newspapers, photographs, postcards flew all the way to P. from that city where the wind was on fire, where the red pencil of fire was filling in the centuries-old crossword of window grids. The unanswerable was answered by fire that morning. Even where there were no questions posed, fire was the answer.

Blood rolled out of bodies like a red rug for the fire to walk on. First, the city, like an enormous elephant, dropped on its knees, and then the buildings bared their hollowed heads and drained themselves into the eye sockets of the sleeping dead on the ground floors. The hungry rushed to the borders where they eagerly gorged on bullets, stuffed themselves with the bullet rice until their weight pulled them down and they could no longer get up.

Vikstya, a heartless woman, since her birth, death stood behind her left shoulder knocking on her body – knock-knock, knock-knock, knock-knock. She learned to trick death by what her body could give without giving itself – her children, newborns, handed over one after another. She cried on top of their graves until they came into her dreams begging not to drown them in her tears. She took you, among other orphaned relatives and for four straight years fed you boiled water.

In four years you could not make a step by yourself. The rot showed from underneath the bluish knee like the tumid face of your drowned father flowing slowly under the still waters. A beautiful man, even bloated with water and blood of horses and soldiers, a woman washing herself in the river could have taken his face for her own reflection and smiled to herself in peace. In the kitchen of the blue house in M. his unframed portrait hangs alongside a reproduction of Vasnetsov's *Alyonushka*.

All the furniture is painted white, with brown shades of dirt along the brushstrokes. From the crack between a mirror and its frame, sticks a yellow bouquet of curve-edged photographs, leaving no space for reflection. Every curtain on the windows and in the doorways, every sofa, apron and napkin, every rug and mat, every cup, kettle, and every inch of the wallpaper are densely covered with a flowery pattern, a variety of flowers of every shape: roses, lilies, dahlias, daisies of every size and color, the lifeless blooming of my youth, of my secret, my truth, my desire, the pattern that offends nobody, the pattern that means nothing, the fastest answer to the request of beauty.

While the blooming is transported inside of the house, the front yard and the garden are cramped with the indoor furniture: in the tall grass a big armchair stands swollen with rainwater. Rainwater also comes to the brim of a large rusty bathtub which has no other purpose than catching falling leaves. While in the kitchen, cupboard doors and drawers open and close, making their own distinct moans, releasing tea cup, plates, sugar bowls, and cutlery, the two women inventory our extended family, mentioning their Aunt Anna only briefly — so evasive is Aunt Anna's body, it is impossible to hold a thought of it for longer than an instant. The plastic tablecloth has a pattern of exotic fruit. I eat sausage and stare through a many-faceted glass.

A century ago Aunt Anna got married in M. Hard to believe there was once a train going through that village. It was on the train that they put Aunt Anna with her handsome and wealthy husband Adolf — that same Adolf who, bitten by a bee in one eye, would, out of natural aesthetic inclination, catch another bee to restore the symmetry of his face — and all she managed to do was to pass little Jadzenka into Kazik's hands through the compartment window. It was Jadzenka's second birth — her skinny genderless body pushed by her young mother through the window gap towards her not-that-much-older cousin — out and, this time, truly away from the womb. Whether Jadzenka gave a long newborn's scream towards the leaving train, I cannot say. Kazik brought Jadzenka to the house, his parents already in hiding, the removal committee walked upon six children sitting on the cold stove-couch, asked for somebody to sign the removal papers, but none of them could write. Thus they remained in P. while Aunt Anna's train went all the way to Tyumen and beyond it, into the Siberian woods which Aunt Anna learned to cut, grab up, saw, hew, drag and pile. On the cleared land they sowed millet and, returning to the barracks after work, Aunt Anna covertly plucked the spikelet, rubbed it between her palms and cooked into a soup. When Adolf and their newborn died of hunger, Aunt Anna decided to run away.

Aunt Anna, who once married into M. and had walked three miles from P. to M. every weekend, walked 1730 miles from Tyumen back to P. This time she walked there for no man, for no village girl's dreams of the neighboring village; this time she walked for the memory of that pubis, for what it concealed — the source that her mouth was so hungry to embrace. When she came into her mother's backyard, all she wanted to do was to eat. Cast iron barrels were filled with beets and potatoes for pigs, and Aunt Anna ate with pigs, standing before the barrels with pigs, on her knees with pigs; knees, small and sharp like two millet grains fertilely planted into the dirt and manure. She ate so much that her belly couldn't stop growing — it swelled larger and larger, until it became Aunt

Anna's younger brother. Aunt Anna walked from house to house complaining about her brother's bad health. When she got stronger, somebody wised her up to take her brother and go straight to M. to claim Adolf's house. In M. both of them were arrested and taken to jail, and from the jail – to the train that went 1596 miles towards the Urals.

In Nizhny Tagil, Aunt Anna worked at a Railroad Car Works, manufacturing freight cars that were to transport people and lumber across the incomprehensible country. Later she remarried and at family kitchen tables was inventoried as free and happy. She had another child, maybe even two, but as for Jadzenka – Aunt Anna never wanted her back. After the war Anna returned and moved from one house, like this blue one, to another, until she settled down and started working at a calf barn. Janak went on foot to P. from Berlin. Instead of a usual triangular envelope with a hand drawn airplane and inscription, "Greetings from Air," a telegram arrived from an aviation college somewhere in Russia: "at the hospital, unwell, alone, please come."

Janak, without washing blood and foul off his feet, without picking splinters out of his heels, without waiting until skin grew back on his soles, went jumping from one freight train heading to Moscow to another, Vaclav dying alone, in pain and hunger (in far off lands there lived a King and his Princess daughter for whose hand competed three Princes – the eldest Solitude, the middle Hunger and the youngest brother Death). Kazik announced that for several nights he had been waking up to see Yusefa sit at the edge of his bed stroking his feet, and shortly, when running across the street, was hit by a car. Yanak died fifty years later, beaten and robbed by his own grandson.

You weeded and clipped the rose bush at M.'s cemetery, and, though always calm and collected, you would, just for an instant, break into a lament, short but excruciating, as if you had choked on a flower seed or raised your eyes too high into the unseeable:

> I rest on the pillows embroidered by you, mama,
> while worms embroider your resting body,
> stiff as a doll I'm still small enough to play with,
> to spoon-feed the soil that has been shoveled
> over your young mouth.

II

As I write this, I imagine you are here with me, at the North Sea, on an island shaped like a ballerina, frying potatoes on both hemispheres of a tiny stovetop. At sunset, the birds at the edge of the water are black, but their shadows are purple. A girl jumps cold waves holding her hands up like a candelabrum. Have you ever noticed this about the North? The heat can fit into a tip of coal or a tongue, into one cigarette butt, into one red button that guarantees the eventual boiling of water, into that thromb of a space allocated to it here — this tiny sun, bruised into the lavender neck of the sky with a brute thumb. But, as for the cold, it calls for vastness. Cold needs absence — even speech, a phrase like "how to stop thinking about you without stopping to think," can startle the cold. It needs dunes of bleached vegetation falling down in rows of ivory dominos; it needs dog-rose bushes nailing their buds to the soil with their own thorns; it prefers the flatbreads of fish bodies to the curves of the animals. The cold needs a sea — this polonaise in G-flat minor, this gray flat wing of an injured bird still trying to lift itself up while being pecked relentlessly by its own kind. The sea unburdens the cold, unsaddles it, lets it loose, the sea carries the cold as the cold gains speed, as it stretches, as it unfolds, like a handkerchief rushed to a bleeding child. Stripped of warmth, freed of any expectations to shed itself, the northern light is a separate part of day and night, their third, out of wedlock sibling, the yellow time that docs not illuminate but color. The sun caught into the web of the northern light is merely an insect quivering and struggling for many hours to free itself, until it finally gives up and steps down, and for the rest of the season it hangs across the sea like a cut-off head of a city criminal thrust on a stake on the other side of the Amstel river.

The sea is the land, only bared, skinned. You look away, avoiding my eyes, in such sweet misery — an opera singer catching her breath; then slide your eyes onto your perpetually tanned hands that are already fidgeting the edge of your shrunken pink cardigan. I want to tell you how as a child I dreamed of you being raped in this pink sweater, lying in a ditch behind our summer house, your unbendable leg thrust into your body like a shovel, your mouth opened without a sound and staring at me like your third eye. I didn't even know what rape was back then. All I knew was that your pink sweater was your way of showing others you were not a pauper.

"A poem named after Aunt Anna, pages about Aunt Anna, and not one word about Boleska," — the clock on the wall sounds like a leaking faucet, a drop after drop measured with striking precision. The journey made by your voice is as long as the journey of light. (Boleska, if you are reading this, please find me, everybody is dead.)

"When I'm back, let's go to M. together."

"To M.? What did you forget in M.?"

"Yusefa's grave might need tidying up."

"To go across the country to prune a rose bush?"

"It is a very small country."

The two of us here, on the parting from where the sea is combed in one direction, and the sky — in another, from where the sea casts its shadow — the wind — over the rest of the world, on this scar on the skin of landscape, on this strip of skin showing from under the gray garments of the planet. The waves thrown generously, at no interval, the sea bailing the water out trying to save itself from drowning, but then, at once, rushing to claim its own back. The sea which, in its restlessness, only waits for the right moment when it could get up and walk out of here for good. Your mother who sits on the bench in front of the house and coughs out red crumbs of blood hastily picked up by hungry birds. Your mother rolled up on her deathbed, folded along every joint, ready to be shipped away, ready to be a light load, ready to return everything she has been given — this body, already less believable than its own shadow, while its shadow can still break a window against which it is cast. This face that explains beauty in the simplest lines, these curls — as if somebody had emptied an overscribbled diary over her head; she brushes its words off her face, scratches them off her neck, spits them out of her mouth, her face is already only a fist that death is trying to unclench, her senses already tuned into a different frequency — she is cold when it's hot, and hot when it's cold, sour tastes bitter, bitter tastes salty, but nothing tastes sweet enough. Outside, the saw of the forest line cuts into two the immaculate spring sky. Cows howl smelling through the cracks of the barn the wet mouth of the waking earth.

Boleska, forgive me this time.

GOTTFRIED BENN

Chopin

Not a good conversationalist,
ideas were not his best,
ideas only scratch the surface,
when Delacroix goes on with his theories,
he feels uneasy, he, on his part, cannot
justify the nocturnes.

A poor lover;
a light shadow in Nohant,
where George Sand's children
dismissed his parental advice.
Sickness in the chest

with bleeding and scarring,
that drags on;
silent death as opposed to one
of spasms of pain
or fired weapons:
the grand piano (Erard) was pushed to the door
and Delphine Potocka
sang him a purple song
in his last hours.

He travelled to England with three pianos:
Pleyel, Erard, Broadwood,
played for twenty guineas in the evenings
a quarter hour
at the Rothschild's, Wellington's, in the Strafford House
dark with fatigue and nearing death,
he went home
to the Square d'Orleans.

He then burns his sketches
and manuscripts,
wants no remnants, fragments, notes,

those deceptive insights –
in the end he says:
"I have taken my experiment as far as it was possible to go."

Each finger is to play
no more than its natural strength,
the fourth one is the weakest
(siamese only to the middle finger).
When he begins, they lie
on E, F-sharp, G-sharp, H, C.

Anyone hearing certain of his Preludes
in country houses or
at altitude
or through open patio doors,
say, of a sanatorium,
will not easily forget it.

He composed not one opera,
no symphonies,
only these tragic progressions
from artistic conviction
and with a small hand.

Adapted from the German by Monika Zobel

STEVE SCAFIDI

PORTFOLIO

In the City of My Childhood

In the city of shimmer and birds, birds
   in gabardine stroll the boulevard
pointing at the sky with their canes.
   Crows mostly as tall and strange
as young men or young women.

And the streets are heaped with hay,
   twigs, turds and old newspapers.
A robin flicks at her feathers
   on the steps of the Stock Exchange.
A goose by the water limps slowly

toward the water heavy and stately
   thinking god knows what.
On a beautiful day once I heard
   the flap of sail-boats going
in the bay and laughter and wings

rising in the cobblestone markets
   where a pigeon dove to a crumb.
Nothing happened of significance
   on a daily basis and this made
some nervous. It made some sleepy,

some anxious, some greedy for loss.
   And the people where I come from
weep and cough when we think of
   what happened that summer day.
A fox. A god. A shadow. A thumb.

Ode to O and K

In the minute and a half it takes
   for a plane to fall from the sky
there is time to pray for all of us
   living now who will in this way
die the excruciating slow fall of

strangers cloud-high and plunging
   down together and there is time
while the lights flicker and the fire
   grows and the human noise stuns
everyone and all certainty disappears

except for the impending one now
   rising up like cornfields or cities
to snatch us back—there is still
   a moment or two in the chaos of
gravity to say something—it's OK—

It's OK.
   Once as a boy my father helped
a sheep give birth and the thing was
   stuck and so he put his hand inside
the body and pulled out a thick bouquet

of flowers—tulips, roses and a spray
   of Queen Anne's lace. He was a boy.
He told me this when I was grown,
   old enough to know better. It's ok.
Breath carries us and we fall away.

To Gaze Is a Ghost

Notice how the curving waves
   of her hair lay across
the pillow and the pillow holds
   the shape of her sleeping
and the face betrays her sleeping.

Notice the eyelashes like hay
   combed after mowing—
Notice the forehead as calm
   as the white of bones. See
the way the line of the nose

descends to the rested valley
   and cliffs of the upper lip.
The way the sheet luffs up
   when she moves a little
from the dream she makes up

as she goes and all the facts
   of that kingdom blind to us.
The way a teacup rests
   in the flat paw of the bear.
The silence of the forest

deepening and the sad ghost
   of her father flying overhead.
Even the mockingbird hunched
   in a nest in the middle branch
of the pine sleeps. We find peace.

The Butcher-block and the Fawn

Here in the wilderness of my room
  deer walk through the quiet
of words on the page on the ash
  butcher-block table of this house
in the woods where we live, love,

and the moon moves and it shines
  and the fox in the tree and the crow
in the stream and the fish dream
  all of them, I believe, of the world
before the world and the one after

this magical one we can see—
  And I share in the old fairytale
shares of the sun and the moon
  that are one and the same tonight
for the lamp in the sky—it warms

as it brightens. For the fear of death
  moves me as it frightens. For love
of energy is clarity and magic
  and the fox in the tree and the crow
in the stream and the deer in the woods

move through the quiet of words here
  in the wilderness of my room.
Let the going on of what is—go on.
  Let the criss-cross old table top
of the butcher-block be. Let the fawn.

The River Away

That tender saying softly spoken—
    something whispered, something broken.
"Here you are, I have looked for you."
    Something whispered, something broken,
something still and hardly spoken.

I don't know you anymore. Something
    whispered, something spoken.
Last night in the crash of light
    the moon made in your eyes
I saw something I'd never seen.

The whole person turning away
    from me. Once one summer day
I saw a horse slowly lower
    its face into the grass to eat
and it moved its heavy body piece

by piece fluidly like a river risen
    patiently to flow away—
like a sleepy ghost—just so,
    I saw something I'd never seen:
your eyes go blank and blinking.

There is no such thing as wings.
    Nor words that sing or open.
You are leaving in the morning.
    Tender saying softly spoken:
Something whispered, something broken.

Words for the Meanwhile

Persian Kings of Persian moons,
   persimmon trees in the afternoon,
watermelon, fig, fog and through
   the days when I wait for you
sad and alone, I think of you.

So the centuries pass and nightly
   new white moths flicker-on-
flicker fast to death flying
   hard to be the street's bright
sizzled paramours of light.

Words too large to ever use—
   I think of love and of death.
Well, one is a thing we'll lose.
   Persian kings of New York City
drive taxicabs in the afternoon

From Brooklyn north to Queens
   from fare to fare all day they move.
It's half past eight and half of eight
   is four and half of that is two.
Love is the random music we make

of everything intentional we do.
   Persian kings of Persian moons,
watermelon, fig, fog and through
   these words I think of you.
Forever also I will wait for you.

BEN RIGGS

Uncle Jim

His feet leapt inches from God-given ground.
His smile was toothy, laugh snapped toothy joy.
His head—his heart—his head was tightly wound:
A big, rambunctious, six-two little boy.

His smile was toothy, laugh snapped toothy joy.
He slipped us all wet-willies Christmas Eves.
A big, rambunctious, six-two little boy
who spilled his heart so sloppily on his sleeves.

He slipped us all wet-willies Christmas Eves.
He'd quick cuss-out a golf ball, whip a club.
He spilled his heart so sloppily on his sleeves.
He made the floorboards shake with every flub.

He'd quick cuss-out a golf ball, whip a club.
My uncle operated in extremes.
He made the floorboards shake with every flub.
He looped rope through the basement ceiling beams.

My uncle operated in extremes.
His neck—his heart—his neck was tightly bound.
He looped rope through the basement ceiling beams.
His feet swept inches from God-given ground.

ROCHELLE HURT

Helen's Confession

They can call it what they want to. Here
is what I know: when the hairs on his forearm
first brushed my wrist, I thought only of bristles
on a giant sunflower's stem, how they prick,
but still are softer than you'd expect—how
willingly they give beneath your fingertips.
I remember the clover, mashed in the grass
with mud, was thick in my palms, like silt,
and the pressure of his chest on my back spread
warmth wider than my husband ever could,
down to the fleshy sunken spots behind
my knees. It welled there like sun.

I know, at home, what they ask one another:
how, but nothing is as simple as that. I could say
my daughter's name like penance, weigh it
like a stone next to his, Paris, but why
not tell them instead, that in the hush that followed
the din of an ocean that rushed from his mouth to the back
of my head, everything was crowned in light—
even the pointed bodies of the wasps, blue-
black at the far lilac bush, were beautiful
in their fickle movements: feed, recoil, feed.

NATE KLUG

Advent

In the middle of December
to start over

to assume again
an order

at the end
of wonder

to conjure
and then to keep

slow dirty sleet
within its streetlight

MICHAEL KRÜGER

In the Forest, After Sunset

At the edge of the forest, below the moss,
a king still slumbers,
he dreams
with thievish words of empires.
His army is composed of mushrooms,
and with blackberry juice
he signs his mandate
of mischief, of salvation and death.
His sole ambassador across the globe—
a strayed echo
out of the tragedy for clarity.
Outside of his palace stones rest,
they know everything from us.
When we enter his realm,
the birds rebel.
At once we are lost, and free.

Translated from the German by Monika Zobel

In Bulgaria

The brown–white doves of Ruse
drag dawn across the river,
and on the sand bars, where fishermen sprout,
the seagulls build a house of dust,
as if to push their luck.
On the elevation a mulberry tree.
Every twig, every leaf pulls me
into a cyrillic conversation over water.
I don't know what I'm searching for.
The people sleep in watermelons,
they squeeze seeds from their eyes.
Here, only children don't sleep,
children follow the water to a parched country.

Translated from the German by Monika Zobel

The Mosquito

Maybe it is excessive
to memorialize the mosquito.
But even the mosquito holds,
by the sip of my blood, a stake in the history of anxiety.

Translated from the German by Monika Zobel

Dog

I love shady pathways,
and the park on the corner,
where bums converse about God and the world.
They may call me dog,
my birth-given name
I recently lost.
I am pleased to roam nameless again
among houses and humans.
God, a poor fellow claimed,
gave out too many names,
now he doesn't know his
way around.
Dog.
Only I know what it disguises.

Translated from the German by Monika Zobel

MICHAEL DUMANIS

State of the Union

We paint the bedroom walls Quixotic Plum.
We paint the bedroom ceiling Foggy Day.

You paint your nails and eyelids Powder Blue.
We drive to photograph the flying buttresses

of the flamboyant oil refinery
and stay through dusk to catch the glimmering

reflections of its lights against the Ship Channel,
and also the striated moon in the water,

rippling alongside, an incontrovertible fact.
You whisper, *How much would it cost*

to reupholster the Chrysler? You are as elegant
as a grand piano. You throw tantrums

for a living. You make a good living.
Everyone is rich, for a little while.

Everyone is happy, for a little while,
even a day is a very long time,

and for a while the spoons and butter knives
continue to reflect our sunburnt masks.

For years we act astonishingly lifelike,
running one's lips across the other's thorax,

painting the stairs and hallways Golden Fleece.
It would be nice to believe in a God.

Children step out of our curtains
and ask us to hold them.

Ours is the only of possible worlds:
femur, pubis, ribcage, sternum, clavicle.

We close our eyes when we get tired
of looking at each other. In my dream,

it is always the same: having painted
my breath Frost and my hair Quicksilver,

I stand with my luggage outside, getting ready
to board the slow train to Albania.

The night is heavy, though her skin is soft.
She comes at me across the lawn until I fall.

She covers my mouth with her novocaine mouth.
Little torpedoes of grass shard my back.

Night paws at me with her five thousand hands,
then rubber-bands her limbs around my neck.

She prays into my ears. They turn to moss.
Possibly, this is the only end: dust,

the star-addled, wind-saddled black
flag of the sky waving over us.

When I grow up, I do not want to be a headstone.
When I grow up, I want to be a book.

CARIBBEAN POETRY

FEATURE

Introduction

If I were to be a little heretical and give the Caribbean muse a name, I think Hybrid would be quite fine. At least, for the eight gifted poets gathered here, this identification is not altogether blasphemous. They all—but for two, Jennifer Rahim and Edward Baugh—live and work outside of their birth islands. They are widely dispersed too: Canada, England, France, USA—self-exiles from the landscape of childhood, they have laboured to create a poetry of memory, splendid fragments grafted onto the foreign regions they now inhabit. These poems resist nostalgia and mere anthropology through a language imbued with the best of oral and scribal traditions. Such attention has fostered a poetry of pristine clarity that, without abstraction and metaphorical obliqueness, fulfills poetry's hardest task: transformation through the recollection of ordinary things: sunlight, the hot sea, a woman convulsing in church. These poets handle features of the Caribbean experience without condescension, but with a truly ecstatic embrace of what it means to be Caribbean:

> I have to praise it. I have to lull it
> with new roses. Run my fingers
> along this sallow river
> of desire. Stuck in the plantation
> kitchen, black ants dying
> in an orgy of honey.
>
> "Lightskinned Id," Christian Campbell

There is an urgent heterogeneous mode running through these poems, voices that are startlingly varied, like the vegetation of the poets' different islands; voices restless in their veiling and unveiling of Caribbean identity and spirit. A voice can be tender and private, coming through a phone line, confessing genealogy never before known:

> There are thirty-three of us reveals the voice
> lodged on the other end of the line, Kieran
> who lives on Church Avenue in Brooklyn,
> keeping count of our father's unclaimed offspring.
> I knew only four before tonight—Faustin, Fara,
> Melvin and Cheryl, faces seen long ago
> but undimmed by memory.
>
> "Kindred," Sassy Ross

Another voice is public, declarative: a tide building to an astonishing beauty and intensity which is characteristic of many of the poems presented here:

> Then all the nations of birds lifted
> together the huge net of the shadows of this
> earth in multitudinous dialects, twittering tongues,
> stitching and crossing it. They lifted up
> the shadows of long pines down trackless slopes,
> the shadows of glass-faced towers down evening streets,
> the shadow of a frail plant on a city sill –
> the net rising soundless at night, the birds' cries soundless, until
> there was no longer dusk, or season, decline, or weather,
> only this passage of phantasmal light
> that not the narrowest shadow dared to sever.
> "The Season of Phantasmal Peace," Derek Walcott

It would be wrong to call the hybridity found in these poems "schizophrenic" or "mongrel." These are poems that speak to the fissured, uneven reality of the Caribbean consciousness, home and abroad. These poets face the challenge of the everyday, writing and speaking the places that have shaped their lives, all that eternal land and sea bound up in their bodies and minds. They speak firmly and assuredly of the singular truth that they are Caribbean, scattered as they may be up and down the Antilles. However their voices come to you, as a whisper through the telephone or prophetic from some unknown place, they arrive with vigour and elegance through a masterful use of artistry. Listen to these voices, return to their pelagic intelligence, their presence like waves striking shore.

> So I break. I break the rule. I break
> the ground we will dance on;
> I break my mother's heart; I break the fast –
> it did not work. I break the chain – lines end
> with me. I break the body, the bread, the words.
> I break the ceiling. I break the bone and the jaw
> and the habit of hiding. I break the stone. I break the curse.
> They are broken. I am written.
> From "The Broken (I)," Kei Miller

Ishion Hutchinson
May 14, 2010

Derek Walcott

The Season of Phantasmal Peace

Then all the nations of birds lifted together
the huge net of the shadows of this earth
in multitudinous dialects, twittering tongues,
stitching and crossing it. They lifted up
the shadows of long pines down trackless slopes,
the shadows of glass-faced towers down evening streets,
the shadow of a frail plant on a city sill –
the net rising soundless at night, the birds' cries soundless, until
there was no longer dusk, or season, decline, or weather,
only this passage of phantasmal light
that not the narrowest shadow dared to sever.

And men could not see, looking up, what the wild geese drew,
what the ospreys trailed behind them in the silvery ropes
that flashed in the icy sunlight; they could not hear
battalions of starlings waging peaceful cries,
bearing the net higher, covering this world
like the vines of an orchard, or a mother drawing
the trembling gauze over the trembling eyes
of a child fluttering to sleep;
                                        it was the light
that you will see at evening on the side of a hill
in yellow October, and no one hearing knew
what change had brought into the raven's cawing,
the killdeer's screech, the ember-circling chough
such an immense, soundless, and high concern
for the fields and cities where the birds belong,
except it was their seasonal passing, Love,
made seasonless, or, from the high privilege of their birth,
something brighter than pity for the wingless ones
below them who shared dark holes in windows and in houses,
and higher they lifted the net with soundless voices
above all change, betrayals of falling suns,
and this season lasted one moment, like the pause
between dusk and darkness, between fury and peace,
but, for such as our earth is now, it lasted long.

Sea Grapes

That sail which leans on light,
tired of islands,
a schooner beating up the Caribbean
for home, could be Odysseus,
home-bound on the Aegean;
that father and husband's
longing, under gnarled sour grapes, is like
the adulterer hearing Nausicaa's name in
every gull's outcry.

This brings nobody peace. The ancient war
between obsession and responsibility will
never finish and has been the same

for the sea-wanderer or the one on shore now
wriggling on his sandals to walk home, since
Troy sighed its last flame,

and the blind giant's boulder heaved the trough from
whose groundswell the great hexameters come to the
conclusions of exhausted surf.

The classics can console. But not enough.

Edward Baugh

A Nineteenth-Century Portrait

When Mister Robert Scarlett, master
of Cambridge and Druckett plantations, stood
for his portrait, the good man made a point
of having his personal slave-boy, Oliver,
beside him, waist high, holding his game bag,
with which he'd ride to hunt wild hog
and occasional runaways. At his other side
his favourite dog. How well the boy's
dark visage serves design,
matching the dark of the trees to cast
in relief the pale, proprietorial white.

Those were the good days; they didn't last.
After the slave revolts of 1831
great houses, factories, everything was gone;
only the family tomb remained.
And what of Oliver? History has left
no afterword; a boy in a picture,
a period-piece, on which poets may stretch out a fiction.

Freeze Warning

for Ralph Thompson

On the second, deceptive day of Spring,
when, unseasonably cold, but bright,
the forecast, thanks to America-on-Line,
reads, in red, quote, FREEZE
WARNING TONIGHT, my poet-friend,
silver-haired, capricious, sends me
from home a new poem. It recalls
a day when, he too far from home,
some other Spring bounded clear
of Winter, bang on time. The old
angora, testosterone thudding in his balls,
configures young girls at skip-rope,
an older one bellying with hope
and promise – 'jig, jiggle, jerk
and jolt,' perennial procreation,
'fish, flesh and fowl,' the lot.
At which he sighs, 'I am afflicted by the sickness
of the country. I have caught the sadness of the land.'
Then springs to mind a song my mother
taught me, about a songbird that sings
at my window; and so, still hearkening,
I click 'Reply,' then type 'Rejoice!'

JACQUELINE BISHOP

Under the Mangoes

Gaugin, this is Martinique
as you wanted it to be:

A woman, her back turned to us,
balancing a basket on her head;

another figure, woman in white,
on a low wooden stump.

You have taken the time to notice
how the folds

of their dresses fall;
elaborately bound headscarves;

careful mixing and re-mixing;
however many revisions:

Unruffled indigo sea, tangle
of wild cane and guavas.

JENNIFER RAHIM

Ground Level

It happened on the sky-god's feast. The sacred came to ground level. Somehow
she had missed it, maybe from straining too long at altars across an eternity of
separation. But how could she, following so faithfully, the seasons of crèche,
communion and crucifixion? She did anyway, missed the spirit of it. That day,
the homeliness of earth welcomed her, in fact, wanted the human touch of
her. It has never left: that burnished surface, pressed to wafer smoothness and
polished to imagination's glow by a living dance of faith. Since then, she has
been busy revising her catechism with lightning strokes and hurricane swirls.
Since then, her people mistakenly weep at her grave; but if they really look,
they will see her walking in step with an insatiable thirst for the homily of
trees.

KEI MILLER

For the girl who died by dancing

"It is a warning to young people that dem mus stop du de Dutty Wine," said one
woman who called the incident a curse on the land. "Is like a demon sen' from de pit
a hell dat is taking the lives of the youth even before dem have time to repent."
                                               –Jamaica Gleaner, October 30, 2006

Forgive the old woman who only sees
confusion in the wild
rotations of your head &
the in/out butterfly of your thighs.
She could not imagine how,
in the helicopter swing of red braids,
you were being lifted high.

Forgive her, the selfish belief
that heaven is reserved for ladies
with names like Agnes or Beryl
& that no *Tanisha* would ever inherit
the kingdom of God.

She will be surprised soon enough
to find you on a wide marble tile
in front of Jesus. She will be surprised
that the savior has given unto you
a tall speakerbox, filled
to its brim with music,
& that you continue your peculiar art –
dancing *dutty wine* with a clean heart.

From **The Broken (I)**

VII.

He has broken every coffin and scattered the feathers.
He has smashed every clock. And what I thought
was wood and nails and varnish and velvet
and hour-hands, turned out to be silence.
So I break. I break the rule. I break
the ground we will dance on;
I break my mother's heart; I break the fast –
it did not work. I break the chain – lines end
with me. I break the body, the bread, the words.
I break the ceiling. I break the bone and the jaw
and the habit of hiding. I break the stone. I break the curse.
They are broken. I am written.

KWAME DAWES

YAP

He was remembered
his name becoming a common
noun and verb in regular parlance:

A yap

(/ˋyap/ *n*. **yap yappist** /ˋya-pest/*vi* **yap yapped** /ˋyap-t/[Youthful
innovation Jamaica College] (1974) 1 :HOMOSEXUAL usually considered
obscene : 2 : battyman and specialist in homosexual practices : 3: the scourge
of school boys : 4 : their secret fear when clandestine hands cause self-inflicted
sticky orgasms; 5 : something no boy admits he is to other boys. (*no longer in*
common usage)

A gentle boy with a sharp tongue;
he played chess quickly, aggressively
winning with a laugh – played football

in a torn yellow shirt and red shorts;
his father sold radios and calculators
in an air-conditioned appliance store

somewhere downtown and made good money.
They lured him into the piss stink toilette
flooded with loose water and shit;

its blue walls scarred with obscenities;
secrets about teachers, yearnings
hieroglyphics of a twisted culture.

Nunez, the short Syrian, was the bait
with his tight pants and benign smile;
securing his heterosexual credentials

despite his lisp and delicate eyes.
And they lured Yap into the toilette
where he thought he'd find a friend.

They beat his head till blood
washed the wet cement floor
and his blue shirt turned purple.

This dizzy day of crows circling
heating to a haze the old cream buildings,
lonely on the feet-worn dust

under the tamarind tree
sat Yap, wiping the blood
from his broken teeth,

tears streaming, frantic to find words
to explain why he wanted to leave
this school and why his shirt was wet

like that. The Citreon sailed in
and stopped. The door opened, swallowed
Yap. The Citreon sailed out.

Kindred

There are thirty-three of us reveals the voice
lodged on the other end of the line, Kieran
who lives on Church Avenue in Brooklyn,
keeping count of our father's unclaimed offspring.
I knew only four before tonight—Faustin, Fara,
Melvin and Cheryl, faces seen long ago
but undimmed by memory.

Birth by birth my brother locates, catalogs our clan.
Malcolm, Brenda, Lionel, Lance. I land, he says,
somewhere in the middle of that number
between a second Cheryl who waits tables in London
and Calixte, gone to Canada to work construction.

I have roamed far from their features,
those hardback notebook nights in New Orleans,
in Santa Fe, in a one-room apartment in LA
inventing my familial mythology, inventing
with the adopted moon accompanying, raised
or rising, halved or waning toward the west
like this one; and a breeze, too, troubling
some tree's limbs—birch, ash, crabapple.

But I would have bartered the secrecy of the wind
for a sister's borrowed ear, the moonlit
pathway for a brother's hand. Rooted, now,
between the dial tone and the dark,
I nurse names until siblings gather,
bridging the absence in my mouth.
Marcus, Germaine, Josephine, Din
and all the brave ones who wanted to be born,
to be formed of matter, the substance
with which the gods clothe themselves.

CHRISTIAN CAMPBELL

Bucking Up on Evening

When the whole of the sky
is beside me, and all live things
are clearing away,

I run through the small
valleys of sand searching.

Time to time I dare
myself to race the sun
and when I think

I am in the lead,
I see my shadow ahead
pacing me step for step,

already in the blue hour,
around my shoulders
like a shawl.

Flash between wake and sleep,
sound of a proud man passing,

one turn of the body
and there it is.

How you send me
deep into forgetting—

where I am, what I want,
the name of someone I love.

Oregon Elegy
for I. H.

I once told a friend, who was going
to Oregon for Christmas with his girlfriend,

he'd be the only black person there
and, in fact, if you shuffle *Oregon*,

like a seasoned minstrel, it spells *Negro*
but with an extra *O* as if to make

a groan, nearly a shout, perhaps
a moment of fright: *O Negro in Oregon!*

He died laughing and told me
that's word-lynching, and I wondered

if we could also lynch words,
string them up, sever them,

tattoo them with bullets and knives;
if we could hold a barbecue

for language swaying with the branches,
soon picked to silence by crows—

words soaked in coal oil
then set ablaze, a carnival of words

sacrificed over rivers, from bridges,
from trees, too-ripe words dangling

from branches just beyond our reach.
Like Alonzo Tucker in 1906,

shot twice, then hanged
from the Fourth Street Bridge

by two hundred men arched into one
white arm because (we wonder,

we know) a white woman said
he raped her. I want to tell my boy

blacks weren't wanted in Oregon
at first, but what do I know, I've never

set foot on Nez Perce land where
exactly one hundred years after

Tucker, he could go west to one edge
of America because he loves

his woman enough to be
the very last Negro on Earth.

Lightskinned Id

for Neruda, for The South

It so happens my id is red.
Check the clues—my lightskinned
parts: underneath my underwear,
if you pull the skin taut; on the white
hand side and down my wrist
where the veins branch out
like green pipes; my foot-bottom
and almost my eyes up close. It used
to be my whole self, until I was
six for sure. But a brownness
took over. Started swimming
at nine, how sun and chlorine
kissed the night into my skin.
There was no turning back.

But my id is good
and redboned. Like slicing open
a pear for the surprise
of its flesh. Look hard:
there's a murmur of bronze
in my skin. I'm a peanut-butter oreo,
an apple dipped in molasses;
I'm a broad dish of crème brûlée.
O the chiaroscuro of my self.

Still not freed from Freud, I'm fried
on the outside. What a brown on me!
Since the color beneath my color
is curried. It wants to come out,
my high yellow id. Always on the verge
of beige. It wants me to Ambi my skin,
to blossom peach all over. My id has such
a need. Here it goes with its libido of gold,
clashing with the ego, my I, a browner negro,
and the superego, who's a radiant absence

of white. He thinks he's in charge.
It makes me act like I'm
better than people, my id. It wants
what it wants. It makes me lick
melted margarine and steal copper
coins from bums. Makes me
bathe in mango juice. Pour sour
milk down my ears and sign
checks in blood to prove it.
On the forms I fill in
Other and scribble *Yellow*
on the inside in red ink.
I suck the nectar beneath my skin.

My id's pretty niggerish
(for a mulatto). My id is everyone's
Indian uncle. It's taking me
to Hollywood on an undersong
of cream. My id is colourstruck
with itself. My id is El DeBarge.
My id; its job is to keep it light.
How my id misses the eighties.

If only this amber
at heart were enough.

I have to praise it. I have to lull it
with new roses. Run my fingers
along this sallow river
of desire. Stuck in the plantation
kitchen, black ants dying
in an orgy of honey.

JACQUES PRÉVERT

Barbara

You remember Barbara
It rained without ceasing on Brest that day
You came smiling
Flushed enraptured streaming
With rain
You remember Barbara
It rained without ceasing on Brest that day
I crossed Rue de Siam
I saw you smiling
And I was smiling
You remember
I did not know you
And you did not know me
Remember
Remember that day
Don't forget
A man took cover under a porch
And shouted your name
Barbara
And you ran to him in the rain
Drenched ravished blushing
You threw yourself into his arms
Don't forget that
Don't mind if I call you darling
I say that to everyone I love
Even if I've seen them only once
I say that to all lovers
Even if I don't know them
Remember Barbara
Remember
That wise and happy rain
On your happy face
On that happy city
Rain on the sea
On the arsenal

On the boat bound for Ushant
Oh Barbara
War is such bullshit
Now what's happened to you
Under this iron rain
Of fire steel blood
And whoever held you in his arms
Lovingly
Is he alive or dead or disappeared
Oh Barbara
It rains without ceasing on Brest
As it rained before
But this is not the same
Everything's in ruins
It is a terrible rain of mourning and despair
No longer a storm
Of iron steel and blood
Simply clouds
That die like dogs
Dogs that disappear
Under water in Brest
And rot washed far away
Far away from Brest
Where nothing at all remains.

Adapted from the French by B. H. Boston

TAMARA J. MADISON

Luck of This Irish

By way of Ross Baker
who "bought" Melindy, took her,
(in the biblical sense)
begat Ione who
begat Carlton Dulaney who
begat MariOla who
begat me,
I-rich, I am.
Nothing ado about Shamrock Soup,
dandelion dreams, though I have eaten dandelion greens,
worn their weedy blossoms in my hair
and corned beef and cabbage, potatoes white and yammed
were staples in our homes.
Kontomble know my name, but
I have never seen a leprechaun.
And who is Patrick anyway?

BILLY HUGHES

Erin (23/27)

This is what comes before love,
nudes painted by Bonnard –
one, at the fireplace,
one, in the bath,
one, face down in an unmade bed,
one, in black stockings,
one, picking through spilled
iron filings from a child's board-game,
Erin, you yourself are the fifth.

A list of what is missing,
this is what comes before love:
negatives wrapped in glassine,
a book of matches,
egrets in wet sand,
penciled hatch marks.
These will serve as points of entry:
Erin, you yourself must be the fifth.

This is what comes before love.
Once, paint the cold-water tap red,
once, keep dress shirts in empty soda bottles,
once, shred a napkin while you wait,
once, smear water colors with a brush,
Erin, you yourself must be the fifth.

If you write about what comes
before love, apologize for five things.
One, suspending belief,
one, serving a higher purpose by telling lies,
one, using "it's a simple thing
to know" when it's not,
one, biographical fallacy,
Erin, you yourself are the fifth.

If you wish to survive this
(what comes before love) –
once, pull a nail,
once, stare into the sun,
once, chip a tooth,
once, glue popsicle sticks,
but this may not be enough,
Erin, you yourself must be the fifth.

C.G. HANZLICEK

My Mother's Memory

We're sitting on the porch at Sterling House
(Personalized Assisted Living),
And a song sparrow in the cherry tree
Bursts into his name.
"He seems happy," she says.
"Seems is the right word,"
I say. "He's hard at work,
Building a wall with his voice."
As if verification is his game,
He chases two interlopers away,
And she tells me for the third time in an hour
About a fight she had with her sister.
"That happened 25 years ago;
You've got to let go of it."
She looks at me like I'm a registered member
Of the Know Nothing Party.
"No, no. It was just a couple of months ago."
What can I say but nothing?
We're summoned to the dining room,
And she takes a sip of coffee,
Then leans toward me and almost whispers,
"Just in case I have to introduce you to someone,
What last name do you use?"
I'm flummoxed for a moment, but then I say,
"Hanzlicek."
We live on separate planets now,
And she mulls and mulls,
Wanting to join me in my world,
Where sometimes I'm a son, sometimes not,
At the will of whatever wind.
Finally her face brightens, and she says,
"Oh, that's right.
You're mine."

My Mother's Passing

It was she who taught me early
To love birds and flowers.
We had the first bird feeder on the block:
A 4 x 4 x 2 foot wooden box,
Upside down close to the window,
Spread with sunflower seeds
For her favorites, cardinals
And bouncing chickadees.
Later there were mesh bags of suet
Dangling from maple branches
For downy woodpeckers,
And, just once, a giant pileated.
For long days in autumn,
In blue jeans and red bandana,
She spaded up bulbs and rhizomes
For dormancy in the basement's dark.
After the thaw, they were nested in loam,
And then weeks later, a jubilation,
Sudden ranks of tulips,
Riots of bearded iris;
She held the huge iris heads
Cupped in her hands like a child's face,
And her smile was itself a bloom.
How is it I never thanked her
For passing me the key
To a world outside myself?
Sixty years later,
The phone rang at 1:30.
Deep in Lunesta sleep,
It took me many rings
To reassemble myself and find the talk button.
She was in the ICU and fading fast;
I was in the air all day to cross six states.
When I entered her room,
She asked me to put one right there

And pointed to her cheek.
The nurse told me to wash my hands and mouth:
She was toxic,
Her colon necrotic,
Her belly filled with gangrene.
They stepped-up the morphine and Ativan,
I think she no longer knew me,
But she kept mumbling
That she had a hair appointment on Friday.
At 91, appearances still mattered.
Then came the end of understanding,
Her arms flailing, hands falling
To her face, her forehead,
Heart rate racing, then calming.
The next day I had her moved to the hospice;
All of the tubes came out,
There were no monitors beeping,
There was quiet except for her murmurs,
The world outside her body
Imploded to nothing,
Her mouth became an O
From steady pain and hard drawn breaths,
Her cheeks caved in;
She borrowed the face of another
For her dying.

DERICK BURLESON

from Melt

Her nipples spoke to me only to me
said come here and suck come here
and be whole again as you were
then trailing clouds of glory trailing
clouds before language took its hold.
Her nipples spoke to me only me
they spoke to everyone and their
voices were husky and more red
dark now the daughter had fed
there. I came and sucked too and two
lines ran straight to her center
where the story began one morning
when the sun honed new edges
on everything outside honed clarity.
I sucked and they spoke to me only
to me daughter full and sleeping
they spoke to everyone and the story
they told was long and sad and sweet.

★ ★ ★

The people came together at the farm
and there was salad from the farm
and carrots arugula goat cheese bread
wine the people walked under rain
through the pasture past the poppies
and chicken coop past the broccoli
and greenhouses bursting in rain
and cucumbers past the compost
and potatoes leeks garlic peas sweet
alyssum and borage in azure bloom
in the salad the farm feeds the people
who live here and twenty-nine other
families of people. Past red cabbage
the heifer grazing beneath mountains

invisible in cloud mist rain vanishing
now though so dramatic when you can
see them above the pasture through
the gate to the yurt where they went
to eat and drink and listen to poetry.
The children played and listened
and spoke fell and were hurt crying
for their fathers who kissed the hurts
and took them outside to the pasture.
Their mothers listened to poetry
were moved by its power to transform
wordsound to music to feeling they
felt deep in their bodies the women
who planted these plants. Yes they.

★ ★ ★

My breath rose white into blue
snow and the only sound other
than my breathing was the snow.
No. The birch creaked in breeze
and the snow slanted. And the snow
struck my skull with the sound
of twigs clicking in breeze.
That was all. No. A voice rose up
not my voice not the birches'
nor the snow not the voice
of blue shadow and I heard
it not the words there were
no words and the voice was
not my voice not silence nor birch.

SHADAB ZEEST HASHMI

The Stonemason's Son Contemplates Death

Because my heart
became a kiln
I wished to die

The inscription on the tiles
made a prayer in butterfly script
crowning your well

May the water refresh your soul

The clanging of keys became loud
A soldier stood behind me pissing in the well

Someone sang in the distance
Couldn't tell if she was a Jew
Christian or Muslim

It was a devotional song

ANN ASPELL

The Poet at Seven

examines her conscience:

1. She swallows the watery ends of the drinks
       after her parents have left for their dinner;

2. loves in secret the neighbor boy Mike;
       a. searches the pockets of his coat hoping to find a declaration
       b. multiple times;

3. leaves notes in the dark for the invisible ones demanding proof.

None of these things have been forbidden her,
but she knows, to protect them
                                        she will lie.

Tiziano Fratus

Responsibility

you're more silent than usual today
I can't even manage to offend you

the news is showing hamas militants entering the al fatah headquarters
the dark heads with the green scarves occupy gaza
I know you're worried
you're a good soldier and you'll do whatever needs to be done
the government knows this and for years they have depended on it
so it's abstinence today? I ask peeved
I turn off the tv but you put up some resistance when I undo your trousers

Translated from the Italian by Gail McDowell

From *The Molossus* (*MOUTH II* | *old documents*)
Image II

the turin of seventy-eight with the desks the banners classrooms filled
street theater and the illusion that a laborer could discuss
philosophy with a student
the bombing in piazza fontana the smoke the metal the symbols sewn on the
waving shirts in the voices and in the patterns
the fight for rights that seemed to justify any action
motivated by a moral principal to a certain degree shared
one doesn't kill a commissioner a journalist a police officer without
first consulting a friend
death is born from the vocabulary from the syntax from the breath
a war fought in the columns of daily papers but above all
in the factory dumps in the residences and in the offices of the mayor
pushing the truth from one single point closer to the paradise of robespierre's
        paris
for years enemies and for years families cleansed of the guilt
of being victims
today the offices are bursting with retired military
in the library in the registry in the university
they silently resist with their hope chest of memories of rusted
chisels of relics even if objects of an underground market
to us watching from the apex of a future turned imperfect
lies the hard realization that the past cannot return even if
tattooed on skin

Translated from the Italian by Francesco Levato

Polka

Dancing the polka is like walking
       on a ship's deck
during a storm, water flying into the air,
       sliding in sheets across the gray
wood. Each time the ship
       tilts, you take two hop-like
steps in one direction, and
       then, determined to
keep walking, keep your balance,
       you, with the next wave, hop-skip
another direction. The ocean spray
       blinds you. It ruins your best clothes.
There is someone in your arms, and this is what
       makes it a polka, although she or he
does not look into your eyes, and you
       do not look, either, at your partner,
which would be the waltz, or the tango, which
       you will not dance this side of Heaven,
although to dance the polka is definitely
       to think of death, your partner's shoulder
surprisingly small in your hand. With
       your other hand, you hold aloft
your partner's hand and, arms outstretched,
       the two of you are almost like
the prow of a great ship, those carved,
       streaming-haired, fierce-faced
angels that stare out to sea,
       except the image of that prow, any prow,
too dramatic for you. Drama embarrasses
       anyone who has learned the polka
from grandparents, whose grandparents
       learned it from their grandparents, who left
Petrovavest for Bratislava, Bratislava
       for Prague, for ships that took six days
and five nights to cross the ocean.

They never spoke of the crossing,
not even to each other. Likely, they knew
    that *polka* is from the Czech for "half-step,"
pulka a rapid shift from one foot to the other,
    the basic step of the polka: a starting
and, immediately, a hesitation
    before plunging into the moment
with this person who is in your arms.
    You might as well call the dance
Walking the Ship Deck During a Storm
    that Partly—Holy Mother, Forgive Me—
I Did Not Want to Survive, this dance
    that could more succinctly be known as
Long Marriage, although you
    who were raised on the polka would never
say this, speak of this, this
    rush and near-collapse, over
and over again, this
    two hop-steps this way, two hop-steps that.
God. You're beautiful when your hair is wet.

KARY WAYSON

PORTFOLIO

American Husband

O, Empty-of-Hours, the doctor's a clock. His hand
is a serrated knife. Heavy his books, his
medical meanings,

his pharmacological eyes.

Father Infallible, Doctor Indelible, Goat
you've got, my goad — You, and your mal-
practice suits, your wingtips and tuxedoes.

Doctor Parenthesis, Father
for emphasis, Stepmothers Must
and Because: Doctor dismiss
my dire diagnosis — my god's

a blot — of implausible pause.

Dear Doctor, Dear Proctor, ad-
Minister my test (Your office assigns
your affections.) Dear Doctor, Dear

Forceps, my Father, forget this —
I'll ration your attention.

I'll wait
and I'll wait. I'll compile
and I'll plate
an unending compendium of
juvenile complaints:

American make me, American take me
with you when you go. *You do not do, you do not do* —
Faster, Bastard! American
Fetch! — *you do not do* — you don't.

American Father, My General Boss
I am your lather – and you
are my loss. Professor my lecture, mother
my tongue – I live
with a desk where nothing gets done.
Inhibit my habits and dress me in gauze – my god's
a clot. Of unsolvable cause.

American Husband, American Head, nobody
stopped me, nobody said *Surgeons*
must be very careful / When they take the knife!

Echolocution

I am at home. I am
interviewing the telephone. She says hello

when I say hello: Hello.
The front doorknob fits against a gauge in the wall.

I cough and stop and scratch and stop and listen –
when I listen for long enough I'm lost.

Voices of men recite the radio news. Time
is a travel advertisement.

I hang on to the telephone like a handle.
Fastened to the wood wall of a boat.

She says what I say while I say it.
When I listen for long enough I'm lost.

The light's got rice in it, like after a wedding:
me in my ambulance, you in yours.

More of the Same

But even with my mouth on your thigh
I want my mouth on your thigh.
At the center bite of bread I want the whole loaf
toasted, and an orange. On a sunny day
I want more sun, more skin for the weather.
I'm in Seattle wishing for Seattle,
for this walk along the water, for her hand while I hold it:
I want to tie my wrist to a red balloon.
I'm counting my tips.
I'm counting the tips I could have made.
I want the television on, the television off.
In the ocean, I want to float an inch above it
and when my father finally held me
like a stripe of seaweed over his wet arm,
I was kicking to get away, wishing he'd hold me
like he held me while I was kicking away. Listen to me.
I want to leave when I'm walking out the door.

Federico & Garcia

Green you know I want you Green I want you
Green I want you blue no Green
I want your Green to mean
high mass of trees and trick bamboo.
Good I want your gas. Night
I want your nurse.
Now I know the consequence: my half-slip
grass skirt. Thistle
give me a stick, muscle my bungalow
Green I want you black and green – my ration of pistachios.
Boast I want your best. I'm boats.
I want the shore – Green Jack
and Jill attack
and kill
the Emperor of Ecuador.
Jade-Green grenade, my luck's
been laid: most Irish
of all bridesmaids. Green butter
in the batter, Green plate
upon the platter, Green song I'll sing
your serenade.
Green I'll dot your double-cross, your eyes
are upside down. Your nation is a face I've seen
the water wants to rise around.
O Green you know I love you Green
by Green I mean engrave me.
What color is that? The color of wax –
my littlest light Green craving.
But Green I've got your filagree: your wife was my idea
my yellow buffet, *my* Green array –
Green, I want Garcia!
But answer me as anyone – sell me the telephone.
Hire me.
Fire me.
Tomorrow I will it alone.

Green pear I'll do your dare, I'll wear
your chandelier. Green guillotine, sweet
nicotine, my mirror,
hang me here.

The Mean Time

After San Francisco, after getting back
from going to San Francisco,
I wash one glass while I unpack
and collect the half-eaten apples
of the afternoon I left
all afternoon. All through each room
of the intolerable tract house of the afternoon:
the interim of the airplane,
the interrogation of the seat strap, then out
into the bright humiliation of high noon.
I'm back to the embarrassment of the bathroom
where the one window watches
while I tweeze tiny feathers
from the breast of the bath mat between
twelve and two. I can feel my feet
because I can feel my feet on fire.
Burnt to the slack asphalt
of the black tarmac
staunching the center of the living room.
I am burning because I've been built to burn
and I have been burning
because I've been left to burn
and I am still burning,
built like a boat tied to a float
and I am forbidden to turn.

DAVID WOJAHN

For Tomas Tranströmer

Down Commercial to Land's End, your gait slow,
    rooftop shimmer & the wheeling gulls,
        gable & widow's walk—you're taking it in,

with the almost feral gaze of those
    who store the world under pressure, carbon diamonding.
        The Foc'sle & The Eye of Horus, Town Hall

& the March light intractable, hammered tin
    against the Bay. Beside me half my life ago,
        you amble. My fabulously silly poems had

everything to learn & and you'd just made them
    half as long. & now by the town pier we come to it,
        a crowd of half a dozen, circling the dolphin

beached beside an upturned skiff, some waiters
    from the Mayflower dipping checkered
        tablecloths in seawater & laving them

against the putty-colored flanks. Mostly we are silent;
    mostly we stare. Shallow rise & fall of the wet
        ginghamed skin. Someone from the Coast Guard

will be coming too late. Half a life ago.
    & always the future setting forth, beyond where my pen
        can summon this back, beyond where Tomas

can inch his stroke-straightened frame to a bench
    & flex his one good hand above the keyboard ivory, region
        where the faces are shadow, masked & opaque,

crouching to check the drips & monitors, the bed
    repositioned, where the soul floats clumsy
        as a child's balloon to land

on the banks of a place that is not Styx or Lethe,
    but a tourist town off-season. & the soul
        may linger there at last or always. The wind

off Long Point is rising. Tomas bends down,
    his hand stroking beak & forehead, dorsal fin & spine.
        He's taken off his gloves, the leather jacket,

talking low, in Swedish, almost a whisper, his eye
    against the great black pool of eye, twin gazes affixed,
        the way, when two mirrors are set against each other

they fuse to a single burnished infinity.

ROMANIAN POETRY

FEATURE

Introduction

In Romania, it's something of a cliché to say "every Romanian was born a poet," a saying that traces back to the 19th Century poet Vasile Alecsandri. Alecscandri was born into a Romania far different from today's—in fact, he grew up in the northern region of Moldavia when it wasn't technically Romania at all, but still fighting to emerge from the shadow of Imperial Russia. This informed his eclectic life as writer, folklorist, revolutionary, and finally politician in an uncertain world; in short, he was a typical Romanian poet.

This past winter marked twenty years since the revolution of 1989, and in that time certainly much has changed for Romania and the Romanian poet. Dictatorship and censorship are gone, and along with them well-funded state publishing houses that issued massive press runs of poetry books for a hungry readership. Born poets or not, it's abundantly clear that in 2010, fewer Romanians are reading the stuff. Running websites and bedroom presses on shoestring budgets, contemporary Romanian poets work largely in obscurity and often get dismissed as a marginal, even irrelevant group. Of course, nothing could be further from the truth. A closer look reveals there are more poets than ever in Romania, and good ones—an increasingly diverse and dynamic group doing elegant justice to the country's storied literary tradition.

As many poets as there are, there are nearly as many literary categories to put them in—a compulsion that's distinctly (if not at all uniquely) Romanian. The fascination with categories and manifestos reads as a natural response to the tumult and discord that's characterized the last century of life in Romania. After the 1989 revolution, this trend has only intensified as many poets made a point of signaling a break from the past and became increasingly fixated on "re-inventing" poetry, or at least the language of poetry. These efforts do much to expose the growing pains that poets, and in fact all Romanians, experienced (and continue to experience) while transitioning to a post communist world, though they too often ignore one simple truth: Romanian poets have been re-inventing poetry for as long as they've been writing it. The best Romanian poets have always proved adept at defying categorization while embracing the full complexity of their rich cultural history. Thus one could read Nichita Danilov as a modern surrealist and O. Nimigean as a post-modern one, but really, who cares? Both poets proudly bear the influence of the Surrealist movement (a movement with distinctive, if largely unrecognized, Romanian roots), but more notably, each poet has used that influence to craft a voice that's firmly rooted in tradition and is emphatically new.

The same holds true for Marin Sorescu or Ana Blandiana who, writing under the watchful eye of Communist censorship, obfuscated political satire through allegory and metaphor. These practices have continued, as exhibited by contemporary poets like Radu Vancu and Chris Tanasescu, who practice a similar sleight of hand with a different set of strategies. While Tanasescu wryly inverts the fable, Vancu adeptly refashions Marxist doctrine and confessional forms. In each of these cases, the poet embraces the baggage of the past, using it to liberate rather than encumber their poetry. Rather than seeking to discard or disconnect the past, they make it a tool to re-invent and re-imagine.

And that spirit unifies the poets here, a group of writers from various generations working in various modes who all combine a strong grounding in tradition with the desire to innovate and the will to persevere. Much has changed since Alecscandri's time, but then again, there's so much that never changes. As such, Romania remains a nation of poets, and this section features some of their best work.

—Martin Woodside

MARIN SORESCU

Shakespeare

Shakespeare created the world in seven days.

On the first day he made the heavens, the mountains, and the abyss of the
        soul.
On the second day he made rivers, seas, oceans
and all the other feelings –
giving them to Hamlet, Julius Caesar, Mark Anthony,
Cleopatra and Ophelia,
Othello and the rest,
to master them, and their descendants
for ever more.
On the third day he brought the people together
and taught them about taste
the taste of happiness, of love, of despair
the taste of jealousy, of glory, and still more tastes
until they went through them all.

Then some latecomers arrived.
The creator patted them sadly on the head
explaining the remaining roles were for
literary critics
to challenge his good works.
The fourth and fifth days he kept clear for laughs
clearing way for clowns
turning somersaults,
and leaving the kings, emperors,
and other poor wretches to their fun.
The sixth day he reserved for administrative tasks:
he let loose a tempest
and taught King Lear
to wear a crown of straw.

Some spare parts remained from the world's creation
And so he made Richard III.
On the seventh day he looked about for something to do.

Theatre directors had plastered the land with posters
And Shakespeare decided after all his hard work
he deserved to see a show.

But first, tired down to the bone,
he went off to die a little.

Translated from the Romanian by Martin Woodside

Nichita Stănescu

Winter Ritual

Always a cupola,
another one always.
Taking on a halo like a saint,
or only a rainbow.
Your straight body, my straight body
as during a wedding.
A wise priest made of air
is facing us with two wedding bands.
You lift your left hand, I lift my left arm:
our smiles mirror each other.
Your friends and my friends are crying
syllabic tears like Christmas carols.
They take pictures as we kiss.
Lightning. Darkness. Lightning. Darkness.
I lower one knee and fall on my arms.
I kiss your ankle with sadness.
I take your shoulder, you take my waist,
and majestically we enter the winter.
Your friends and my friends step aside.
A ton of snow overturns on us.
We die freezing. And once again, only the locks of hair
adorn our skeletons in spring.

Translated from the Romanian by Mark Irwin and Mariana Carpinisan

lesson on the circle

On the sand you draw a circle

which you divide in two,

with the same stick of almond you divide that in two.

Then you fall on your knees,

and then you fall on your arms.

And after that you strike your forehead on the sand

and ask the circle to forgive you.

So much.

Translated from the Romanian by Mark Irwin and Mariana Carpinisan

Radu Vancu

Kapital

Fourteen beers is bad, fourteen beers plus a pint of vodka is better.
Clearly, Marx was right:
500 ml makes for an ideal demonstration
that, after a point,
quantity transforms quality.
The souses had Marx in their soul,

whether they know it or not.
That's why discussions in the pubs of Romania
so closely resemble those in Dostoevsky's "The Possessed,"
and for the same reason true drunkards are anti-communist—
any socialist atheist who drinks with purpose
becomes, after a certain threshold, a mystic anarchist.

When you find the guts to stop drinking, it's over.
You've reached the end, the landmark where quantity
can no longer transform quality.
You are already, in all likelihood, a perfect mystic
with the appropriate set of regrets at hand.
It's bad not to have the guts. And much better, after the first shot of vodka.

Translated from the Romanian by Martin Woodside

Summa ethilica

Once I wished with all my heart, almost religiously,
to become a committed vodka drinker.
I would have given even my soul for this.

My alcoholism reared from the most respectable cultural sources:
each glass of vodka made me think,
above all, of Thomas Aquinas:
40 percent liquid hell in iridescent light
forced me to see the meaning of
integritas, consonantia, claritas.

Then suddenly you appeared before me,
Cami, you painful teetotaler.
Your missionary ways converted me to the monotheism of hops.
Alcohol would now cap off at five percent;
I resigned myself to this ethylene ice age
because our love prefers proletarian sand in the urethra,
cultivating in its place class hatred for the aristocratic cirrhosis.
The only Marxist accent of a mystic love.

I remember more of Thomas Aquinas
having only my ever expansive belly
to seriously rival the Angelic Doctor.
But I accept this in good graces,
because I have gone far enough to desire
to be a good man, not an interesting one.
For that, now, I would surely give my soul.

Translated from the Romanian by Martin Woodside

ANA BLANDIANA

Soot

What do you think when you see
an archangel blackened with soot?
Of pollution of pollution in space, of course.
And what else?
The habits of angels
to poke their nose into everything.
And what else?
Of stoves that start
to smoke, to stop up in the spring.
And what else?
Oh, if I really think hard,
it might be an archangel
who set himself on fire
forgetting that
he could not burn.

Translated from the Romanian by Martin Woodside

Do you remember the beach?

Littered with bitter pieces of glass
That beach
Where we couldn't walk barefoot?
The way you would stare at the sea
And say you were listening to me?
Do you remember
Hysterical seagulls
Roiled in the ringing
Of unseen church bells,
Behind us somewhere,
Churches that keep fish
As patron saints,
And how you moved quickly
Towards the surf, yelling
Back that you needed
Distance to be able to see me?
The snow
Blown out
Tangled with birds
In the water,
I would look on
With a kind of joyful despair
As your feet marked the sea
And the sea,
Where I waited,
Would close like an eyelid.

Translated from the Romanian by Martin Woodside

CONSTANTIN ACOSMEI

Cardiac Weekend

(there's no devil in me – until Monday.
I stand by the counter where
I get my change close my hand
into a tight fist and give way

a woman slaps a child
sucking on his thumb –
until the crowded tram arrives and I
stick my shoulder in her ribs)

Translated from the Romanian by Martin Woodside and Chris Tanasescu

CHRIS TANASESCU

from How was Ion Iliescu not Assassinated?

11. Envoy

There once was a gifted girl, but a bit homely
a bit of sucker, a bit of a stutterer, called
Romania, and one day she woke up to find something
growing on her forehead, and it kept growing today
and tomorrow when the pimple became
a boil, and began to move, taking on life
becoming a little man stuck there
a beauty mark named Ilici (Iliescu), and then the old
cancer relapses, infecting
the brain. Today, tomorrow, she endured
pitiful girl—shouldn't be pitied!
But finally she finds the courage and goes
one day to see the surgeon. There,
Ilici (Iliescu): good doctor, look what's grown out of my ass!

Translated from the Romanian by Martin Woodside

O. NIMIGEAN

from Intermezzo

3.
ovidean nimigean
then lights up a smoke
to meditate
on how the nation goes.

ovidean nimigean
as I can see
is more a patriot
than he seems to be.

ovidean nimigean
weeps all over the page
feeling pity
for this golden age.

ovidean nimigean
a childish old man
fills with grief
for the Romanian.

ovidean nimigean
after jotting this down
finishes his cigarette
and shoves off to town
this the only way around?
meenie-minie-mo

Oh mosquitoes! Mosquitoes!
Blood of mine
buzzing around the dim room.

Translated from the Romanian by Martin Woodside and Chris Tanasescu

Note: the original arrangement presents numbered sections on one page with a haiku on the
bottom of the next page.

ANGELA MARINESCU

Dadaism vs. Surrealism

Put your fingers between my legs.
I can no longer stand the act of sex
which seems to me dadaist, whereas
fingers wander a precise surrealist
collection agent what I hate the most
but I need pleasure like I need air, now, when
thrust on the peak of solitude
and all my generation stays in You

like a lead soldier on duty

I don't know what else to do
but to write slow and free
like the soft rain
of spring.

Translated from the Romanian by Martin Woodside

NICHITA DANILOV

The Void

He made a hole in the sky
through which to speak with the void.
Hello there: What is evil?
Truth? Good?
After three days the answer comes:
a thin peal
of laughter followed by short sniggers.
Again: What is wisdom?
Love? The soul?
After three days the answer comes:
a thin billy-goat bleat
accompanied by a horse
cackling, an ox squealing
a dog croaking, and so on.

…he asks: Who are You?
After three days the answer comes:
a billy-goat bleating
followed by a horse cackling,
a dog croaking, a pig squealing,
an ox meowing, and so on.

Translated from the Romanian by Martin Woodside

FRED MORAMARCO

Elegy for Kenneth Koch
d. July 6, 2002

It seems too crazy, like one of your mad, funny poems,
that you're not with us any more, not here to point out
the *thisness* of things, like mountains, circuses, and fresh air.
You were always the court jester of poets,
toppling pretension from its granite and marble heights.
"Look," you would say, about this or that,
"how absolutely strange, marvelous, and ordinary it is,
like everything else you will meet on your daily rounds."
You noticed the blueness of blue, the curvature of the round,
the still beats of silence within seconds.
One of my favorites of your lines is
"To learn of cunnilingus at fifty
Argues a wasted life." This from your poem,
"Some General Instructions," which pings in my head even today.
Ah, Kenneth, the obit said it was leukemia and you were 77.
Hard to imagine either. You, a frail old man, eaten by blood cells.
I rarely saw you when you weren't laughing, darting here and there.
I remember we wrote a sestina in your class,
each student writing a line as the poem went around the room.
I wrote the last line of that poem, and remember it forty years later
because you thought it was the perfect ending:
"Who would have guessed at such a meaning for summer?"
And I say that again, for this summer, when you're no longer here:
Who would have guessed at such a meaning for summer?

Midas

I dug the hole. Not you, wife. Not the barber.
It was I, hauled myself wretched to a meadow
damp and purple with morning, scored with seed.
I dug the hole, purged myself of what
lay sharp and heavy, a stone in my chest, mouthed
it to the dark earth, buried it in mud.
No one told me seeds bear ears, mouths,
feet, seek a purpose beyond groping
for sun. Necessity prescribes that now,
as my wife bends nearer to our monstrous
roses, to their thousand fulsome heads,
I must pretend—that they aren't whispering
what I can't admit: Wife, I tell you
I have ass's ears. Reeds slander. Grass speaks.

DANIELLE CHAPMAN

Rituxan Spring

Known as a "chimeric antibody," Rituxan is a drug made of tissues from two different species.

As derricks draw ink
from parched plains
we've struck

Time, silky and game
as a stick streaming
snake roe.

This must be a dream—

spring singing slime
through snail stones,

membranous hollows,
trembling tadpoles'
fatigue greens,

truffle caps fretted
as girdles of whale-bone,

musk like the civet's
resurrected in cologne.

Oh love, let me kiss
the rodent
who died for this.

KATE BERNHEIMER

My Other Self

I don't feel like an adult yet. My other self—inside of me, like a cage. My other self—more in my dreams. A child-girl. Nightmares. Buttons and flies. I feel my day more in my dreams. It is a wilder field of vision. I don't feel like an adult yet. I'm sorry. Art is my refuge, my golden cage. Hard to destroy—like a tree. These other girls I feel inside of me. I don't understand the question, I'm sorry. I feel fine in my life. I don't feel like an adult yet. My mother, she taught me to fight. To live with this world. My other self—inside of me—a child-girl. Framed. I feel these girls. I always dreamed that I would live in this world, I'm sorry. I have some toys and dolls, in real life. Girls and dolls. I feel my day is more real in my dreams. I have fallen in love—I always felt the wish. Dark and lovely. The perfect dimension. Pink. Like a tree. Loving is cruelty. That is a dream. No, I don't feel like an adult yet—it is like a cage. More in my dreams than in my days. Of course vanity is ancient. A giraffe. Cruelty and beauty are inside of me. Naturally. I don't understand the question, sorry. I don't feel like an adult yet—surrounded. The ones I love. Green. Spiders, a girl. Underwater. In the real world? Roots—but floating. I don't understand the question. I don't feel like an adult yet—more like a severed limb—or doll. I don't understand the question, I'm sorry. My refuge, my golden cage. Yes, the perfect dimension. Morning sunlight. Loneliness. Dolls. I've always been very shy, I'm sorry. My father worked in wood. I always dreamed I would be real. That horse, that rider. Mice are delicate too. Nostalgic—like a dream-child. I do have some dolls, I'm sorry. The vanity. These girls, my other self. Riding, the girls inside of me. Like a cage. I don't feel like an adult yet. I don't understand the question. Naturally, I'm sorry. I feel fine, hard to destroy. I feel fine.

MALENA MÖRLING

PORTFOLIO

From *Ocean Avenue*
Visiting

In the shape of a human body
I am visiting the earth;
the trees visit
in the shapes of trees.
Standing between the onions
and the dandelions
near the ailanthus and the bus stop,
I don't live more thoroughly
inside the mucilage of my own skull
than outside of it
and not more behind my eyes
than in what I can see with them.
I inhale whatever air
the grates breathe in the street.
My arms and legs still work,
I can run if I have to
or sit motionless purposefully
until I am here and I am not here
the way death is present
in things that are alive
like salsa music
and the shrill laughter of the bride
as she leaves the wedding
or the bald child playing jacks
outside the wigshop.

The Couple

When Emil fell away inside himself,
Greta put her forehead to his
and shouted: "Vi träfas hos Gud."
What she said was untranslatable.
She could have meant they would meet somewhere
or in the earth
where humans decay faster than dolls,
where the happiness of trees begins.

For the Woman with the Radio

Everywhere we are either moving away from
    or toward one another,
in cars, on buses or bicycles.

        We are either moving
or not moving. But yesterday in one
    of the interminable hallways of the hospital

I suddenly heard Bach
        and when I looked up
the music was arcing

    about the paralyzed, middle-aged body
of a woman rolling face first toward me
        on a bed with wheels.

The soprano was endlessly falling
    into the well
of her voice and we were on the earth

        and this was this life
when we would meet
    and depart there in the hall

where the hectic dust particles were mixing
        in the sunlight
in the air, between the green tiles on the walls.

Standing on the Earth Among the Cows

For Elena

When I was driving through Wyoming
past fields of just-overturned earth
black in the noon sun
and past thousands of cows
totally at home in the open,
I stopped the car to stop moving
and got out to stand among them
and I said nothing in English or Swedish.
Now I want to be whoever I was at that moment
when I discovered my own breathing
among the cows' breathing in the field
and studied their satin bellies
and udders slowly filling with milk.
I was not separate from anything living, I was
equally there and there was nothing to wait for.

An Entrance
For Max

If you want to give thanks
but this time not to the labyrinth
of cause and effect—
Give thanks to the palm sweetness of a day
when it's as if everywhere you turn
there is an entrance—
when it's as if even the air is a door—

And your child is a door
afloat on invisible hinges.
"The world is a house," he says,
over lunch as if to give you a clue—
And before the words dissolve
Above his plate of eggs and rice
you suddenly see how we are in it—
How everywhere the air
is holding his hands with the air—
How everyone is connected
to everyone else by breathing.

MARK McMORRIS

from Suite for an Irish Girl
Alders Grow Everywhere in Ireland

An Irish girl makes every man a hero
they're not easy to get, and you want to
be equal to the poetry in her blood

the bare arms under covers, the breathing
you imagine is the wind in an alder
whispering a message for your insomnia

eyes like the leaves of an alder, touched
with droplets from the rain that always
falls in poems like this one, to a girl

I imagine hiding in the cells
of prayer and the veins of nationalists
a girl to straddle the brute sunlight

a girl meant to stroll beside a river
in autumn weather, when dark falls secretly
across the fields and the farmhouses.

Free Fall in Negative Curvature

If I could write a poem as well as that poet
why then I would write a poem for you
the Irish girl I saw in a cabin beside the sea

What would I say in this poem that the mind
takes on the shape of certain indelible bodies
negative curvature in gravity's free-fall

birdless flutter or hollow arms like pipes
I would talk about my obsession with your neck
the scarf you wore, or the drop of sweat

the only girl of whom I can say, tactfully,
she causes me to breathe the feelings of delirium
without any medical symptoms to report

As you can see, I have nothing to say about her
this girl I call my own Beatrice my only Lara
and she's neither mine, nor is she a girl

but a name and a scent lingering about her neck
which beckons, how her hair falls, I confess
her face gives me a hollow the Greeks call πόθος.

There's something manly about going weak-kneed for an Irish girl
having the blood bent inside the ribcage
an empty flow through the abdomen and, yes, the—

cut that, the body wanders to her melody
falters, as in, my limbs falter in her company
O roses in her glance, at random intervals.

Robin Blaser, 1925–2009

You weren't wanted here anyhow &
You haven't been missed for years
No one is quite sure what you've been up to
Up there
Canada
You must have been too busy to call & all
No one here has written for months now
You'll never understand us why we can't
See the trees
For the forest.

Listen

Samples: JT Stewart

Listen to the waves
Listen to the wind in full sails
To paddles against the sea
Listen to disbelief the distance
You put before me
Listen to the breakers
The hard times ahead
"Our own emotions will scare
Us shitless" listen
To that.

WILLIAM HEYEN

PORTFOLIO

The Steadying

Where we are & at what speed: I know
we're spinning 14 miles a minute around the axis
of the earth; 1080 miles a minute in orbit
around our sun, 700 miles a second
straight out toward the constellation Virgo,
& now Custer is charging maybe a half-
mile a minute into an Indian village; but
from many eye-witnesses we know
Crazy Horse dismounted to fire his gun.
He steadied himself, & did not waste ammo.

Where we are, & what speed: I saw
on display at Ford's Theatre in Washington D.C.,
the black boots & tophat Lincoln wore that night;
at Auschwitz, a pile of thousands of eyeglasses also
behind glass to slow their disintegration;
in a Toronto museum, ancient mummies, ditto;
in Waikiki, some glittering dud once worn by Elvis; but
from many eye-witnesses we know
Crazy Horse dismounted to fire his gun.
He steadied himself, & did not waste ammo.

Where we are, & what speed: I remember,
in Montana, a tumbleweed striking the back of my knees;
when I was a boy, a flock of blackbirds & starlings
beating past Nesconset for the whole morning;
at Westminster Abbey, in some corner, a poet's rose
for just a second, drinking a steak of snow;
cattlecars of redwoods vowelling to Gotham in my dream; but
from many eyewitnesses we know
Crazy Horse dismounted to fire his gun.
He steadied himself, & did not waste ammo.

Trance

He wanted nothing, except that, but what was it,
but no matter. When he fingered hailstones onto his chest,
his nipples filled & tightened. The Oglala language
sputtered a few last syllables behind his eyes,
& then that, but what was it, but no matter....

Part of his horse as he rode, part of the air, invisible....

Later, he remembered the riding toward, the arrival
wherein challenge-cries & death rattles
& the snorting of horses all threaded the shawl
of the Great Mystery of the single word of being, & he
wanted nothing, except that, but what of that other

part of it, the falling out of it? Because of that,

he would not celebrate with the others, would not
talk around the fire, describe, explain, boast,
but took himself away. Alone under the sky
of yellow wolf-howl & scents of green smoke,
this Crazy Horse, the Strange One, slept himself awake.

Fugue for *Kristallnacht*

Around the corner where I lived a beautiful synagogue was burning.
Around the corner where I lived. Around the corner.
A beautiful synagogue. Was burning. Where I lived.
Around the corner where I lived a beautiful synagogue was burning....

My father came home in the evening I didn't recognize him.
He didn't want to talk and didn't talk what happened to him.
Was burning. He didn't want to talk and didn't talk.
What happened to him. A beautiful synagogue where I lived.
He didn't want to talk and didn't talk what happened to him....

Will they kill me is not so easy to forget either.
I didn't recognize him. Came home in the evening.
Around the corner where I lived will they kill me. Was burning.
He didn't want to talk. What happened to him.
Will they kill me is not so easy to forget either.
A beautiful synagogue was burning. What happened to him....

We packed the little things what we could carry.
My father said we didn't know where we are going who
will live will die. He didn't want to talk.
My father came home in the evening I didn't recognize him.
Will they kill me. Around the corner where I lived.
What we could carry. We packed. Who will live
will die. Around the corner a beautiful synagogue....

I didn't recognize him. My father. What happened to him.
Was burning. Will they kill me is not so easy.
The little things what we could carry. Was burning.
Around the corner where I lived a beautiful synagogue was burning....

(For Angie Sus-Paul)

The Bear

Was alone, was carrying her bear with her.
Was alone, was carrying her bear with her.
Was alone, was carrying her bear with her,
bear to counsel, comfort, & protect her.

Arrived with a thousand other children
given toys to keep them quiet.
Was alone, was carrying her bear with her.
Was alone, was carrying her bear with her.

In the gas, her bear clawed free of her.
In the gas, her bear clawed free of her.
She held her bear tightly as she could,
but in the gas her bear clawed free of her.

The mind & heart of her bear are wool.
The mind & heart of her bear are wool.
Its eyes black & shiny as tiny mirrors,
her bear is stuffed with wool.

Was alone, was carrying her bear with her,
its eyes black & shiny as tiny mirrors,
its heart wool, its mind wool.
Was along, was carrying her bear with her.

Jarosław Mikołajewski

My Wife's Spine

And when my wife's pregnant
her spine is a bough
breaking under the weight of apples

humble all the way down to earth
from lack of resistance

On nights of keeping watch
her spine is a scarf
tightened around a slender neck

On nights of animal love
it is the zipper in a suitcase
that won't close, even under a knee

On nights of human love
it is the steel rope
rustling in the wind, at the highest voltage

On the noon walk
my wife's spine is the flag
carried by the pilgrims' guide in a crowded church

In the evening, reduced by the march,
her spine is a bunch of frightened kids
who broke the kindergarten's piano
it is the keyboard
of the broken piano

When she takes a shower
her spine is a viper
lazing watchfully on a sizzling road

Under the midnight comforter
my wife's spine is like a splinter burning in the oven
from which I'll pull out warm bread at dawn

Translated from the Polish by Piotr Florczyk

PAUL CELAN

Memory of France

Recall with me: the sky of Paris, the giant autumn crocus...
We went shopping for hearts from the flower girls:
they were blue and they opened up in the water.
It began to rain in our living room,
and our neighbor came in, Monsieur Le Songe, a haggard little man.
We played cards, I lost the irises of my eyes;
you lent me your hair, I lost it, he struck us down.
He left through the door, the rain followed him.
We were dead and were able to breathe.

Translated from the German by Monika Zobel

José Saramago

Technique

Of the simplest words, the most common,
The ones to bring home and to trade,
When converting to the language of another land:
It's enough that the eyes of the poet, fierce
With the sunlight, clarify them.

Translated from the Portuguese by Margo Berdeshevsky

If I have no other voice...

If I have no other voice that doubles me,
This silence of echoes of other sounds,
It is to speak, speak again, until I flay
The hidden speech of what I believe.

It is, shattered, the said between detours
From the arrow that has poisoned itself,
Or a high sea coagulated with ships
Where the drowned arm beckons us.

It's to force a root to its base
When the rigid stone cuts off the way,
It's to hurl all that one says
Because the more a tree is a stump—the more lonely.

It will tell, its words discovered,
Tales of the habit of living,
This hour that tightens and loosens,
The not seen, the not had, the almost being.

Translated from the Portuguese by Margo Berdeshevsky

RICHARD FROST

PORTFOLIO

Judas

Lord, loyalty is one thing,

but *this*—me betray you?

And worse, for money? So you can hang

until your knees wear out and your weight chokes you

for everyone's sins? I can't do it.

I think you realize what it will do to my name.

Get John to do it, or Simon—

and don't say again I'm more intelligent.

That may be true, but this is too much to understand.

Don't look at me with your gentle eyes

and talk of your dying to prove anything.

I'm decent and practical, with too much to lose.

After To Fu (c.12th C.)

You, omniscient bean of my larder,

remonstrate with roasted birds.

Moon cake, curd of suppleness, I keep you,

serve you deep in my feverish maw.

Oh! aspic of extraordinary friendliness!

Translator of gastric disturbance,

heir of common senses, senseless

savior of girth, runt of unmurder,

quarreler with catastrophic measurements,

leveler,

wait in my long drawer,

season, lean, simplify, coagulate.

Photograph: Jews Being Forced to Scrub
the Streets of Vienna, 1938
for Max and Kyle

In the foreground five men with buckets
and brushes and what appear to be washcloths
or towels or maybe their handkerchiefs
are scrubbing the pavement.
Around them a crowd has gathered. In front
are three officers in perfectly tailored uniforms
with beautiful highly polished black boots,
and another man in a common soldier's jacket
belted at the waist, looking spiffy and proud.
Beside them is a man in a hunting jacket
with a swastika pin on his necktie.
The Jews are also well attired.
One wears a fedora and neat tweed jacket.
He is a professor or maybe a doctor and bends
carefully over his work. The man nearest us
in a cap and back-belted jacket is balancing himself
on his feet, in a semi-sitting posture,
so that he will not get his knees soaked and filthy.
The other three, in their fine clothes, are spread out
in no particular order. The purpose of all this
does not seem to be a systematic cleaning.
Most interesting, you find, is the crowd
gathered around the men washing. Of course, nearly everyone
is smiling or laughing, as if they've waited for this
a long time, and now here it is!
The Jews are doing what they should have all along,
and soon they'll pay their fares to the East
and never contaminate the city again.
But look more carefully at the crowd.
Some are not laughing or even smiling. Some
look worried. A little girl on the left
is frightened. You wonder if they've heard
that intermarriage has continued for centuries,
differentiation on racial grounds is largely fictitious,
and there must be Jewish blood in almost every

Central European family. Has anyone
told them that, or is it a secret?
Probably they don't know it.
Most likely they're simply disturbed by the commotion
and will soon recover, even decide to join in,
or at least tacitly accept the whole necessary business
this year and the next and the next and the next
and the next and the next and the next and the next.

The Chase

Death is a knight, a worm, an old whore,
a sallow gentleman, a clown, a doctor,
a cocked revolver, a cock, a rotten cell.
Death is what we do but don't do well.
We'd put a foot through death, our highest garden,
what we follow, love, last-minute pardon.
Death is our stripped bones, our babies, wrecks
on shoulders. Death is tantamount to sex
or separation, change in government,
appendix, river, turret, unpaid rent,
a footrace, spinning wheel, a blanket, bomb,
balm, a cozy ride. Death is Mom,
the dollar, pill, a notice, social function,
sun, rain, air, extreme unction,
funny, black, white, the full moon,
a season, song, met with a long spoon,
flame, frame, fish, a fine distinction,
obvious as hell, a wish, prediction,
wave, waking, wandering in a fog,
a pitch, a promise kept, a cat, a hog,
a teacher. Death has sour breath
and gets us all fagged out. Death is death.

Drummer Responds

"I'm waiting to read
your old-age poems."
—Carol Frost

Having had sex earlier tonight,
I have mastered lust
the way I have mastered gluttony.
Tolstoy said it bothered him until his eighties.
Jazz music and sex, I tell you,
have taken a lot of my time.
Music I could do without
for maybe a month.
                              Now the weather
is improving. Here on the back porch
I stare at a field of stars
and think, *tits*.

FIVE POEMS FROM

JORGE ACCAME'S FOUR POETS

Translated from the Spanish by Mark Weiss

Translator's Note: The four poets of the title (three of whom are in this selection) are heteronyms (to borrow Pessoa's term), not pseudonyms, Accame insists: three independent voices, with distinct biographies and ways of writing. One of them, Marcelo Atanassi, is also a translator, as represented here by his translation of the fictional Italian poet Gino Gogli's "Today some kids…". Atanassi has not provided a biographical note for Gogli.

Photo by Bruce H. Boston

Marcelo Atanassi was born in Viedma, Río Negro, in 1959. He studied English translation and other subjects at the College of Philosophy and Literature in Buenos Aires. Afterwards he moved to Salta, where he worked as an instructor in high schools and teacher's colleges. He translated contemporary American and Italian poets and compiled various anthologies of their work. In his own poetry one can detect the influence of Ungaretti, Montale and Quasimodo and the North American "dirty realism." He published three collections of poems: *Landing* (1983), *Predatory Species* (1989), and *Blues* (1993).

Deer

I look out at the park and the river
from the ninth floor
where I've lived for three months.
It's snowed this past two nights
and everything is white.

I'd never seen anything surprising in the park before
but today I awoke at dawn
and looked out the window:
A deer and its fawn had come
from the forest and stopped calmly
at the edge of the street.
Their bodies were two flames
waving in the darkness.

I grabbed the phone
and picked at random an apartment
in the building. A woman
answered. "There are two deer in the park,"
I told her, shaking with emotion.
"What?"
"Two deer," I repeated
and listened as she rested the phone on a table
Silence
After a few seconds
she picked up the phone
"Thank you," she said, and hung up.

I went back to the window.
The deer, curious, watched the passing cars
for a while, their breath streaming in the frozen air,
and wandered off into the woods again.

Who had I met
for moments
over their living bodies.

Gino Gogli

"Today some kids..."

Today some kids threw stones from the street
towards the place where I taught my class.
My assistant caught them
when they turned the corner.
He brought them to me, he said that he'd take them
to jail. They looked puzzled. More than criminals
they looked like those who practice
incomprehensible rituals
that they'd seen others practice.
They were as natural as trees bent by the wind
until they broke, never questioning
their being.
A soft jealousy spread through me for a ritual
unconscious life, far from awareness of self or others,
finally cured of always seeking answers.
Like those boys, like trees, like their seeds, destined to become
more trees bent by the wind.

Translated by Marcelo Atanassi

Gabriela Sánchez was born in Buenos Aires in 1949. Each of her books of poems, *Classical Verses* (1972) and *Ausenda* (1983), bear the subtitle *Poems and Translations*, which suggests that Sánchez conceived of her poems as a translation of other texts (her own and those of others). In her strenuous work as a poet, she has attempted everything from the most difficult renaissance forms to the complex, personal strophic verse in which her most recent work is realized. Since 1990 she has lived in Salta, where she practices law.

"I don't want to talk about myself"

I don't want to talk about myself

except to say
that I would travel miles
to find new places
for a cup of coffee
in cafés where no one knows me
and watch the warm steam rising
towards the evening light

I could say that I search those cafés
in quest of a woman
whose hair
gives birth to storms at sea
when she shakes it

or merely to be
what I'm not

But I don't want to talk about myself

"I imagine my parents..."

I imagine my parents
at their first dances
looking into each other's
eyes, the orchestra's music
giving their lives new meaning.
He would say some pretty words
and she would blush with gratitude
or not:
silent
their young bodies
twirling through the glittering room

Oh God while they watch each other
it will always be spring
they will always dance
and the world seem a paradise

it would always be always

Afterwards things would happen
as they tend to and perhaps for the good

Still some nights
they exchange glances
and I hear the music
in those rooms
the rustle of my mother's skirt
twirling around her
as she danced, radiant with happiness

Evaristo Soler was born in 1955, in San Ignacio, Misiones. His mother, of Bavarian descent, taught him German, which he learned before he spoke Spanish. He was educated in Rosario de Santa Fe, after which he moved to Córdoba where he worked as an itinerant evangelical preacher. *Correspondences* (1978), his first book, named for Baudelaire's famous poem, consists of translations of painters and composers, among them Stravinsky, Bosch, Henry, Moore, Arp, Brancusi, Mousorgski, and Tamayo. He also published *Dreams* (1983), a book of prose poems.

A Sleeping Boy

Slowly the canoe crosses the marsh. No one paddles. No one steers. Only a sleeping boy within it. The reeds caress and seem to stop it, but after a moment of hesitation the canoe resumes its voyage.

In the dream the boy has no parents, no brothers, no friends. He floats alone through the ripples of the marsh, while fish in search of insects leap from the water.

The fish break the dark surface, display their shining bodies and fall sideways, opening circles around them that widen until they kiss the canoe's body.

The canoe is like another fish, a big fish making its way to some goal, but nobody guides the canoe and there's only a sleeping boy within it.

On one of the shores the alders part revealing a channel that's like a door. The canoe enters and continues its journey.

The colors are still, one could almost say that they too slept.

Beneath the water there's an animal that no one has ever seen, an animal that lies in wait, taking note of everything that happens, a terrible and beautiful animal, an unknown animal.

The animal and all creatures watch over the boy who floats in the canoe.

It's neither night nor morning. The light is locked within, it waits for the boy to awaken before coming forth.

The animal in the depths breathes deeply and the waters rise and fall.

The skin of the boy is dark and soft; his eyelids flicker when the waves shake the canoe.

From the shore of the channel a fawn watches the boy passing.

The forest takes care of the orphan boy, the shadows bear him up and the canoe will not sink.

The channel widens, emptying into a large lake that resembles music. Silent birds fly over it.

Suddenly for a few moments clouds of steam erupt, as if from volcanoes beneath the water; they spread sideways through the air and overflow onto the surface of the lake.

The boy curls up and the steam covers him. Perhaps someone is waiting for him, but the shoreline is barely visible through the mist.

CAROL FROST

PORTFOLIO

It was August, it was August

and she was dancing, no, we three were dancing.
Her paranoia wasn't yet Thracian.
I thought of the greenhouse in Vienna,

my grandmother, her mother, dancing
while her partner's wife sat stone-lipped
among roses in the Viennese greenhouse.

I was young, what do the young know
of forgivable sin? I was stone-lipped.
My husband was singing, while dancing,

his sin his innocence—how old must one be to know
that sexual beauty is dangerous at any age?
My husband sang *Embraceable You* and danced,

mother dipped toward him, and he turned
to her. She'd want to tear him to pieces,
but she didn't know that

until in the end he spurned her—
her mind jangled like bees in a sac.
But she didn't know that.
It was August, it was only August.

What makes her quiet

when they hand her a doll?
What is the doll to her? She's no fool
in this old colony
where half can't wipe up
after themselves. She must know
this May morning in the enclosed
court yard, a tree white-veiled,
there's no return
to a day when mother
takes her first up in arms.

The doll is naked.
She sees that and maybe hears
inside her head someone crooning,
someone else she can't name.
It's hard to ask her. Her hair is loosened,
her blouse food-bedabbled,
and she no longer apprehends
or doesn't mind the murderous stealth
of shade just starting to break
a bough. Now, *now*,
let her rock her doll.
I watched her sleep then went to the window.

Morning light, cool, honey-hungry,
kept vigil in the garden,
and I thought the gigantic mind that is suddenly
consumed is not less planetary. Star, stone-rooted
rose, and the winds speak paradise,
speak grave. Knowing this turned me back
to her with final calm.

Erring   shoe and sour bib

her dress, wild hair, the woman
is following the turning path.
About her attendants in white
in a parallel world   wait.
One keeps the drug cart.
One writes on palimpest
of another fretting mind.

They have not brought her
or kept her from the clamorous
world to the labyrinth,
whose entrance   is age,
for reprimand though she feels
it, but simply
to give her a place freely   to move

past season and sun and change
inside coded doors   and honeyed
paneling. At the center
is the courtyard   for activity.
Tuesdays a piano plays
and all may dance.

It is no more joyous for them
or for the family   until
having walked so long among
the turnings, she loses sense
of direction and   all trace
of what it was like before.
It is not easy to be free
forever of a wish never
to go back instead to whirl   naked
in a bare world.

The mind is no tunnel deepening

to a pent element, perhaps an underground lake
of undrinkable waters,
bottom silted over
with names of objects and the people
she has known all her life. She can recite
Die Loreli and recognizes the Dali Lama
but not you. Sure, you want to know how
she can talk politics and laugh
but not ladle up a family memory.
It helps to read a book,
change her prescription,
see in her clouded eyes
breezes of light,
think of the myth of the mantis,
who in its exhaustion was laid
on a floating flower. In its thigh
a seed was left, the bee flew on,
all people came to life,
and nothing yet themselves
drank minutes shut in the water.
"Why am I here?" they asked,
and answered then, "To see what comes,
beginning first faintly to look like
something, some parts missing,
fish fins, for instance. We *almost* see it:
turning into gilly, or red butterfly
in water, on black sand. Crisp gills,
insect petals, rose-red, and the even darker,
accurate rose of blood. Then words
rooted at the bottom of the lake,
or agitating the heart."
Said so (their heads dripping with water),
it will be hard to turn away.
But remember the woman
in her dementia who is half dead.
The myth is too pretty.

Light clear in a window, morning

finding white flowers, herself climbing
in the Alps alone to the meadow
of edelweiss and descending
at dusk—rock and field slurring. . .
In her corner room she sleeps and grieves,
bedclothes like dirty plumage.
Light and lamp now drug her.
She was the child Sorrow
in *Madama Butterfly*.   Stattsoper
Haus.   Bombs, strafing,
gut of some war? Where are stones
that were her city?
Who kissed her?
I want to hear those stories,
but she may as well be lyre
and head on a black river, singing
to no one.
A hundred answers within her burn.
When I (*You look like me who are you?*) tell her
the words Marlene Dietrich,
the Marlene she loves, sings,
the melody won't coax the hours.
Her mind's a bedraggled swan on a black river.

You suddenly wearied. You had to sit

under the sun's force, chilled and sweating,
that hot afternoon in Key West. I think it was 1997.

Your eyes grew very bright. Like two zig-zag butterflies,
time and your sense of it spiraled out
over the water. (I'm not sure of the date.)

A ship rumbled in the harbor,
the burning sky was intent on the water.
I'll try to remember the exact date.

You couldn't follow their course
past a certain point, but this was the onset
of your forgetfulness. I told you—Key West in 1997.

What date (not to all, but to you and to me
the year is of importance)? Remember. It was
a hot afternoon in Key West. 1997.

A little problem with space and time, we used to say,
when the diagnosis sounded too harsh.
What year was it, you ask? 1997.

It couldn't have been hotter.
Yes, Key West. No, not honeybees—two butterflies.
You know the year.
1997.

The honeycomb is made from flowers

and the materials for wax bees gather
from the resinous gum of trees,
while honey is distilled from dew.

At the rising of the constellations
or when a rainbow is in the sky,
the dew is deposited in the comb.
Dew from sweet-tasted flowers.

This, mother, is my song for you
pretending to sleep with open eyes.
As odor and dance lead bees to nectar,
though you're far away I will come to you.

That was the mind's wild swarm trapezing
from an oak limb,

odor of honey and blue sky ablaze—until the regress.
Only what's inmost is left and darkened past language,
and she is like a tiny star that Space no longer notices,
unillumined, hushed, and by herself, her course no longer
in the scheme of planets, suns, and lunar systems.
But she is still here. What breaks the archetypic
stone and starves the honeybees moves toward her slowly.

Tyrannus tyrannus

That bird towering: late summer
garden: who senses the burring wings
deep inside roses and like the angel
before all nectar's sipped
before gold scatters in bright air
descends from its high height
to lift away the bee. . .
not a honey eater: though looking so:
bee after bee disappearing
into incandescence::
Only the metaphysic flower
feels the approach: and emptying.

(Ursinus)

Gold helm scent of honey and the drowsing bear:
golden: begotten of honey: bee larvae
chokeberry sweet clover carrion::
leaving the den in the undergrowth
for sweet-thaw sun-thaw above:
shut out from all the world within:
The valleys and hills feel its feet:
shambling when the sun is low:
slow mouth: Didn't mother say she felt
its presence a long time?
thought small as atoms,
and aromatic as honey ales:
body manacled—body preserving
small sweetnesses?
until the bear groaned and stretched:
entered there and deeply ate?

If her falling to quiet

after harsh years reversed, where
would it start if not before irony,
hurt, want, sex?
Time's soft machine goes past
spring, and last, past
Lascaux and the first magnifications
on stone, before the first look in a pool
the first I am, and back
before tongues licked
nectar, wings fanning honey, and body
carrying sexual powders
through conifer forests
to begin the abominable diversification
of flowers:: to rain,
to one drop crashing.

As small lamps drift with river tide

and against the wind, her reverie keeps wavering,
her gaze inward. Beyond is the dark, chopped bay,
beyond no lights at all. Couldn't she step
ashore to a place with its own name
and return, knowing the difference
between there and here? She has told me
of the sea in legendary depth and darkness,
the moon's huge black bulk, apparitional
salt lilies in the blind valleys of the ocean's floor
brain blots—no stars at all, no, no
spindrift light, no nearness
that in sudden whirlpool
doesn't sink and cease to remember.

Amid a menagerie she sleeps as in a lair—

lion, bear, and wolf bedded in rich darkness,
the air sweet with opiates—and when she wakes
refreshed, small lights in her clear animal eyes,
it's easy to imagine that the animals have spoken
in a dream of the allegorical life:
Out of the wounded side honey issues.
In light, dementia exposes the sweet lie.
She gazes but rarely speaks—tree names, German
flowers haltingly knot on the string
she once could string without thought.
The question of her being, of whether she was,
insisted on being asked. If once
the beauty in photos
all knew, how could she be
this other—fervorless and gaunt   or wasn't
the mirror cracked? And with the stinging truth
came her need for more and more sleep
in flowered bedclothes, with the animals
with fixed eyes who seemed to have been
waiting for her still sexual scent and weight
to dream them again all into life.

All things are taken from us

and in a little while our cares
are numb. Lotus pollen wafts
through the valleys and shadows.

Our bodies outlast us, sleep-
wandering in the spiced mist,
even as we sit. We sip the cup
if it is offered. Is it milk?

Is it honey? To taste would be
a simple perfection of thought—
the brain's wild bee that grows
honey seeking bee and rose.

Swollen with dust and rain
and rumor, our eyes grow inward.
It is restful knowing nothing
more, knowing no one any more.

Photo by Bruce H. Boston

Louis Aragon

from **The War and What Followed**

Section IV

In front of the cross   a bottle stuck in the ground
Inside a rolled letter   can it be true   addressed to me
What if I *am* dead What if this is hell Everything would be
A lie an illusion Even I and my whole story   all of History
A demonic game   a mere trick of sleep   grotesquely profound

How else can I explain this feeling   these unshakeable fears
My entire life   and the world   who can ever believe in it again
If all of this is only hell juggling in front of its own reflection
I died in August nineteen eighteen at this rural intersection
So for me everything's been over for almost thirty-eight years

No soldiers ever came to drink on horseback in our bars
No couples ever danced upon our roofs night and day   no train
Packed with munitions burst   no town ever haunted us this way
Hurlers of multi-colored stars   masters of fire that falls like rain
The drums of Armistice at dawn never beat along our boulevards

It never snowed that time we left a hunter dead from the cold
In the attic of a sawmill near Sainte Odile   nor did the eyes
Of our quartermaster shine swapping Deutsche Marks at a bloated price
No flags   yellow and white   flew hysterically as we passed by
Alsace and the swollen Rhine never stopped our carts where they rolled

And no place like Roeschwogg ever existed   nor the green-eyed
Girl in the house across the street who recited German poems to me
As she wrapped wool placidly around my outstretched arms
God knows how we passed that cruel winter between us quietly
While I watched her fingers play Schubert's *The Trout* on the keyboard

There was no Sarrebrück   no coal strike in the mines on the ridge
Or officers shouting contradictory orders in the heat of the fray
No suspects arrested in the suburbs and interrogated

The band never struck up the *Freischütz* at the Wittelsbach Café
And that mess corporal was never bludgeoned under the arch of a bridge

None of this ever happened   even in the years that followed

I tell you that we are dead in our uniforms   completely spent
The world rolled over like a car   sunk like a ship the waves swallowed
Versailles Your shared dreams of empire proved hollow
Companions in hell   we can both laugh and bear our sorrow
Peace never occurred   there was no Dada movement

Translated from the French by Laure-Anne Bosselaar and Kurt Brown

Kirun Kapur

Chapter and Verse

Now Abel was keeper
of sheep, and Cain
a tiller of the ground.

And from that sentence my own began.

Who teaches
a boy to keep
sheep or a man to plow?

It's not as though this was wholly my plan.

But when I saw

the girlish legs of early carrots,
the bent wheat shake
its head as it lunged upright again,

when my mother ran out with her feet still bare
in search of the first
purple irises, then

I became guilty of anything.

In the course of time
Cain brought to the Lord
an offering of the fruit of the ground

And Abel brought
the firstlings
of his flock, their fat portions.

I remember

every bulb and shoot.
A garland of last year's
onion; barley, spelt.

And the Lord had
regard for Abel and his offering,
but for Cain he had no

regard. Garlic
in a braid; two fists of dill,
the fronds like finch feathers.

So Cain was very angry and his countenance fell.
The Lord said to Cain,
"Why are you angry?"

Pomegranates, quince; rocket, celery root!

If you do well, will you not be accepted? And if you do not well,
sin is lurking at the door; its desire
is for you, but you must master it.

I was arguing
for dahlias and sorrel,
lemons on their squat, blunt trees.

It was the first I knew of who I was.

ALEX LEMON

Boundless

Let's go my little paradise,
My little heart attack—
The city is unwinding.
Roots are busting through
Concrete. Soon, it will no
Longer be the epoch of racing
In circles. There'll be no more
Sleeping in the Xerox machine.
All those disposable hours
Where we sat around wondering
How many times you could
Tell someone that you loved
Them before they'd explode
Instead of leaning into
Their warmth & actually saying
It. Soon, no one will want unlimited
Texts because it will be known—
This here right now, this,
Exactly what you mean—
Is brought to you by
Every second that happens
Hereafter & how the sunrise
Holds your closed eyes.
Any time is the best time
For us to go. Please, hold my hand.
It is such a pleasure to be
Not-dead & walking through
This place with you.

G.C. WALDREP

After Music

In the moment after music
we are instructed not to remember
the sounds the children made
as the bombs kept falling, & then,
after, the dripping of rainwater
from the copper eaves, the boughs
of splintered plane trees.

Instead, recall the way the bridges
at dusk seemed to join
mathematics with some other
country, all the people out walking
backwards & forwards like tourists,
Touch not, taste not, handle not.

After music, we look into the mirror
and see thieves dispossessing
the republic of its treasures, then
taking trolleys out to where
the suburbs are about to begin.
Relax, murmur the pharmacologists
from their black-box cafés,
the policemen from their kiosks.

There is this enormous silence
inside music, where the people
in photographs go when we
are no longer there to watch them,
where the dreams of small houses
keep awaiting new shoes.

A bridge requires a body, a human
form sealed inside like an IOU
or a letter from a lover you will never

open. The bombs stop falling, & then
all the people come out walking:

Look, they say, *This was a river,*
this was a school. The sunlight chants
There is no suburb, there is no other side.

Another Day at the Festival
—in memoriam Craig Arnold, 1967-2009

The tour guide walks up to you
and asks, politely, Do you want to die by falling
or do you want to die by drowning
or do you want to die by burning.

You say, I want to eat healthier foods,
get more exercise.
I want to spend more time with the kids,
thinking about the environment.

The tour guide nods, and gestures
towards the deep wooden bins
where they're throwing the corpses of dogs.
The shadows from the bins,
from what's in the bins, look just like
other shadows, you notice.

The wind is picking up again.
You can hear the stridor of the steel cables
attached to the bridge, that hold it up.

In your wallet you find photographs,
but they're all of things
you don't feel any special relationship to:
empty beaches, conveyor belts,
rice left over from someone else's wedding.

The tour guide is walking
away from you, in the direction
of the large building
to your left. You follow the tour guide.

It was a long time ago
when we began to mistake the motions

children made
for the children themselves.

Yes, you call out after the tour guide,
but she doesn't turn around.
You're running after where she used to be.

It's spring. Nobody knows where you are.

And as They Waited in Their Baskets
on the Hillsides It Began to Rain

I meant to write "saved from drowning"
but wrote "drowned from saving"
instead. When I look up from my notebook,
I realize I am writing
once again at the desk made out of the war.

Later, after the lights are turned off,
I hear the jake brakes of passing trucks and litanies
the crickets make. It's as if
at some point, or maybe in some other,
earlier life, they'd all been weavers, artisans of great skill,
but then, somehow, forgot how that all went.

In the fields outside town,
the crickets are trying to piece something
impossibly complex together,
only this time it's going to work, this time
it's going to be about acoustics
and devotion, rather than about covering the body.

It's the war, I tell myself—in the dream—
before letting each fragment drop.

Come down to the water, whisper the cripples
on the tall banks of the levee.
We call what we're doing dancing
because we like that word better than some other words.
It's the sort of thing a god might do,
a god in the shape of a river, in the shape of a bird,
in the shape of a bone tucked inside a scar.

Ideal Boating Conditions

You open the box and see yourself staring back.
"Cool," you think, and then you realize
it's just a mirror at the bottom of the box.

The wind shifts. The little boats go this way
& that in the harbor. You watch them.

Somewhere on board each of the boats
is a mirror, from which you watch yourself
watching the boats. The self you're going to be
sends postcards back to the self you are now,
only the self you are now won't get them
until it's too late, until you're different.

You think the part of you that is out there,
in the harbor, must be happier than you are now.

There's this wedding you're missing,
or this anniversary. The music cycles backward,
past Chopin, Bruckner, Buxtehude even.
See, this city isn't even built yet.

You want to use every word you hear
as a verb: "neon," "medical student," "Talmud."
"Persimmon." "Volkswagen." "Aramaic."

You read the postcards one by one
like cadavers inside of which cloudy coils
of ocean have just gone missing.
A gentle breeze off the water ruffles your hair.

Someone's excavating Troy, someone's
living there—the little shops, the excise tax,
a furnished room near the college,
baskets of blue eggs in the marketplace.

The searchlights launch themselves into the void
music's left, hatchlings on the riprap.

The you that's on the boats misses the you
that's here, with the box. You understand this
much. Someone else's Troy is burning.

MICHAEL WATERS

Amateur Night

The Dugout
Iowa City / 1972
for Norman Dubie

Whereupon they shed street clothes,
Cutoffs then tees, to reveal
Nipples latexed with gum
Chewed and stretched, then thumbed
To conform to the law of the state,
Nipples pinker now, less nubby—
Bazooka better than Band-Aids
As more flesh-like and easier to peel—
Though spotlights sometimes dried the wads
Enough to make the star-specks fall
When hopefuls flaunted gawky routines.
Two cops waited to hustle them off.
Still they'd return before last call
To quarter the juke for hip-synced tunes,
Angling bones to jump-start the jitter.
Long Cool Woman in a Black Dress
Thumped speakers, off came the tie-dye.
Tease. Coeds raising tuition, single moms
Squirreling rent, a few ringers
Feigning shyness—we cheered them all,
Admiring the combo of clunk and bravura,
Shimmy and halt, funk and chic,
Then rushed home to shabby rooms
To nail it all down in stories and poems
Those early years when we didn't know
That we didn't know how to dance or speak.

History Lesson

My wife asks if I'm going to stand around with my thumb up my ass
While she lugs groceries from trunk to table, then laughs—
The phrase so American, so coarse.

What a comical people we are!—I mean in contrast
To Eastern Europeans—though such
Thinking may be wrong—

Zhivkov   Ceauşescu   Milošević
Her point all along.

LEONARDO SINISGALLI

PORTFOLIO

Translated and introduced by W. S. Di Piero

Poems by Leonardo Sinisgalli

The Italian poet Leonardo Sinisgalli, born in 1908, shared with several of his contemporaries—Eugenio Montale, Giuseppe Ungaretti, Alfonso Gatto, and others—a new kind of unadorned anti-eloquence that spoke, sometimes ecstatically, of intimate commonplaces. The subject of what came to be called "Hermetic poetry" was often a privileged instant of perception: a good Hermetic poem taught the eye to see ordinary things under extraordinary aspects. Sinisgalli preferred small-scale subjects and believed poetry to be a reckoning with what's incidental or inconspicuous, yet consequential. In his autobiographical essay, "On the Figure of the Poet," he said that while the poet may experience heightened perceptions, he remains a member of the lower orders, kin to scorpion, fly, and ant. Poetry is localized speech, a recording of instances snatched from the phenomenal world, not a grid of sentimental explanations. The poet asks nothing of the world; he accepts and articulates the grace of the moment. He cannot "exclude himself from the world, visible or invisible, that stands around him. He is possessed by all things."

Sinisgalli brought to his work a rich and rather eccentric personal history. Born in Montemurro, a small town southeast of Naples in the rather barren mountainous region of Lucania, he left in 1926 to study engineering in Rome, his head filled with poetry and mathematics. He so distinguished himself at the university that the physicist Enrico Fermi invited him in 1929 to attend the illustrious *Istituto di Fisica*. Sinisgalli refused, preferring the company of poets and painters. While publishing his first poems in the late 1920s, he pursued his interests in architecture, painting, and graphics. His skills in the design arts led him into industry. In 1937 he became advertising director for Olivetti and spent the rest of his working life in advertising and design. In 1953, he founded *Civiltà delle macchine*, the most influential journal of graphics and design arts in its time, which he directed until 1959. All the while he continued to exhibit his art work and publish poems, stories, and essays on the arts and mathematics. When he died in 1981, he was working on a new collection of poems and preparing a show of watercolors for a gallery in Rome.

This spare chronology barely suggests the faculties and preoccupations that shaped his work. Sinisgalli was very caught up in the architectonics of a poem. He wanted a design for seeing, an architecture of vision. His poems are often acts of exquisite arrangement, dispositions of word-objects that comprise figures of sentiment. His ambition was to make poems that spoke with Cartesian precision, to distribute words as one distributes the terms of an equation, though all the words finally converge, as he liked to say, on the elusive "i," the imaginary number. The result is a poetry that's denotative and spectral. Sinisgalli was fascinated by the capacity of mathematics to imagine and quantify the invisible, to calculate a something beyond nothingness—he said that in his youth mathematics was a form of mystical experience—and wanted to carry that over into poetry. Grammar, he said, is a "physics of words," and in his poems he seeks to calibrate moments past and present as they gravitate around him so that the unseen, the numinous, can be released. His scientific learning led him not to certitude but to a cultivation of innocence, of "unwisdom." His temperament inclined toward chance and error, toward the promise of the unknown held out by instinct and idle wish, while he remained completely aware of what he called "the symbiotic relationship between intellect and instinct, reason and passion, the real and the imaginary."

He also placed a lot of importance on precise detail, the naming and placement of creature, locale, and event. This denotative accuracy, and the even tone that is its medium, give his poems their stripped down appearance and led some critics to regard his poetry as *gelida* or *fredda*—cool, remote. But he was the first to admit he didn't write a poetry of blood and tears. We seldom hear a petulant "I" or overheated Self. His poems direct a steady disinterested gaze at the story the world tells. The two crucial locales for him are Lucania and the Italian metropolis—Village and City. In the Village, a virtually pre-Christian culture, lives the Tribe; in the City are wife, job, friends. The poet is the Pilgrim, village son and city citizen, whose words trace a career between the two. Lucania seems a place outside history. People there live mostly outdoors; indoors, they keep so close to the threshold that the village air fills with kitchen odors and family cries. Children use animal bones as toys. Custom is fixed and ancient as stone outcrop. Lives turn inside seasons, roughened by the demands of an eternally vivid present. Needs are simple and cherished—a slice of pear, a fig, a sprig of mint, a bundle of firewood. The Tribe may lay claim to the earth only because they know that the earth at every point claims them. Sinisgalli doesn't glamorize this world—no plump peasants dance, no golden glow skirts the image. If the Village issues from earth, the City is man-made time, the architecture of intellect dressed in stone and glass. He has written poems about famous citizens like Descartes and Goethe whose powers of hypothesizing have always claimed his imagination, in part because their seriousness coalesces with the highest forms of play.

Most of Sinisgalli's poems fall under the rubric "Roads, Streets, Rooms." He's quite literally a pilgrim, on the move past rivers, shop-fronts, railways, trees, and houses. When at rest in secluded rooms or at café tables, he registers movements around him. In many poems a present occasion trips a memory of overlapping instants. In his physics of words the most important function is verb tense. The present conjures the past, the remote past floods the future. The grammar of time lets him build tiers of memory, slabs of things and moments, while he seeks his own place among the layers. He shares with Dante a passion for the geometry of vision and for a way of walking through or pausing in concentric figures of place and time. It's there, in the scansion of the moment, that the energies of mind and imagination fuse with energies radiating from the phenomenal world.

W. S. Di Piero

I'll Remember This Autumn

I'll remember this autumn
Gleaming and skittish in the migrant light
That curves in the wind across the slouching reeds.
The canals at floodtime swelled waist high—
Shriveled by the dry heat, I plunged in.
When I'm with friends at night in the city
I'll tell the story of these privileged days,
Of my father whose feet turned red
Treading grapes,
Of my shy mother
Carrying a warm egg in her hand,
Happier than any bride.
My father talked of that cherry tree
Planted on their wedding day. It hasn't
Bloomed this year, he told me. He dreamed
It would someday be their firstborn's wedding bed—mine.
The north wind blew open the sky
To the quarter moon. A moon
With a calf's pinkish budding horns!
Tomorrow we'll be able to plant, he said.
I looked at his open palm, its creases
Sharpened by the firelight, I heard
The seed explode in his heart,
I saw blazing in his eyes
The corn-ripened conch.

To My Father

The man returning alone
From the vineyard late at night
Rattles turnips in the tub,
Turns off the footpath with straw
Smeared bluegreen.
Fresh loam on his shoes,
Clean evening odor
In his clothes, the man
Stops by a fountain, talks
To the gardener picking fennel.
I watch the man, the small
Man, from a distance.
He's a moving point on the horizon.
Maybe tonight
His eye will catch fire
Beside the fishpond
Where he wipes his forehead.

Village

We walked all around the village
while the donkeys were coming back loaded with wood
from the sweet-smelling heights of the Serra,
scraping their hairy ears against the rough
walls of the houses. A bell tinkled on the neck
of a kid-goat, led by an old man
through the darkness like a dog. Someone
sitting in front of a door said goodnight.
The streets are so narrow and furniture
crowded so close to the doorways
that when the moon rose we smelled peppers
sizzling in pools of oil.
The color of the mountains excited you.
"Maybe they've been under water for thousands of years."
"Down here even the stones look withered,
even the leaves look worn out."
Women walked from houses with burning brands.
"In our villages the sun sinks fast,
night begins when the noon bells ring."
Horses returning from the watering troughs
snorted, dogs prowled the doorways.
We were alone, treading the airborne ashes.
"It's as if everybody goes underground
to sleep then comes back to life
each morning." The street was quiet,
wrapped in rags, colorless.
In one locked house the tribe's billygoat
sneezed in Margherita's bed.

"Let's go visit the old folks. My aunt
and uncle always set aside something good
for me." We sit in the kitchen and see
the magical family of keys hanging on the wall:
the small garden key, the gigantic cellar key
over a hundred years old. "My grandfather

used to quiet all the screaming kids
by whistling through the keys." Here's the silvery key
to the rabbit hutch, and the oil lamps, lanterns, wicks.
I watch my family profiled,
magnified on the walls, and the enormous
shadows of flies creeping like mice.
"My grandmother, Cosima Diesbach, sailed around the world."
"My ancestors probably saw Atlantis."
At night Domenico comes to lock the churches
and bolt the gates of the dead.
"They used to tell us kids
that he talked to the owl, on the rooftops, up there.
The bellman is stone deaf
and sleeps hard. To lay out the dead
(he's better at it than anyone)
you had to call for hours
in the middle of the night and whistle loudly
through the keys." Domenico stands there,
strikes a match on his trousers, smokes his pipe,
engrossed on the edge of the deep ravine
where one night long ago I saw them set down
the casket of the dead Christ, by the railing.
Down in the valley Crescenzio goads his lame
mule. "I take things as they come."

September 16, 1943

Moments before she died at midnight
on September 16, my mother said
a flea was biting her back,
a flea heavy as a horse.
A dark hoof pressed her on the bed.
She sweated and tried to fight it,
gasping, face down, too weak
to say a prayer.
The flowers on the porch have bloomed
though nobody's watered them.
The colts have been reshod,
the days have burnt away.
The ugly cat still mews
in the cracks of the old house.
One night in August
we were out on the terrace
watching the huge wasp nest in the sky.
The August wind that whisks the chaff
from wheat and dizzies the hooded
threshers on the threshing floor
and polishes the blades on the straw,
blew before our eyes the hope
of a hard-earned peace. My father
fell asleep on a chair
in that soft rustling air.

Mother spoke to me while I smoked:
Foul water always runs before clear, she said.
The river brings truth.
Each night from the cracks in the walls
comes the song of some unhoused beast.
Barn owl, weasel, screech owl, stone marten,
half mammal, half bird,
killing the hens, tearing sheets stored in chests.
Not a cat, not a rooster, but some demon

hiding in the lofts
wanting smoke, shadow, plaster peelings,
but spooked by leaves:
beast bound to the folds in clothes,
to the smell of the dead.
Early in the morning my father
sits on the hearthstone.
People come and go with bottles
wrapped in shawls, asking for vinegar
to cure thrush.
The women talk to one another
about pigs, pigs clean as dogs,
living under their beds.
Epidemics among cows, sheep, chickens.
Signs that the end is near?
The women list them one by one
while they squat on bundled twigs
around the fire, remembering my mother.

As Soon as They Arrive

As soon as they arrive
the swallows fly away again,
dazzled and twisting against
a plaster sky.
The balconies are empty,
the windows still bolted.
A fly hovers silently
near us
in these awful days,
this awful destiny.
It whimpers softly,
nips our hands,
nuzzles our forehead.

Holy Saturday in Manfredonia

There's no one here now.
The ducks go gliding one
by one
toward the dark shore.
Our friends are founding a celestial city.
They leave us here by windows
facing the sea, brown
as a mountain.
Couriers between life and death,
the children
dive for worms
and the old fisherman
waits for them to surface
with a twig of blood
in their fingers.

The Visit

Something barely visible
is slipping in the order of things.
A dog nuzzles the stump
of his cropped tail,
a crow looks for the feathers
of his clipped wings.
A small boy behind a door
asks me for his mother.

Autumn

The flies seem glad
to see me again.
They inch along the stems
of my glasses, pounce
on the tips of my ears.
The white paper fascinates them.
I talk, I pet them,
gather them in my fist,
call them by name,
Fantina, Filomena, Felicetta.
I fool myself thinking
it's always them.
One checks his reflection in my fingernail,
the others hide so that
he'll have to find them.

The Windows on Via Rubens

1.

It's late Sunday afternoon
and I feel I can sit and watch
the swallows forever.
I've opened all the stops
to air out the empty house.
I hear the palm rustling,
it lifts its wings, flutters,
then settles down, motionless,
hiding inside its silence.
I've been watching it for years. Celebration
never lasts long
here. A brief game
of swallows playing at twilight.
They enter the sky two by two,
coasting the rooftops near the pines,
then shoot back like arrows.
Suddenly the whistling stops.
Silent, they fly another moment,
then the sky is blank again.
I write quickly
while there's still light on the paper.

2.

I give up the pleasure
of staying late at the café.
I give up the smiles of the sky.
I run home to sketch.
These nights the moon
is waning.
Its journey is brief,
a short walk.
I follow it step by step.
It rises in the dark
and slants across the sky.

I catch it on deep blue paper,
then in a corner I rough in
a distant star.
One stroke is all it takes
to write history without regrets.
I've excluded passion from my work.
All I want is to watch,
to watch like a halfwit.

3.
The worm that makes
fruit and flowers rot
squirms from a hole in the wall
or a cleft in the heart.
Moons and swallows stay outside.

Anniversary

Blackberry brambles
around the cemetery.
My mother
remembered by a pale inscription
on a headstone.
Thirty-three years now
since they laid her out
in bed. Soldiers were fleeing
through the valley. We barely
found men to remove
her corpse.
The other evening in Piazzetta
San Nicola, Adelina said to me:
"Your mother died lost in thought,
it was hard to shut her eyes,
she looked unconvinced."
"If you could see me
you'd feel pity, you can't cure
my ills, they're older
than you."

In My House

In my house you
talk to the flies
you live among the flies
winter and summer and
when you come home you shout
where's that fly
is the fly all right
and the fly's all gone.

STEPHEN DOBYNS

Spring

Out at the lighthouse a man with a yellow slicker
and a boy in a red jacket walk along the rocks
as I watch from my truck. The boy is about six—
father and son with their backs to me, hand in hand
and walking slowly, not talking—a scene repeated
maybe a trillion times since time began. My son
and I did that too. When they negotiate the corner
to the front of the lighthouse, the boy looks back
to his mother waiting in the parking lot and makes
a small wave just to let her know he's okay. Today
is April 1st. At one point I started to shout: Hey, kid,
your pants are on fire! But then I thought I'd better
not, the parents might get upset, maybe report me.
You can never tell these days. Everyone is looking
at everyone else, wondering what they'll do next,
like pull a knife, and if that doesn't worry them,
maybe it should. The water is gunmetal blue and
as flat as a blanket, some fog on the horizon keeps
the foghorn busy. And today is a friend's birthday,
maybe a former friend. I last saw her and her husband
in Rome, meeting in front of the Pantheon. The day
was hot, the square crowded. We had coffee and
discussed old friends, who was well, who was not.
My wife and I had just spent a month in Florence,
a daily round of paintings and cappuccinos. Now
we're bickering about money. That's how it goes,
a pendulum giving what's called character to a face,
or carving a roadmap to a place not worth the trip.
From my truck I can see the tip of Long Island.
I've a friend over there I haven't seen for a while,
maybe a former friend. I'm afraid I've got too many
of those. The ones who remain, the ones who are gone,
those in between—I miss them all. Once my feelings
fix on a person, they stay bright pictures in my mind,
they always stay fresh even if I never see them again.

Often that feels like a weight. In Florence I saw that
Savonarola and Anna Akhmatova had the same nose,
long with a distinctive bend a third of the way down.
Akhmatova felt that Florence represented everything
opposite to Russia under Stalin and this protected her
and her poetry. She began to write at the age of eleven
and Savonarola, too, wrote poetry when young, but then
told his father he couldn't stand "the blind wickedness
of the people of Italy," which led him into the church
and to Florence as a puritan preacher where he created
a democracy, a gift too costly for the city's wealthy
and the pleasure-seeking church. When the pope tried
to bribe him with a cardinal's hat, Savonarola replied:
"A red hat? I want a hat of blood." And so he was hung
with two others and the bodies burned in the Piazza
della Signoria. My wife's niece visited us in Florence,
a woman so lovely that men stumbled over their feet
as she passed. She liked having her photo taken in front
of public statues, other places also, often asking people
to take her picture with her camera, which made me see
the spot that moved me most was the plaque showing
where Savonarola had been burned, because she didn't
want her picture taken there—it being only a metal
circle set into the stones. Staring down at the plaque,
I was sure I felt the preacher and former poet burn.
This morning two men in a boat set out lobster pots.
The Block Island ferry from New London cruises past
on a straight line, a no nonsense sort of work. I can see
few birds: one resembling a miniature goose, practicing
dives, and some gulls hunting for snacks. A movie I saw
last night about East Germans spying on one another
in the early eighties was about complicity, how everyone
was guilty in a system that ensnared them and everyone
they loved as hostage. Hard not to squeal like a stuck pig
and sell out your neighbors and lovers and best friends

with your own life on the line. Even Anna Akhmatova
at last caved in. Her poetry condemned; accused of being
half harlot, half nun; her first husband shot as a traitor,
another husband rotting in prison. Then, with her son
in Siberia, she sought to get him back by writing poems
in praise of Stalin: "Where Stalin is, we have Freedom,
Peace and grandeur on earth." Was her betrayal of what
led her to write a knife in her gut all the rest of her life?
Or did she say: I was forced to do it because of my son.
That's the trouble with complicity, the lesser of two evils
may be only a bit better than the greater. Even Savonarola
bargained with the Pope and shut his mouth to protect
his work, which did little good since he still got hung.
But both were lucky to have identifiable villains. Here
we're bought by having sugar poured down our throats
in a country distrusted by every other country on earth
and a widening program of spying on our own people.
This just begins the list as we say complicity doesn't exist.
Yet all my actions reek of complicitous acceptance. Is it
wrong to live in comfort when so many die in Darfur? I
expect it is. Today I've little room in my heart for anything
but complaint; it becomes my illness and great discontent.
The smoke from Savonarola's corpse must have coated
the windows of that lovely square with a greasy film.
When I looked from the Palazzo Vecchio, I was sure
the distortions in the glass were caused by the smoke
from the victims burned below. I'd think of it at night
till I thought I was going nuts. Freud said the neurosis
of thinking the wretchedness around us doesn't exist
lets us stay sane, although at times it seems that sanity
comes at too great a cost, so even the joy of walking
with one's son along the ocean's edge extracts its price
in drops of blood. A year before being hung, Savonarola
held a bonfire of the vanities at the same spot: books,
silk dresses, musical instruments all went up in smoke.

Botticelli even tossed in two of his own paintings.
This excess rivals the excess of Savonarola being hung,
one more pendulum swing to give character to a face.
Isn't a withdrawal from friends a withdrawal from life
and a denial of time's assaults? Better to preserve them
as bright pictures in my mind, than to see them vanish
into the dark. Akhmatova's love of Florence included
Dante and his poetry, and this, too, she set against Stalin,
not that it justified her complicity, but it offered relief.
Don't say it was only a distraction, only another vanity.
Perhaps it formed the gift that let her gain back Freud's
cleansing neurosis, to live in the presence of the horror
even if it meant pretending that the horror didn't exist.
If answers are excuses, is art a more acceptable excuse,
or is it just a twig I put down to tiptoe across the muck?
Now the boy in the red coat has worked his way around
the lighthouse and comes running back to his mother,
imagining her concern, as his father comes trailing after.
For a while she is the boy's whole world till he graduates
to the larger world that year by year will carve his story
across his face. What compromises will he have to make
with how he wants to live? But today my hopes are set
on the start of spring as the gods of a hundred religions
are being reborn, yearly visitors who give the world
a penetrating look, receive our praise and briefly offer
their consoling warmth, before they once again depart.

CHARLES PRATT

This Apple

I picked in sharp September –
Taut skin, firm flesh, a keeper –

And taste now in May's
Tremulous mist of blossoms,

Puckered, yes, grown softish,
Still is the apple I wish.

Skiers

We break an old trail through new snow
Under high, snow-heavy trees
Cautious on the hush of skis.
This, I think, is how we go,
Still and still, slow and slow,

Pushing down a trail we know,
New again in fallen snow,
You ahead and I behind,
I ahead and you behind.
This, I think, is how we go.

This, I think, is how we go,
I ahead and you behind,
You ahead and I behind,
New again in fallen snow,
Pushing down a trail we know,

Still and still, slow and slow.
This, I think, is how we go –
Cautious on the hush of skis
Under high, snow-heavy trees
We break an old trail through new snow.

Marital Sex

1)

Watching the Eclipse from the Bedroom Window

Three spheres slide precisely into place.
Shadow of earth brings blood to the pale moon's face.
Celestial rhyming! What metaphor for this
Collusion of heavenly bodies but heavenly kiss?

   A distant kiss. And perverse – three pairs of lips.

Five, counting ours. Love, let's eclipse the eclipse.

2)

Gestures of Love

Now that we've made love, you turn your back
And settle into sleep. I lie alone.
My fingers trace you, curving like a hook
Hung in deep waters, all its soft bait gone.

3)

Aubade after Twenty-five Years

Somewhere halfway down the closet, my pants turn to your pants.
Mine on top, yours on top, our sweaters have sex on the shelves.
My foot pokes a hole in your sock, you're lost in my shirt
As laughing in half-light we try to unscramble ourselves.

J. Hope Stein

The Auctioneer:

Ladies & Gentlemen The apparatus
you see before you
isn't quite a phonograph or telephone line to the dead
nor a movie screen to project their lives
It works more like a breathalyzer What is inhaled
is never quite What is exhaled is personality
Is words to your neighbors Is touching
your tongue to your nose Is blowing
out your candles Hiccups yawns & laughter

Ladies & Gentlemen The body
is the soul's model T
A factory of microscopic men tug the diaphragm We breathe
into stomach not chest Ladies & Gentlemen
these are the principles that guide the machine
you see before you The Inventor's final secret
found by the great-great-granddaughter
of the mistress of the Inventor Ladies & Gentleman if
we were to voluntarily stop breathing we would
lose consciousness and the tiny men would take over

Ladies & Gentlemen The test tube
you see before you
contains the Inventor's last breath A larva
in a jar since 1931 A soft vapor or vibration
at the cork's edge Not unlike
Galileo's middle finger
in a glass case still
pointing up The story of a man
can be told in a single breath A unique
chord struck by tiny starfish Tonight
we release the man into the machine
Ladies & Gentlemen All there is
to know about a man is in his breath

FRIENDSHIP & POETRY:

ELEANOR WILNER & BETTY ADCOCK

Editor's Note: In a new feature section that celebrates friendships between poets, we will ask two practicing poets to make independent selection from each other's work, and present it to our readers.

BETTY ADCOCK

I was much taken with the idea of having one poet choose another, and then having each of us choose fifteen pages of the other's poems. I chose Betty Adcock because she is of my generation, but comes from a very different world; I came to her work late, and it was a wonder to me. She represents to me the living voice of the Southern poetic tradition, though as only a woman schooled early in loss and unafraid to embrace contradictions could have carried it forward, and with such eloquent, grieving and clear-eyed attachment to the common ground. These poems are from books spanning a thirty-five-year period.

—Eleanor Wilner

Things Left Standing

That summer I trailed the creek
every day daring to come
to the end of what I knew
with thin August water beside me,
the sun on the fields almost audible.

The last day, I turned with the creek
where a pine grove I had never seen
held a ruined country school, gutted
not by fire but by children
grown tall and permitted
their will among the unused.

In a coat of shadow and dead paint,
the walls seemed to fade, leaving outlines,
leaving one intact pane of glass
where the sun struck and gathered a shape
like the tow head of a child,
one who was left or whose ghost stayed
to study the seasons of corn.

Drawn in through a doorway of splinters,
I touched broken desks, touched
the smell of wasps, housedust, pine needles.
The back wall was gone,
the room left open and legible.
Names were cut deep in three walls,
and shapes: every sexual part, all things
male and female carved outsized,
whole new animals
in a wooden impossible book.

In the movement of shadow, that place
trembled with ritual, with the finding
that always is personless.
I spoke to the fields
severed names, fragments, forbidden
words notched crookedly, correct.

I lay down near a tree, slept,
and my dream shaped a man,
made simply of summer and grass,
who would take on a face, who would hold me
speaking the tongue of the touched.
I woke with the grass on my dress,
sharp stain that would stay.
The ghost that clouds any window
only at one angle of vision
was gone when I turned for home.

That which is given once
or thrown like a curse or a weapon
came both ways in the ruins of August.
I knew the dead child in the glass,
knew the sun with its open knife
and I stood up in the smell of the future
to wear as time had given
the green, deep scars of the light.

From *Walking Out* (LSU, 1975)

At the Fair

Before even the glorious ferris wheel,
we wanted the animals. "Wild!
Exotic!" yelled the menagerie man.
Inside, we watched the molting hawk ignore
for the third year in a row,
boys and their sticks. The fox
caressed his cage door with a furious muzzle.
He was new, unused to noise.
We counted splinters in his nose.
The giant bat uncloaked himself, a mouse-mouthed yawn
and wing-tips touching wire on either side.
One old wildcat stalked his shadow
while his eyes stood still.
When we had seen them all,
we moved to the music and wheeling lights
where people were passing each other.
Behind each fixed look something quick walked,
jerked at the end of its chain, turned
to cross a face again.

From *Walking Out* (LSU, 1975)

Clearing Out, 1974

After this kind of death, sudden and violent,
there's difference forever in the light.
Here's the sun I'll see from now on
aslant and keeping nothing
in its backward look. I have become rich
with disappearance. I have become this light

pooled now on my father's desk,
his grandfather's—rolltop sturdy as a boat
and ice-locked in a century of deepening afternoon.
I have to open it and take the cargo on
myself. There's no one else.

Forget the pigeonholes with their indifferently kept
papers waiting to fly out and be important.
They were never important, the cash and receipts,
leases, royalties, mortgages wadded here like trash.
Forget the checkbook that was awash with blood,
and the wallet, its pictures crusted dark.
Everything in his pockets was afloat.
A man shot in the stomach drowns
what's on him. Let the *personal effects*
stay in their labeled plastic sack. Go on

as if this were a forest with a path.
It's like him to have kept a jay's flightfeather,
old now to crumbling, though it holds to blue
like a blind man's memory of sky;
and a terrapin shell bleached of all camouflage,
white dome of cyclopean masonry in scale,
packed with the shape of silence as a bell;
a wild boar's intact lower jaw, the yellowed tusks
like twists of evil weather caught in sculpture,
dusty in a scatter of red cartouches,
the shotgun cartridges gone soft as cloth.

One drawer's half filled with pocketknives,
all sizes, jumble of dark hafts like a cache
of dried fish. Opened, these could still
swim through to sapling heart. To bone.
He had a good eye. With any kind of blade
he'd make a creature walk straight out of wood
into your hand. The few he didn't give away
are gathered here, votive and reliquary:

bear with her hitch-legged cub,
dove in a tree, wild turkey open-winged,
two deer with antlers slightly off
—imperfect the way antlers really are—
and a razorback, a bobcat in a leap.
And then the horses.
My mother gave him real woodcarver's knives,
cherished in their box and not once used.

The best of the figures is the bucking horse,
body like a hauled-back bow.
Even on this scale the strain, the shine
of muscle showing, wind in a flung stirrup.
And all the intricate heave of wished-for power
is drawn down to a block two inches square,
four hooves and the head locked on the moment
arching off that little ground.

Drawerful of keys, marbles, arrowheads, rocks
he saw some form in. Keys to nothing standing.
There's a grace to the thin-shanked instruments
whose ends look like dull claws, the kind old houses
had for every room; blunter keys for barn lots,
cabins that held the violated lives of slaves,
cotton houses, lawyers' offices, stores
that ran on barter.

A peace comes to this sorting.
When my grandmother was a girl, she raised a fawn.
It went wild afterward in our woods. Later,
a buck full-grown thumped up the steps one night
onto the porch outside this very window,
slipping and knocking antlers on the rail.
Framed in the lamplight for one still moment,
the strange known eyes looked in,
and the young woman looked out at him.
It's the part of every story we remember,
the dream lost track of, changed
and coming back.

Distance has webbed my eyes like cataracts,
thickening like an ice sheet I must lift.
Heavy with damp,
here is the Teal Bible, 1815,
brought to Texas with the first encampment
of Anglo settlers. It's pure living mystery
why they came. Unless mystery's what they came for
after all, with no way to answer it
except the ways to kill; and no new dream enough
to staunch the stubborn longing to recover
what vanished in their footprints.

My great-grandfather's whistle carved of horn.

A cedar knot, deep turn in the red heart
heavy and separate. Nick it, and the scent
of cedar pours out like a sound, that thick.

Wild turkey caller whittled out of pine,
all confirmation gone.

The hunter's horn with one note for the lost.

And a perfect doll-sized real cane-bottomed
chair in a bottle.

That's the lot. I'll take what matters,
blood and documents, to the life I made elsewhere,
that place so far different in this light
you could get the bends between here and there.
The animals in wood, the stones, the silence caught
in terrapin's shell and turkey's pine voicebox,
this desk itself—a beholding full
of time before the tree was cut to build it—
I set all adrift, dismantled vessel, log raft,
rough-layered rings of association
like a language widening.
And the loosed river takes it
toward the turning sawblades of our dawn.

A Greek poet said it. Thémelis:
What would death have been without us?

From *Beholdings* (LSU, 1988)

Ays

I.

The name softens in the bayou,
borne on that murmur, and anchors in wrong letters
on the black bridge marker: the local mispronunciation
   Ayish—anyhow
  it goes on being gone.

  And it must have sounded, said right,
like a cry, like something between a cry and ashes,
   what wind and earth will take.
    So little
   is known of the people who spoke
themselves in it, the spell of their living,
   I think my father—
I think my father with his boyhood's hoard
of scrapers, handaxes, bowls, and arrowheads,
must have held the heavy unhearable echo
   of all that was left to know.

  From the fields at the broken foot
of our farm, from the stony rise that's still
   called Mission Hill,
  he fished their village up,
hearthsites and graves blindsided lightward
   by the shovel-load and scrabble
of a boy's dream-ridden hands in 1915, imagining,
given to imagine, another kind of Indian—
   plains-eyed, horseback and dangerous.

  And when the ceremonial stones
in their perfect pairs, and the points of every size,
the pipes and awls and quick-fired shards
   were stolen in turn from him,
   in his seventieth year taken

by persons unknown, persons unknowing, who must have sold
the lot to a back-street dealer in Dallas or Houston
       where there'd be no questions about origin,

       then I think my father crying
as one might cry for kin, and not for the simple
serious forms but for unknown echoes around them,
       something never unearthed of his own,
a firesite blackened and fine-sifted as sorrow is
when it cannot be spoken, having become the ground,
       and the longing forgotten:

those magical far-eyed horses that never came.

From *Beholdings* (LSU, 1988)

To a Young Feminist Who Wants To Be Free

You describe your grandmothers walking straight
off the boats from Finland, Latvia
too late, early in this century, to bear blame
for sins we're bound to expiate:
in their funny hats, a potato in each pocket,
what possible American shame
could they hand down to me? You have your own
angers, you say. So much for the nineteenth
century's slavery, lynchings, native massacre, and the teeth
of cities still gnawing off the feet of survivors,
those gigantic traps still set.
You blame the men and free yourself of time
and fathers, displaced from more
than countries lost. Or never claimed.

I can't help thinking of the miserably hot summer
I taught in Michigan, where a July Fourth
was the whole *treasury of virtue* hammered home
in speeches praising Michigan and the lever of the war
that undid slavery and joined the union back.
Yet that whole campus was the record of a severing:
not one face in any class was black.
And only a few miles distant, our Detroit
was roiling and afire.
The students laughed at my slow southern accent,
joked that I'd brought the unaccustomed heat.

Perhaps I know too much, living as I must
with the lives (in letters) of great- and twice-great-
grandmothers,
southern women talking about their slaves
as if it were ordinary. It was. Sometimes the wills are there:
whole black families listed with the mules. It's terrible enough
to die about, and people did: the saviors and the guilty
and the simple poor. Never believe it's gone.

The stain is mine and I can't pass it anywhere but on,
and to my own. I live with what the past will not stop
proffering. I think it makes me wiser than you are,
who measure by the careful inch your accident
of time here and your innocence.
It lets you be only the victim,
lets you find the gold–
eyed goat still waiting in the bushes
to be bled.

Anyone who came here anytime
came here to take this country's gifts.
Not even you may refuse this one:
what's built on darkness rests on it.
And there is wisdom yet, though hard to see
in this peculiar light. It is the only light
we've got. And when was it *not* the case
(except in hell) that land and history
wear another's face?
Here is the necessary, fearsome, precious,
backward whole embrace.

From *The Difficult Wheel* (LSU, 1995)

Four From the Spider

Enact yourself between fixed points,
but loosely—let the wind anoint
clarity with death, and death with light.
Live on the sheerest opposites.

Dance in a thin but working order.
Choreograph a net that severs
with just such difficulty as
makes it worth the making-over.

Take what comes, food or the random blown,
with indiscriminate self outspun.
The world is everything that sticks.
Choose. Then count illusion's tricks.

In the season's final filament be caught.
Nothing—not saving grace nor closing argument—
attaches to your having been
the wheel you turned in.

From *The Difficult Wheel* (LSU, 1995)

Fallen

The space shuttle *Columbia* broke up over several East Texas counties,
including sparsely populated San Augustine County, on the morning of
February 1, 2003.

Silver the winter morning, silver
the early sun downpouring
on to columns of pine and oak, miles
of birdsong-piercing silence silver
in the hour just before the rain;
and our shining myth oncoming, loosening
piecemeal overhead a ghastly charivari
in the high branches, mayhem broken
from the seared-off caul of cold space.

Imagine the torn, deer-haunted woods
where a severed foot still in its boot
was driven into mud. Imagine rags of flesh,
the heart found near a logging road,
the arm in underbrush, insignia beside
an upended helmet filling with icy rain.

Buzzards led the searchers—

                        don't recoil—do
not imagine this a story to be tamed by naming
heroes who died for country and some further bourne
worth dying for.

                Don't imagine this as anything
beyond the old arc snapped, covenant entirely
broken, our ships no more than silver needles
trying the boundless haystacks of the stars.

Those shadow-stories people lived within
(when we were only hurt and poorly wise)
have hardened into nightmare: heaven

as fleshly destination, hell a fire
we make on earth where myth and science
change partners in the dance.

Only thin February light could plumb the deep
East Texas forests, men combing miles of underbrush
for the whole bloody puzzle, every shard
of failed metal and all the flesh it failed.
Among enormous trees, on a red clay road,
Chinquapin Baptist Church—chosen
beyond all prophecy and imagining—became
receiving station for the shattered dead.

Of course exhausted searchers didn't exhaust
that arboreous dark, its snarled thickets,
its hawk-sharpened air.
                                        Light-footed foxes live there,
wildcats, the invisible cougar, wild boar
winter-thin and hungry, and shuffling armadillos
better armored than the astronauts sent out
as latter knights to press
our argument with airlessness
and make a grail of the mirage our image is,
among the novas and the planetary shrugs.

Disarticulate as temples seized by jungle,
this journey too will disappear. For a while
a mangled piece of the spaceship's hull
swung high in a shagbark hickory,
            bell calling what faithful
                            to the altar of the owl?

From *Slantwise* (LSU, 2008)

Rare

Leavenworthia texana . . . found only in the southeast
corner of San Augustine County, Texas.
–*Nature Conservancy* notes

Losing ground, this obscure East Texas county's
gone into its past like a wintering plant,
its one town shrinking inward, root-cut.

Beyond the empty streets, one farm—enisled—
rests on strange erosions, outcrops of the Eocene,
greensand clay under calcareous sediment

that holds more fossils from the ancient seas
than any place on this Deep Southern coast.
What died here was immense, was measureless.

What dies here now is negligible to compare:
songs, a forest, a lilt of speech, and violence
in the ways to farm and worship, to kill, to cure

the meat. Churches and small stores once bloomed
with people and raw goods on a roiling sea
of the dark history that lived on. Now

the depths are gone. The South's crooked anomalies,
like beached creations of another world, have built
in dying a land no one can till.

Now, on my great-grandfather's farm, on fossilized
remains of the longest prologue, this
unspectacular blossom: Texas golden gladecress.

Leavenworthia texana flowers in February,
a tiny yellow burgeoning for the narrow
days between winter and spring. Sharply bright,

endangered, useless, almost too low to see,
it's visible only on close inspection
of the common ground; is found in this one archival

soil, nowhere else on earth. Like poetry,
it thrives in contradiction,
one of the small, acute survivals.

From *Slantwise* (LSU, 2008)

ELEANOR WILNER

Eleanor Wilner and I share an era though we are from utterly different worlds. I met her only during the last decade, but I had loved her poems from the moment I read her first collection, *maya,* the year it was published (its title poem appears here). Singularly intense, rich with the material of the world and with re-visionings of the narratives that have shaped us, Eleanor's work serves as celebration and warning at once. She is sorceress of the word, a wise woman, and I am honored to choose poems to represent her compelling presence in our literature.

—Betty Adcock

Of a Sun She Can Remember

After they had been in the woods,
after the living tongue woke Helen's
hand, afterwards they went back
to the little house of exile, Annie and
Helen, who had lived in the silent
dark, like a bat without radar in
the back of a cave, and she picked up
the broken doll she had dismembered
that morning in her rage, and limb
by limb, her agile fingers moving
with their fine intelligence over each
part, she re-membered the little figure
of the human, and, though she
was inside now, and it was still dark,
she remembered the missing sun
with a slow wash of warmth
on her shoulders, on her back –
as when you step shivering out of
a dank shade into the sun's sudden
balm – and as the warmth spread,
it felt like the other side of water,

and that is when she knew how
light on water looks, and she put
her outspread hands into the idea
of it, and she lifted the lines of light,
crosshatched like a web, out of
the water, and dripping, stretched
the golden net of meaning in the light.

From *Reversing the Spell: New and Selected Poems* (Copper Canyon Press, 1998)

What It Hinges On

When everything is going
just one way, and seems to be
headed for a cul-de-sac
or some stunning culmination…
all at once, a creak (as a rusty hinge
warns of an intruder in the night)—

the wind from another quarter
takes the sail, the cage door opens
or the lid slams shut: and all our
plans are so much smoke, a handful
of torn paper, confetti in the air
that swirls—a letter here, a sentence
there, years of work litter the field
that lies outside the town that flood
or fire took back, as the great tectonic
plates grind out their harmonies
below the sea, and the earth turns
in its restless sleep, spun
by what we cannot see, the hand
that is no hand, but brings us calm
to think it so, and think it ours
to smite our enemies,
forgetting
as we turn it to a fist,
it is ourselves curled, blind
as newborn kittens, in the palm.

From *Tourist in Hell* (University of Chicago Press, 2010)

American Atlas

This morning the mountains were moving again,
        the train sliding across the northern steppes
            of America, clouds clinging to the peaks
                as they disappeared behind the glass, one
                    after the next. The trees, up close, went first,
                just green streamers at this speed,
            and, it is true, the mountains lasted longer
        to the view – but still they went. The roof
of the train was glass, and the windows
        huge, so that the moving landscape was
            the sheath of our cocoon – everywhere we
                looked, the world streaked by. At night, safe
                    in the rocking bassinets of berths, we
                could forget how the world was fleeting,
            a fugitive from our gaze – the fields turning
        to malls and parking lots, then those a blur
of asphalt and of lights; the forests
        rushing past on the flatbeds of logging trucks;
            the transient cities were a smear of
                toxic gold, a yellow pall that flowered by us
                    like buttery, liquid smoke. The Vs
                of geese retreated through the skies;
            we saw no animals at all, and if, out there,
        birds called or insects chirped,
we heard nothing through the walls
        of glass. Sometimes we wandered down
            the narrow swaying line of cars,
                the tubules of our sealed world; a blast or two
                    of air would hit us as we swung between
                the cars – freezing air, and thin, that forced
            us quickly back inside. Days passed,
        and months, and then the years, as we
watched the world fly by, and disappear;
        and lately we have noticed that the blur
            out there is getting worse, but whether

this is a symptom of our failing eyes, or
the earth itself is going dry, its thick loam
turned to dust and blowing in the wind, a desert
where the woods and farms once stood, or
the world outside is somehow growing shy –
at times it seems to abruptly turn away – the train on a hairpin curve,
the fleeing world the products of our speed.
But it is when the mountains shift on their great
pedestals of stone and, one by one, begin
to slip away, that a desolate thought
will rear its head – as if a giant had grown tired of
its burden of the sky … a cry goes down the cars
and here and there we hear the fists
beating helplessly against the panes, for knuckle-
bones will shatter long before the glass gives way.
Someone pulled the high red handle of the emergency brake.
The handle came off in her hand. We hurtle on.
The mountains are going now, faster and faster
they seem to race away from us, like waves
in a strong ebb tide from a fading coast –
we stare at what is happening out there;
as daylight will dispel a ghost, nothing now
impedes our view, and someone shouts:
A toast! Let's drink to that. Prosit! and lifts
an empty glass to the empty air.

From *The Girl with Bees in Her Hair* (Copper Canyon Press, 2004)

Fetish

Fetish is defined by
Slavoj Žižek (a philosopher
writing from Vienna)
as the embodiment of the Lie
that enables us to sustain
an unbearable truth. We cling
to the disavowal of what is so
in the shape of an object
that we love and can't let go –
this object lets us go on
as it keeps the full impact
of what is real
from reaching us. Though
he says so, in the fetish of his
nomenclature, he too is hiding
from the nature of the sentient
beast. Mind-numbing
numbers massacred, year
after year, by our own kind,
more kin than kind – how
live with what we know
without the Fetish, pale
as hope, evanescent
as the foam, translucent wings
made in the image factory
of that recurrent dream
where madness is staved off
another day. While real
cities fall in burning chunks
of concrete, melted steel
and flesh, who dares
(philosopher or not)
to mock the glued-together
toothpick cities of the heart,
where the soul, that cricket,

lives and chirps, and leans
against the brittle wood,
and, as a Fetish should, even
in the twilight of the gods, folds
back its little wings, and rubs
its skinny legs against
the odds, and sings.

From *The Girl with Bees in Her Hair* (Copper Canyon Press, 2004)

"Wreck" and "rise above"

Because of the first, the fear of wreck,
which they taught us to fear (though we learned
at once, and easily),
                              because of the wreck
that was expected (and metal given velocity
and heft to assure it) —
                              we became adepts in
rise above: how many versions: the church
steeple that took the eye straight up to
heaven (though it seemed snagged on
the cross-beam of that cross, torn blue
at the top, where sense leaked out). And
rise above, transcendence, on that higher
plane, the vertical direction of virtue (a bony
finger pointing up to where matter dissolves
into distaste for it);
                              the space program, expensive
tons of rocket (soon to be debris) fired off
the planet's crust at anything out there, pocked
moon, red rocky Mars, *ever the upward
urge*, carved in the marble arch of the old library
door under which generations passed,
hoping to rise above it all —

like the woman the magician levitates
over the table, her body floating an unlikely
inch or two above the velvet-draped plateau…
watch her hovering, weightless,
                              the crowd staring
in wonder, the trick of the thing still hidden,
and the magician doing something now
with his hands, a flurry of brilliant
silk in the air, as she floats
in the endlessness of art,
                              the magician

still waving his scarves, the air a bright
shatter of wings, doves from a hat,
our disbelief suspended,
while below, the wrecks accumulate:
scrap yard, broken concrete slabs, and
all those bodies not exempt from gravity,
beneath our notice as we ride
above it all, like froth on a wave
that will be water falling by the ton,
soon, when the tide turns.

From *Tourist in Hell* (University of Chicago Press, 2010)

In That Dawn

"Bliss was it in that dawn to be alive,
  But to be young was very Heaven!..."

  —Wordsworth

We thought if we brought the statue down, the bronze
        man on a horse, the tyrant-hero, if we held the old
            armor up to the light, till it faded to a ghostly
scrim, then the sun would pour through, the doors
        swing open, the window shades fly up of their own accord
            and all would be well in the public square, the buckets
lifted from the central fountain would overflow
        with a clear water, the man on the cross would step down,
            put on his clothes, and – a feather in his jaunty hat
and walking stick for the mountains – wave goodbye,
        taking with him and away forever the bleeding ikon
            of tortured flesh as an object of veneration. And the bells,
the bells would play Mozart in the towers, and a fresh breeze
        would set the wind chimes playing, and – of course –
            birds, not seen in decades, would nest again
in the blossoming branches – oh, it was a good
        dream, really, though now it lies in a child's book,
            and the library in which the book stood, on a low
shelf that a child could reach, is burned to the ground,
        and the child with it; the city is under curfew, helmeted men
            patrol the ruined streets, where nothing stands but
the bunkers – not the statues of the old founders,
        not the wall made entirely of mosaic tiles, not
            the firehouse with its great carved doors, nor the sandwich
shop on the corner where, on his blanket, the little
        terrier slept, nose in his paws, and his dreams sweet.

From *Tourist in Hell* (University of Chicago Press, 2010)

Beauty and the Beast

Her fur new-licked, the whitetail fawn
peers wide-eyed through the screen
of field grass, her ears outspread
to catch the slightest sound. Even asleep,
her ears are pricked and ready, as if
to catch intruders in her dreams.
But breathe her name, she's gone.

"These things in which we have seen
ourselves and spoken" turn from us now;
even the rocks, in which we glimpsed
enduring things, obscure themselves,
perhaps deliberately, in mist.
As deer, when caged in zoos or
put to other abstract uses,
lose their thick plush of russet
brown, the wetness of their
noses, their special way of stopping
at a sound—so when we fling our net
of thought, the living silver
of the ocean clots. To what
pass have we come, when hope
is no more than desire
to share in their oblivion,
when what seemed brute and dumb
till we had loaned it beauty's
tongue, seems now as eloquent
as silent heaven?

We, who burned our brand
into the uncomplaining flank
of the creation, begin to hope
for what may yet survive us . . .
and as the animals grow
smaller, moving off into a blue, inhuman

distance, we dare not call out
after them: "Good luck!"
for fear our best meant words, straight
from the heart, will follow them
as they depart, and curse them.

From *Sarah's Choice* (University of Chicago Press, 1989)

A Moralized Nature Is Like a Garden Without Flowers

In the Garden, as the Bible tells it,
there were: two trees – forbidden;
the snake of a former cult – demoted;
one man, one woman – her appetite,
their famous shame. And nowhere
in the shade of those *verboten* trees
was there the feel of cool moss underfoot, never the veils of water, gravity-
flung, over the edge of granite
into the dark that pools below;
no restless hours, no bug-eyed frog
unfurling its tongue, no insect hum
of propagation, no busy messengers
of change; nowhere the silken bowers of
desire into which bees plunge, drunk
on nectar and remembrance
of the larval honey-lust –
no flowers in Eden, not even one.
So beauty had no figure, no sacred
symmetry, centripetal, slowly opening
to a half-glimpsed nuclear core –
hot enough to melt the arctic,
icebound heart of God.

One flower in Eden
and they would have known
beauty, and knowing that,
would know how beauty fades.
But Eden was flowerless, and from
that lack come flaming swords,
and words like *everlasting, absolute,*
and parting seas, and burning towns,
and fear of looking back.

From *The Girl with Bees in Her Hair* (Copper Canyon Press, 2004)

maya

The yogi sits on the burning rock, a drying skin
that has shed its snake. His beggar's bowl
is empty as a skull; the sky *nir-vana*, without the wind.
His eyes are waterless and shed
tears neither for the dead nor those
who drag themselves through doors
to start the daily round again.
He is vacant as the space between two stars.
He lets the lion claws of sun
rake him unopposed. Chameleons, mistaking him
for stone, stretch out on him to take the sun
and lose their color to his own.
And still he sits, transparent soul,
a blister on the earth's brown back.

The woman, says the holy man, can never
escape from *maya*; it grows in her like maggots
in tainted meat, and drives her from his holy ground.

She runs, down the grassy path by which she came;
her passage stirs the grass to dancing. *maya
maya*…as she goes down, the growth thickens
the green and tangled forest takes her in.
Her skin is like the fawn's – indelibly marked
with sun and shade: in safety, ornament;
in danger, camouflage. When she sinks down
among the twisted vines and sleeps,
the darkness gathers at the center
of her eyes, the pupil of the moon
under a covering of cloud. *maya, maya*…
everything is close to everything, the stars
hang among the woven branches of the trees,
the moon is a lantern overgrown with leaves.
The first light rises from the steaming
earth; a heron lifts his head, his long legs

reeds that awkwardly step
out of their roots and walk, as the sun
opens his great yellow eye and lowers
his gaze, veiled by the lashes of the ferns.
A fish with golden scales leaps
through the shadow of the woman
as she bends to drink.

maya, maya…this veil is my skin
that hides me from him
who sees nothing.

From *maya* (University of Massachusetts Press, 1979)

"Never Apologize for Poetry"
—for my students

Despite the times, the cursèd spite
there is still music
in the leaves and magic in the cunning
spiral of a snail, and falling water
with its lovely, ruinous cascade of sound,
all this that beggars speech and yet
gives tongue. And when we say, "I, too, hate
poetry," it is not modesty forbids
the brag of art, but this abundant
wily earth our words must fail. Yet
in this union with the word, the long reach
of our little minds that compass
galaxies and quail before the corners
of a room at night, can still
ignite what otherwise might just go
      darkly
            on
as a fox deep in the hedgerow
brings its eyes to light
the otherwise too blank a green
and gazing out, gives that strange
brilliance to the dark luxuriance of leaves—
though here the trope must fail before
the fox, who suddenly gets up, swerves out
of our conceit to go its own
unhuman way, and yet the last
red blaze of tail, defiant plume
that waves off in the closing grass, turns back
into an emblem of our concealment,
red flag to warn the others off, meanwhile
our eyes will go on burning, stay
when all the world goes on its accidental
artful way—a double vision
bright inside the hedge, nature
given memory and pause…

as sun pays homage to the solid world
by laying shadows at its feet, as sky
lies looking up from the reflecting ponds
and clouds rest easily among
the lily pads, the sky and water, blue
and green, are so at one
that those two realms they say the gods
divided at the start, are mixed again
along these shaded paths, so far
from war, where leaves command
their ancient speech and falling water
telling its passage in the hand
has its own cool blue renewed
by touching us, the spell is cast
and joyful and assured
of our defeat, we spell it back
(*adieu*) into another hand.

From *Sarah's Choice* (University of Chicago Press, 1989)

Margo Berdeshevsky

For a Festival of Women
After Louise Bourgeois' "Seven in a Bed"

Louise has seven in a bed.   Her lonely pink litter of pups.
Dear women: I'm so unsure of a body,   as a life.

My four—
Are unknowns in my own   bed, in the dawn-dream,

Are in a man's skin, in a woman's skin,   flesh, are
Trance-dim are hemmed in the sheets' flat heat, faceless

Flesh. Are my wants, are my skins, are two and two, are
Me, are all me,   in the—

— That third body-boy is   too—
Young for me, is   just a baby tow-head boy   is

Me in my middle years midriff softened by kisses, cream,
He, a body I could want, see. —Is he looking at aging, at mine?

While my red vines climb. While they wiggle like
Hearts in flames. Humming.   Bodies and bodies. Mine.

Well, we are four. We are thousands. Of flesh.
Louise's are two headed and kissing. Are sculpted and seven in a bed,

Are cotton stitched limbs, twisted pink. One
Is singing soprano—*Put your head on my shoulder.* Thousands,

I can hear it,   their lives looped into lives like the vines. Louise's
Are the color of a dying old lady bathtub pink I ripped out for a better

Boudoir, late in summer. Seven, for Louise. Lives.
Mine—all ready for an orgy that hasn't begun. Hers

Have exorcist-neck-twists, hers are joined in being joined, hers are
Stitch and stuffing. Are more human than mine. Entwining.

Flesh, they pretend. Flesh is lonely, I say. Not so pretty,
I say. You know, I say, Dear women, I'm so un-

Sure of a body, as a life. Are you? Her clinging pink litter of pups.
Her coition. Her softened by crying, her by woman-stitches. Her by

Flesh stretched, by neck twist—entering. In my
Dream of an un-begun orgy—we're ready.

We're waiting soil, and fallow. We are not moving.
My four in a bed. And she has seven.

My not-mine tow-head boy—eyes my pale—shakes his
No, Not touching it, says No, not your softened

—I can hear it. Humming-humbled, am
Too old. Soft, am too

Not. In Louise's bed they're wrapped around and blind as worms.
Crying, maybe. A family, maybe, a full litter of

Pups in dying old lady pink embrace. Are loved.
Are disturbingly loved, and living like that. Joined.

In my house—it's yes autumn nearly, the ivy's fire-draping, now,
Virginia-creeper flaming, now, mounting walls like bats,
All passion-color brights, and—

I know so many women, aging, waiting, we—
All unsure of a body. Now, and later.

Oh my dear festival of women.
Gazelle again and young again. Yes. Tossing my yes, mirrored,
Yes,

About to be wooed and
Climbed yes, naked newly

Yes, or dead newly—to live newly,
Metal–spider–slowly.

How the fallow field is patient. One in a bed. Dear
Woman. I'm so unsure of a body as my life. Entwined. I.

KAREN AN-HWEI LEE

Sliced Casaba Until Three

Flat banana leaves in the ice box. Later on the street, a truckload of cut palm–
date leaves. Bright orange dates still cling, rustling in the exhaust. An open
window. Summer. Bottles of benzaldehyde or almond extract. A transparent
drop of amaretto burns a flutist's tongue. She presses a cool embouchure plate to
her mouth, no sound. Imagines a smooth song rippling in hot weather. Sets the
flute lengthwise on a table. Thinks about all the loved ones she's hurt.

Sun streams through the window, color of pressed guava.

Monday is a man with a fish bone in his name. Tuesday is sliced casaba until
three. Wednesday, a man sliced open an orange-fleshed melon so I could taste it,
says the woman. It's not a santa melon or casaba, is it. Friday is a vendor selling
brown cones of cane sugar and fried sliced plaintain, manzanos, memory of a
girlhood carried around in letters.

Requiem: Four Chrysanthemums

You would love to swim not in the way of transparent women who rest in the estuary, rather, from a region of blindness to bright surf roiling in your open mouth, from one fevered place to another. Four blue chrysanthemums aflame in your face. The gas stove clicks. Your voice sounds like a trio of smooth white stones the blind woman found outside her house. She washed the stones and put them out in the sun. Thinned hair white as a paper carp, not lush dark as years ago. A persimmon tree nurses bloodied fruit. Your soul was a permeable boundary, an open door for strangers. You are the angel with a dictionary. You write your own eulogy with the images of your hours, whispers this transparent woman. At your funeral, you inscribe the eulogy with your own life, your unsaved chrysanthemums.

POLINA BARSKOVA

Motherhood and Childhood
Another impression of Prague

Not too far from the place where Doctor Kafka is at rest,
Where one could fathom souvenirs, tourists, a press,
There's emptiness, a shop beset with emerald ivy-tresses.
I'll sit a little while and go.
Left right directly straight-ahead.
A worn-out cross, a wretched cat, a pit.
Lieutenant So-and-so, Averchenko, and next to him – the mother
Of one of our favorite (mine and yours)
Thought humidifiers, enshrouders
Of the *dull* truth about life (which they say is like pus),
Lies here at the edge of Prague. Alone, poor thing.
Above her is a grave – a slouch and scatterbrain,
Above her, scratching its belly, sits a mongrel,
And from afar Prague bellows with mysterious babel.
She lies here at the edge of Prague, beneath wet needles.
It is so dark and quiet. I believe Daphnis and Chloe
Would without hindrance here surrender to their joys
Atop a resin-perfumed carpet, alive and rusty.
On the outskirts of Prague lies his mother, the one who
Washed him in a basin, pouring water from a pitcher and singing.
And it seemed to him that all of her – was like a tower,
The body of a giantess soared, billowed, faded out
Into the darkness, while he was just a gob, a wad, a lump
Beneath her hand – a gob, a wad, a lump.
Her hand emitted warmth, the smell of home,
Up to that time when nowhere smelled of home
To him. But even this warmth and charm,
And her transparency, uneasiness, and burr,
Like any form of love, proved, finally, a real bore,
Nothing was left.
She died alone – he could not come,
Regarding such an impulse – as an impulse, as a whim.
And he stayed where he sat: at the table, *in his little glasses*,
The cat dug glumly through the pieces left to it,
The bird stared straight ahead with its round, lifeless eye,

And they told him that in Prague his mother died.
Sorrow sorrow and sorrow – he lies nude upon white,
And she laughs at her height, like a tower,
And with her pearly body and her stellar body and her snowy body
Shields him from the word *odd* and the word *horrid*.

Translated from the Russian by Boris Dralyuk and David Stromberg

Virginie Lalucq and Jean-Luc Nancy

From *Fortino Sámano* *(Les débordements du poème)*

Translator's Note: This translation is excerpted from the co-authored poetry collection, *Fortino Sámano (Les débordements du poème)*, poems by the poet, Virginie Lalucq, and prose commentary by the philosopher, Jean-Luc Nancy.

The excerpt is from a section in which Lalucq moves away from contemplating the execution of the Mexican revolutionary and counterfeiter, Fortino Sámano, to explore the function of language and image. The prose poetics commentary in italics by Jean-Luc Nancy is alive to the lyric aspects of Lalucq's poetry, as well as to the essence of the Lyric, which it theorizes. In the original, the poems appear separately, first, and then are reproduced in tandem with the commentaries afterwards. The Centre d'études poétiques (ENS) in Lyons, where Nancy and Lalucq held a colloquium, described their dialogue in *Fortino Sámano (Les débordements du poème)* as a work in three parts: "the poem, its duplication, and its overflowing." Taken together, their work transcends the division between poetry and philosophy: "there's no schism between the two sections, but interaction. It's about a trans-mission, a trans-position or an exchange of knowledges." The two sections are separate and connected, distinct and intertwined, mutually illuminating.

Not gone out / however / if I contemplate
under the lens / blades of grass / or snowflakes / in that instant / the window /
flowers / with frost /

    Suddenly it is elsewhere, it is not the execution anymore, it is a scene of interiority and observation – but no, it's the same: here, she regards the photograph and also the grass and snowflakes. It is only an optical chamber, a camera obscura *from where she is making her observations – and suddenly what is made visible is a glazing of frost prepared for by the assonance of blade and flake. What freezes then, what is glazed with frost, what frosty and what icy? It is always about the image, the glaze on the film or the window's frosted glass.*

    But also, flowers of frost cover the windows, this is a glazing-over of vision, a glaciation: what is cold in the image is like death. Fortino Sámano has been iced, as gangsters say (and he is one to the Feds). Iced while his cigar still burns. The question of the image is the question of frost just as the shadow is cold and just as everything freezes over in this scene of the summary execution of an impassive, sardonic hero. I understand the poem as being like these windows covered with frost flowers; as soon as there are flowers, poetry is taken to court; and appears as a "poetic image," one might say. What else is poetry making, if not an image? But what else is the image making, if not frost, ice, the cold glass of a magnifying lens or of windows?

    Remember: the image says nothing – it is in saying nothing that it becomes an image, it is in speech freezing over it. It is in photographing the dried blood of meaning.

Would you like to know something else?

All right, if I spend all my time writing
words, at times very intricate ones, with
pieces of ice, it's because I love to play
a game of cold reason.

*Now she addresses us, clearly speaking in the first person in her own name
as a poet or at least as a writer of words. Virginie Lalucq in person, whose name came
before the title, came before Fortino Sámano's name, shadow before a shadow, image-
maker opening the image up or observing it through a lens. "Virginie Lalucq" is a very
cold name, as cold as the name of Fortino Sámano — with his cigar between his lips — is
scorched.*

*Virginie sets and freezes Fortino, and then she comes and tells us what we did
not ask to know: her reason for writing. It is not clear, however, that we never asked
silently. What one calls a "poem" is a machine intended to provoke the question: why
was this written? While any other text responds to expectations, the poem devotes itself
to creating the expectation of its own reason. And here is its answer: "cold reason." This
is a tautology. Coldness is not an attribute contingent on reason, but an essential quality.
One might say it is a topos: "cold reason." Virginie turns and drops the epithet in like
an unexpected end, a final accident. There might be hot reason, and that is what is being
chilled down. Like Fortino, like the embers of his cigar. From hot smoke to cold shadow
a good game gone down is chill. The purpose of the poem is to freeze the image and frost
over its meaning. To freeze what burns is the necessary and sufficient reason for the poem.
The frozen fire, the dried blood of meaning, this is the reason.*

*After all, both the flame and the ice are burning, and perhaps ice can retain,
contain and maintain the fire's flames: the gun shot, the blood, the cigar.*

/ STOP / I'll stop you / and in reverse / eat
my language / I'll make you / speak / STOP /
as others / make / song / I won't leave you /
alone / STOP / stage / by / stage / hard palate /
after / soft / STOP / I'll make you speak /

i / ẹ / ę̣ / a / ü / œ / œ̨ / u / ọ / ų / â : repeat /
after me /

    Language in itself, in you as in me, language from you to me, language with stops like a telegram: a halting transmission of strokes, phonemes, voices, vocalics, spasmodic stream of bits of the desire to speak, it is an internal rage to externalize, to speak outside without stopping at each syllable that collides with the "hard palate," which, at the same time, deconstructs itself "floor / by / floor" like the poem tumbling down its own scaffolding but then, at the same time, always sharpening the flint that chips it (I want to say language) as much as shapes it. Here I am reading Virginie, I write "I want to say," but who's "I" and what do "I" want? She makes me speak and—in the end—prevents me from making comments, because she forces me to repeat after her exactly as she wrote it, and she does this to stop me, which is to say to forbid me from delivering my exegesis, since there is no way around the fact that what makes me speak is her. That is, poetry.

    But stop is also a homonym that means to shore; to stay (keep in place, prop up). She shores up my language like a stay, like a brace.

    I must understand that, in effect, the poem—and this is why it overflows— makes us speak more than it says. A poem glides onto the tongue and down the throat of its readers / listeners and makes us speak, takes hold of our jaws, lips, larynx and consumes us from the inside out. A poem that does nothing but speak in front of us and at us, without forcing us in turn to speak, has not overflowed and has missed the mark.

    So I repeat. I repeat after her, or do I repeat "after me"?

    "After me, the deluge," this is what happens in the end by repeating "after me": this is what happens with language; the deluge of language comes, rivers and seas overflow, the whole earth drowns; when we are brought on board language, there is no more terra firma; language is an ark to which no dove brings an olive branch; there is no relief from this endless flooding: the poem never lets go of us.

    These voices never let go of us, these vowels, vocations, invocations, convocations. To what are we convened? To repeat the whole of language, element by element, the whole of language vowelled and consonanted in the face of an obstinate silence.

In the Andersen fairytale, snowflakes
hover like white bees around their
queen, tall, beautiful and cold. Before
returning to her realm, The Snow Queen
walks down one of the streets in the tale
and every window blooms with flowers
of frost. Riding a sled with internal snow-
flake propulsion, swathed in a large, black-
iced cape, The Snow Queen has never
actually been taken as a model of warmth
(being snuggled in her arms is a risky
bet with death, on pain of immediately
freezing). Her regiments of frost protect her in tight ranks (white hedgehogs,
rotund bears, packs of snakes: in short
an army of living snow). Her castle is
built of powdery snow with no doors no
windows. In the center of this fortress
as light and airy as chaff, a frozen lake
serves as her throne.

*The legend becomes a fairytale, and the fairytale is the story of ice. It is clear, it
is a bet with death. A bet lost, a bet won in the losing: the legend freezes with the Queen
it holds tight. We hear in the assonance of the words "frozen" and "throne" a stalactite
of words like "tongue," "lexicon" or "glossary"—not far from "gloss," which is nothing
more than I am trying to do here. Frozen legend: here is the work of silencing. We do
not care about the story of Sámano, about his heroic death or his reckless insolence, we care
about how this death freezes speech inside us, stops our words, chaps our lips, rids us of all
comfortable and sensational literature. Rose water freezes, and reflective thought does, too.*

*Fairytales are for children. Children are the ones who do not speak. Fairytales
are not meant to be held true, but to be swallowed whole, like language.*

Translated from the French by Sylvain Gallais and Cynthia Hogue

ALICIA OSTRIKER

from **Approaching Seventy**

Lying in the tub after a smoke I remark
economics doesn't interest me
the three things I care about are individual

human lives, then art and beauty
then politics and cultural history and mythology
I'm thinking: apart from the personal stuff

on the other side of the tub my rational man
says truth then fun then honor, by honor he means
both reputation and doing what is right

head to foot we recline in the warm steam
and I remember a few summers ago
the peachy tangy cool night air

that blew in through the bathroom window
as we stood in the tub looking out
side by side trying to locate the comet

with the double tail, ah there it was
off to northwest over the neighbors' charcoal trees
difficult to see, like the lightest pencil touch

Poem Beginning With a Line by Fitzgerald/Hemingway

The very rich are different from us, they
Have more money, fewer scruples. The very

Attractive have more lovers, the very sensitive
Go mad more easily, and the very brave

Distress a coward like myself, so listen
Scott, listen Ernest, and you also can

Listen, Walt Whitman. I understand the large
Language of rhetoricians, but not the large

Hearts of the heroes. I am reading up.
I want someone to tell me what solvent saves

Their cardiac chambers from sediment, what is
The shovel that cuts the sluice

Straight from the obvious mottoes, such as *Love
Your neighbor as yourself*, or *I am human, therefore*

Nothing human is alien, to the physical arm
In the immaculate ambassadorial shirtsleeves

—We are in Budapest, '44—that waves
Off the muddy Gestapo in the railroad yard

With an imperious, an impatient flourish,
And is handing Swedish passports to anonymous

Yellow-starred arms reaching from the very boxcars
That are packed and ready to glide with a shrill

Whistle and grate on steel, out of the town,
Like God's biceps and triceps gesturing

Across the void to Adam: Live. In Cracow
A drinking, wenching German businessman

Bribes and cajoles, laughs and negotiates
Over the workers, spends several times a fortune,

Saves upward of a thousand Jews, including
One man he wins at cards, whom he sets to work

In his kitchenware factory. A summer twilight
Soaks a plateau in southern France, the mountains

Mildly visible, and beyond them Switzerland,
As the policeman climbs from the khaki bus

To Le Chambon square, where the tall pastor
Refuses to give names of refugees;

Meanwhile young men slip through the plotted streets,
Fan out to the farms—it is '42—

So that the houses empty and the cool woods fill
With Jews and their false papers, so that the morning

Search finds no soul to arrest. It happens
Over and over, but how? The handsome Swede

Was rich, was bored, one might have said. The pastor
Had his habit of hugging and kissing, and was good

At organizing peasants, intellectuals
And bible students. The profiteer intended

To amass wealth. He did, lived steep, and ended
Penniless, though the day the war ended,

The day they heard, over the whistling wireless,
The distant voice of Churchill barking victory

As the Russians advanced, his Schindlerjuden
Still in the plant, still safe, as he moved to flee,

Made him a small present. Jerets provided
His mouth's gold bridgework, Licht melted it down,

Engraved the circle of the ring with what
One reads in Talmud: *Who saves a single life,*

It is as if he saved the universe; and Schindler
The German took it; he wears it in his grave;

I am reading up on this. I did not know
Life had undone so many deaths. *Now go*

And do likewise snaps every repercussion
Of my embarrassed heart, which is like a child

Alone in a classroom full of strangers, thinking
She would like to run away. Let me repeat,

Though I do not forget ovens or guns,
Their names: Raoul Wallenberg, Oskar Schindler,

André Trocmé. Europe was full of others
As empty space is full of burning suns;

Not equally massive or luminous,
Creating heat, nevertheless, and light,

Creating what we may plausibly write
Up as the sky, a that without which nothing;

We cannot guess how many, only that they
Were subject to arrest each bloody day

And managed. Maybe it's like the muse, incalculable,
What you can pray in private for. Or a man

You distantly adore, who may someday love you
In the very cave of loneliness. We are afraid—

Yet as no pregnant woman knows beforehand
If she will go through labor strong, undrugged,

Unscreaming, and no shivering soldier knows
During pre-combat terror who will retreat,

Who stand and fight, so we cannot predict
Who among us will risk the fat that clings

Sweetly to our own bones—
None sweeter, Whitman promises—

Our life, to save doomed lives, and none of us
Can know before the very day arrives.

CASSANDRA J. CLEGHORN

Emperor Select

Question is how many
oolong buds I can snatch

from the bauxite cliffs before you,
craning, recall me to the verge.

Cypress shade you
make my rest.

Task me, trapeze me,
more fetch and trove

clamor, reach, fingertip tweeze,
not one bruised leaf, never

pay: day basket bulge,
crooked way home where I,

sleeping, dream the steeps, as you,
steeping, wait to sip.

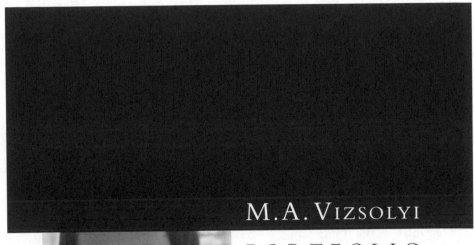

M.A. VIZSOLYI
PORTFOLIO

M. A. VIZSOLYI

[look i am king of the happy poets]

look i am king of the happy poets
& spend all my days where i am
buried i will leave a baby on the steps
of your door where the little field mouse
licks its tail in the mirror of the nail
i will leave a baby who will grow
to tell you i am just a stranger
he will ask you to teach him things
like how to whistle through two
fingers & make love to a girl so
she likes it it will take him time
to get at what you are hearing & he
will learn to say the things you
love & be king of the happy poets

[your stubby slavic fingers be not far]

your stubby slavic fingers be not far
from my mouth when i'm saying something
that will make everyone in the room
close their eyes & shake their heads
& one girl kiss me on the cheek & grab
my hand & take me to her room & say
what big beautiful gloves you bought
your fingers are so slavic there are
tiny hairs on the knuckles i want to
part them down the middle & draw tiny
sunglasses on each one & introduce them
to my zipper they will mess up their
hair & grow tiny wings & they will
carry me from this world to burger king

[all the kings are dead they lost to image]

all the kings are dead they lost to image
who has many children one called peter who
went to the track to watch his true love run
he loves runner's shorts & tuesdays
because no one else loves tuesdays & because
who wouldn't love a woman's hand i trimmed
my pubic hair he told her smiling joy
recurs between the legs of lovers &
sometimes you can never summon it &
people go to the doctor for this kind
of thing or learn how their tongues
disappear into the sea when i left my
country i came to your body & tasted
the sweat pooled in your belly–button

M.A. VIZSOLYI

[and now you must follow ah snowfall is]

and now you must follow ah snowfall is
gone we no longer need prayers the junk
floating about the ocean yesterday
when your mother strolled down
to meet us we were lying in the sand
in the picture you can see it floating
past us in the picture you tightened
your little woman muscles &
kissed them i lifted you up & the sun was
behind you in the picture the question
i never asked i meant to ask your mother
to take her shirt off i meant to see
what your breasts would look like
in forty years i may not live that long

[consider anal eroticism like a small breeze]

consider anal eroticism like a small breeze
lovely in its ends my small hands point to
the direction of lovely matter & it will
stretch out like a dream upon waking the
memory of your kiss is another way to live
near the edge of water in the place where
god is suffering i desire my love-stick to
be in your hands & what is it dear you desire
in various selves which perch along my sill
& bear silence like a doll with its own visible
history your sweetness and pretty bones
step into the room & knock on the door &
call out my name & I take you by the hips
& yell out sweet jesus those are tight pants

[in the heart of pennsylvania there]

in the heart of pennsylvania there
is no evening world bears prey upon
the sparks from sleeping flags &
the deer have learned to bite their nails
resting beside a blood-stained engine
in the forest when you enter the room
in your evening dress the heart of
pennsylvania turns away from the bullet
so it pierces the ribs & sends it
running through the woods shoeless &
brilliant we will scarcely lift its head
when we find it in the river
without realizing its weight
& you will look at me & i at you

[to be a poet you must understand how]

to be a poet you must understand how
to install a window i'm not speaking
metaphorically anymore there are books
on this kind of thing they are so
uninteresting you will find yourself
writing constantly on everything having
nothing to do with windows & sure
you can make extra money on the side
but that's beside the point you can
start a journal call it broken window
or lead a workshop on how-to manuals
& when a famous poet-mentor asks you
what you've been reading you can smile
& say in-depth window repair &
you can wink at her & she at you

[i wanted to write a ballad today i]

i wanted to write a ballad today i
would have called it the ballad of
apollinaire the pooh he would have been
such a simple man he would have lived
alone with his cat & he would have watched
women pass by his window on the rue des
fantômes the only thing he would have
eaten was honey to keep his skin shining he
would have been thrown into deep fits of
melancholy & touted a pop-cap gun & shot
at his reflection in the mirror wearing
his pajamas & humming a little sad tune
that faded out into the sound of rain i didn't write
this so i could write you this poem my love

[a woman loves to see her man with his]

a woman loves to see her man with his
dick out walk into the room & relax
on the couch his balls softly resting on
the cover i am building a ladder i told
her a ladder to my penis so you may climb
up to it & hang blue christmas lights
from it to the window to the table
& back again we will drink virgin
eggnog & watch it's a wonderful life
every time a bell rings my dick will
get hard & the wire will tighten
the window will open slightly the table
will move & a tiny angel
will fly out of my penis and sing out your name.

[i don't believe the old when they walk]

i don't believe the old when they walk
by me holding hands how can they love
each other's bodies when the young
girl with breasts as soft and bouncy as
the breasts of stars walks past them in a tank
top they smile at her this happened
today i was upset i asked them about her
they didn't notice the girl i was
upset i asked if they had any
identification they looked down & shook
their heads i arrested them both they
were sent to separate prisons my name
is radko yakovich soviet guard
budapest october 15 1968

[pleasure forever what a funny thing]

pleasure forever what a funny thing
to say i thought as you scratched my
back what would it mean to my cat &
the dead i realized you mean heaven
the place i always imagined would mean
no more carrying cakes just the cakes
a productive place you meant this is
communism do you like it & grabbed
the oil so i rub the knots
off your back which i did in the spots
you pointed out to me you said no
this is hell i turned to my cat & said
run for it i'm going to make love
to her & you don't belong here

[i'd follow you nowhere which is a place you]

i'd follow you nowhere which is a place you
call home here is the stage door of what
water does i've never named a thing but
that place on your body only i could ever
touch is source & is that every night when
i kiss it angels have no voices the one
in my car i think they might be blind &
deaf & bitter the one in my car
tomorrow i'll love you more i
promise as i approach your bed still i
will set down getting somewhere on your
pillow i am making a second promise to be
between your breasts & legs & to name my
first child the first word you whisper tonight

Tamara Kamenszain

Skullcap

It's not Toledo
it's not even in Spain
I don't know that city
where without a casket
they buried Buber.
They're all men
I see them coming
a procession of heads
retraced in circles
feminine little hat
along the fabric
I advance
to the open grave
I don't understand why
if I'm a woman they let me
glimpse the black hole
I'm long gone
I walk now
through the neighborhood of a hundred doors—
it's not Toledo
it's not even in Spain—
they're all men
from curb to curb
covering their eyes with their forearms
not even crazy
would they look at me
and I don't understand
how I'm suddenly a sin
that young prostitute on the Malecón
shouting I is another
young girl in Hebrew sandals
holding the bible in hand
men ignore me
use their language to scurry off
like New York cockroaches

—it's not Toledo
it's not even in Spain—
they want to return
to their black holes
their pigsties of rumination
their tongues at their fingertips
as they scan unnumbered pages
in the crumpled crotches of books
they don't even read
because that's not reading,
I'm ignorant of that city
—it's not in Spain
less so New York—
of texts as robed scrolls
of philosophers biting at dust
where *thou art*
where *thou shalt return*
sand slipping through fingers
ideas without a casket
aren't ideas
they're Friday's shooting stars
Saturday's obligations
you must wash away all of your sins
they saw me they looked at me
I was for them
another's woman
better I abandon them
in their ritual bath
they won't baptize themselves
so far from Toledo
expelled from Spain
extant since eras long before their own
and now what
now it's my turn
I'll deliver them in time

return to the future
shut with a key the hundred renovations
in the secular ghetto
of my indoor neighborhood.

Translated from the Spanish by Seth Michelson

SUSAN RICH

There is no substance that does not carry one inside of it

The real story is that she is a piece of light.
The real story is that light turns to flame
Turns to ember, then ash of burned
Sagebrush and city. The real story is
Sebastian remains behind to save the black
Mare with a bucket, a spiraling circle
Of stones. No one believes the real story
When the strangers politely repeat *fire*, state *evacuate*,
Stress *please*. Instead the hotelier at the front desk spits
Foreigners. Demands credit cards, passports, car keys.
Curses the tourists who create work after midnight,
Curses Isabella and the ships she sent out to sea.
Which leads the man to look up past the courtyard,
The mountains ringed with fire beads, the little
Flames clearly flirtatious, clearly beyond belief.

Here Are the Photographs Taken When We Were Alive

Here are the photographs of the fire, peach-colored and pleasing.
Here are the mountaintops, the houses in the distance, orchards
Caught in the cross breezes. Here are the helicopters heard
All around us—appearing like over-fed birds dragging their
Bird-baths of water. Here are the fire trucks filling up by the fountains.
The army, the Red Cross, the chaotic hum. Here snap, here click
How about that? heard continents away. Hail the award-winning images.

Don't Tell It To Go Away

There's a ghost in the room.
Call it *us*.

If we court it,
it will not stay. If we fail

to court it, it will not stay,
but it is here now

so we name it,
you and I, in the empty world

we warm with these old words,
your sleep talk,

incomprehensible,
and my simple unanswered questions.

I lie along the length of your body—
an old habit

reacquired. In contact
we remake this visitor together,

forged like a long-handled fork
to help sate a hunger

or a pure-hulled ship
meant for freighting what we knew and know again.

SAM TAYLOR

PORTFOLIO

Grand Opening

With flowers in your hair streaming
from slavery's indigo vats, come to me.
With elegies written in purple flames
on the white, brown, and black asses
of inner city tattoo parlors, come to me.
With an infinite regression of hands
over mouths, and mouths over azaleas,
with fists of subway concrete, with a cry
for autumn and for Ford Motor Company,
come to me. Come to me with my cunt on fire
with churchsick touchdowns of despair
with neon organs carpeted with newsprint
and three-minute music videos of cherry hoses.
Come to me like a bereft cocktail waitress
drunk in a trailer in the Florida Keys,
and I will come like a monster truck driver
with a six-pack of stars and Jim Beam,
I will come with a Library of Congress
chained to a collar and sworn to its knees.
And I will cry the pumping soulless cry
against your rosy cheek in the modern
vacant vacant and televised, my working mom.

Confession

I don't know about Grace. I know
about last night's snow puddling now
under the eaves in the global sun,
about Lucky Strikes and mathematics
and the neighbor's tv like the background
sound of the universe, careening.
I know about slot machines

and the odds that somewhere in infinity
a beetle will crawl along the underside
of water like a glass ceiling
and then somewhere there will be me—
feet and hands, you know the rest,
except this one will be me—really, me!
And one July 4th I will be thirsty

wishing someone would offer me a drink
and just then a chubby homely stranger,
unnoticed on the next sheet,
will turn and ask if I want a Sprite
and I will tremble with love, as we look up
at the sky scrawled secular religion
of America—fiery flowers spurting

colored semen across the heavens.
I know another night I will be
terribly alone, and racked with chill
and no one will call or knock
and the bombs bursting in air will fall
upon the hovels of permutations, people,
a few digits off from my home phone.

I know last night she turned over in her sleep
and said, "Go back and get the horses, John"
as I lay clueless with the moon

and hum of highway traffic. I know
Mexico borders Romania in the heart
of the atom, and China is on our back,
and some sweet young girl sewed this shirt for me.

I know a seed can blow sheer across
the wasteland to the other side of earth
and just as easily, the wind
can bury our words between our two mouths.
But, this morning after I had the thought
for her to place a piece of the dark
chocolate she was eating on my sunbare

dick, she did. She did. One moment
and then another. A sparrow rose to its branch
and looked around, snow fell from our roof
and then from another six miles away,
then four. I know there is always
something we are forgetting and something else
we have remembered too long. The river

rages day and night with the affluence of Spring
and not just here or on one continent.
The sea of grass goes on and on, until it joins
the sea of trees, or the sea of streets,
and I am lost in my own name
for happiness: the sky following me wherever I go
even into Conoco-Phillips. Last night, someone painted

my ceiling blue. Today, they want to make me treasurer
and give me 5,000 frequent flier miles
for a risk free 30 day trial offer. I know my fifteen minutes
will be eighty years, or maybe end tomorrow,
so thank you, I say, while my body can say,
checkmated into silence, wondering who will argue
where there is no grace, there is no grace.

Testimony

I have given up meaning, order, religion, but there are still constellations:
Your cunt. Your cunt and the sun. Your cunt and the sun and your face and
the table.

Your cunt and the moon and the sun and the street.
I travel these pathways again and again, Tuesday at noon and Thursday at dusk,

with a little song, a song and a jig, with laughter and sorrow.
I raise the cup to my arm raising the cup. I raise the cup to your cup

and to the cup of snow and the chalice of earth in the hand
of a crippled God who cannot raise a cup. Because he cannot,

I raise the cup to your arm raising the cup, and to the forest
of your arm showering its scents on an undeserving and hostile world.

I raise the cup to the impossibility of living—have you found it otherwise?—
and to the moral imperative of dying

and to shaving with a dull blade in the fountains of Madrid
and to the black sky that will cover us with pitchfuls of dirt

and to bouquets of frightened voices for sale in a clown's hand
and to my baby sister awake in the night like a sculpture of milk.

I have given up meaning, but there are still constellations:
the cup and the cup and the cup and the cup

and the stars falling into a black mug that no one will drink,
and me falling into your body these hours appointed by no God

and the moon and the sun, and tomorrow, and your cunt, and today.
And not your cunt, but your face. And not the moon, but this tear.

And not the street it carves, but a life. And not a life, but a cunt
telling a story to the face of the dark. Saying: *Listen, come here.*

And not on Thursday, but Today. And not in the Spring, but the Summer.
Not the Summer, but the kitchen. Not in the kitchen, but the warm bread.

Not in the bread, but the fingers and the tongue.
Not in the tongue, but the song, in the elegy sung.

And not the elegy, but each thing we did not know was loved.
And not love, but two bodies in Winter. And not the song, but the song.

Walt

Amid the bustling shipyards, he walks:
crates and bare-chested men, that's all he sees.
Slowly, I have to tell him,
point out how all the men are fully dressed,
everything hefted by a giant crane.

But already he has run ahead.
When I find him in the market, he is clapping his hands
watching children dance around a fiddler.
Walt, I say, like someone who must tell
a friend his mother has just died,
we are in a modern shopping mall.
No one is happy. No one alive.

I watch them disappear from his face.
We are standing in Hot Topic;
someone is selling a thirteen-year-old girl
a studded dog neck collar and a midriff.
We walk on through the Gap, Penney's:
glittering handbags, lingerie, cargo pants.
In the electronics aisle of Sears, he collapses
to the floor, before a bank of TVs.

I look at him, a broken man now
like the rest of us, crying, ashamed.
He tells me he wants to be alone.
I don't know where he goes
wandering—through a single rose,
through a kelson of grief,
through the avenues of the nineteenth century.
When he returns, he tells me we must sing.

Optical Illusion

Beneath a dark branch of oak, a darker blur
shoots down a pane of bright sky
disappearing into scrub, as if
entering the earth, but it's only a vulture
circling, downhill: unhurried, blue.

They're everywhere today, covering
the cliffs—meander, strong breeze.
This is the day in which yesterday happens
again, but slightly different.
A different man dies in a different car crash.

A different woman's heart is broken,
walks out into a different rain,
a different taxi. A different person cries out
in joy for no reason under a tree,
buys a coke, sits on a washing machine.

Someone different searches the internet.
At a different meeting, different people
discuss nothing from a different angle.
A different sweatshop moves to a different country;
A different woman is beaten with the jeans

she sewed too slowly. The ones
who were fucked yesterday get fucked again
today, but by different sergeants and captains,
different medals, more calloused hands.
Someone different stands in a different city,

holding a different sign. A different crowd
of inattention rushes by. Someone different dies:
Again, again. The poem writes itself in different words.
In the supermarket, we decide to make something
different for dinner: buy Bok Choy, endive.

Walk out into a sunset no one has ever seen.
The supply chain runs about the same.

Like This

The kayak's two blades dipping and rising on each side
like a machine, a propellor, its tan muscles—
trapezius and lats—perfectly timed, in synchronicity,
a calculation of microseconds that never need calculation.
Like this, a person moves down the river.
Like this, a person walks down the street. *Hallelujah*

has been said and resaid, said ironically,
said bitterly, parasitically, unsaid, and said again.
Pass the peas, likewise, said and resaid.
A child spits out his food and a mother frowns.
A word, said too many times, dissolves in the mouth:
Sa-id, suddenly foreign, misspelled, senseless,

is spit out. *Hallelujah. Fuck you. Pass the peas.*
The river flows with its spilled sack of jewels.
A person walks with his bagged up river of jewels, concealed.
A white man worries over how to put together a sentence,
how to say hello. *Hello, Hallelujah, Fuck, God*:
Centers of meaning like overflowing cities

to which all roads lead; granaries of sense, impulse,
contradiction. Every feeling in *fuck*, every in *God*.
Fuck yeah; fuck no. The scripted mantra of porn:
Fuck yeah, fuck yeah, fuck yeah, the yeah
dipthonged. *Oh fuck*: The woman who has locked her keys in her house.
Fuck: the man who has just chopped not kindling, but his thumb.

Fuck: the man at the edge of shuddering as her mouth grows still.
God, we say, in exasperation, in anger, fury.
God, I just want to make you shut up right now;
a man and a woman in a hallway before a mirror.
And in ecstasy—*Oh God*—the same woman perhaps, an hour later.
Oh my God: shock; did you hear Tyson drowned in the Pacific?

Fuck no way, a synonym. A healthier world perhaps
where they are synonyms. Like saying "this"
and meaning it with your whole animal life. This
thing, this life, this us, this. . .
Everything. Without fuck, no life. Without life, no God.
The kayak's two blades dipping and rising on each side.

The Book of Poetry

A friend, in Thailand, helping to build straw bale homes
was riding with four Buddhist monks on the back of a truck
piled high with musky bales. "I love water buffaloes," she burst out
in broken Thai. The monks laughed. *I guess that is*
a strange thing to say, she thought, but insisted.
"No, really, I really love them," trying to unfurl herself
clearly, practicing the Zen Garden of making conversation
with only a few words. "They are so beautiful, so strong.
Don't you love them?" But the monks just kept laughing.

Every traveler in Southeast Asia has her own story
of tonal confusion: the same syllable spoken different ways
becomes four, six, seven words. In China, Ma
means mother, but also hemp, horse, scold—depending if
it is flat, rising, dipping, or falling. Sometimes context helps,
as when ordering food: No one is likely to confuse
"I want to eat" with "I demand an ugly woman,"
unless one is dining in a brothel, and even then "I want eggplant"
though mistoned "whirlpool shake concubine twins"
is likely to produce only strips of sauce-smeared nightshade.

Everyone in China wants to know what you do.
It's not easy, even in English, for a poet to say that.
When they asked, I said first, "I write," *wo xie,*
or sometimes, after I had learned the word, "I am a poet."
Wo shi shi ren. Often, I was met by puzzlement,
strained foreheads, awkward laughter, Chinese people
glancing at each other for cues, uncertain how to react.
Not so different really from the response in America.
"A poet" I'd repeat. *Wo shi shiren.* Then,
"I write poetry," trying to make the most
of my minuscule vocabulary. "I write books of poetry."

Wo shi shi ren: literally, I am a poetry person.
Wo means I; *ren* means person, or man.

Near the end of my travels, someone told me
shi—which is pronounced "sure" and means poetry
in the high flat tone, as well as the verb "to be"
in the falling tone—also means shit
in yet another tone. So, all along I must have been saying
I am a shit man. I write shit. And repeating it.
A shit person. I write books of shit. Understand?

To be—poetry—shit. Something fitting in how these words
were assigned the same syllable, the same address.
Later, looking the word up, I discovered for each tone, *shi*
was ten or twenty words, a whole apartment complex
sharing one mailbox. *Corpse, loss, world, history, time, stone,*
life, to begin, to be, to die, to fail, to be addicted to,
rough silk, persimmons, raincoats, swine, long-tailed marmot,
clear water—all crowded into the same syllable—sure,
sure, sure. It was also coincidentally the word for yes.
So, perhaps I had said something else entirely.
I thought of the combinations I might have said.

I am a shit person. I write life.
I am a death person. I write being. I shit history man.

I history being person. I write time. I write books of failure,
books of corpses, books of loss, books of yes.

I am a being person. I write to be.
I am addicted to being a man.

I write books of shit, books of clear water.
I am a poet.

It seemed all the world could, even should, have one word
for everything—table scales, taxis, bicycles, stones, cities,
time and history and death and life. It was all shit.

It was all poetry. As for my friend, she found out later
water buffalo was a variation of the word for penis.
So, "I love penises" she had confided to the Buddhist monks,
the truck jostling, the potholes throwing her knees
against theirs. "I really love penises," she had insisted,
looking into their celibate eyes. "Penises are
so beautiful, so strong. Don't you love them?"

Since the syllable for monk is also the syllable
of my name on fire in a world of loss, I will answer. Sure,
I love penises and water buffalo and the smell
of wet hay, and vaginas and sautéed eggplant and concubine twins,
and I want to tell the Buddhist monks, and the Chinese bureaucrats,
and the official from Homeland Security
who stopped me in customs to search my computer, and my mother
the Sechezuan horse: I am a shit man writing books of stone
and the clear water has failed, but I am addicted
writing yes in a city of corpses and swine and persimmons,
here at the end of history, now at the beginning of time.

Chocolate Häagen Dazs for Karl Marx and Noah

Who is out in the desert waving the white flag
to the soldier with the sun in his eyes?

Yes, my name is God. Every morning, I shoot myself
in the mirror. It hurts a little, but I'll be alright.

Who prays? The proletariat: pack rats and squirrels
with exotic mushrooms hidden in the roots. And the rich

to clear conscience. A few thousand years is no time at all
to wait for a flood. So when you buy your Tide

and Pine Sol, remember. And as you drive your engine
through the peopled wilderness, remember

God is laughing. And not just because
everyone likes ice cream and shooting off their load.

Ours, ours. This land is ours, we all say;
before that, *ours.* But all of us are never there.

Someone said, in our agreed allegiance to insanity,
let us fight. And fall. Rather than say we've been wrong all along.

Falling is a great pastime. The disposable camera
left on the battlefield—who owns the picture?

My soul is there.

CHARLES BAUDELAIRE

The Albatross

Often, to amuse themselves, mariners on board
Will catch an albatross, that vast bird of the seas,
Indolent companion of their voyage, which soared
Above the ship gliding across blue vacancies.

As soon as the sailors settle the bird on deck
This former king of the air, awkward and ashamed,
Lets his gigantic wings piteously drag back
Along his sides like idling oars, useless, tamed.

How clumsy the winged voyager becomes, and weak!
Once full of grace, he's ugly now—comical too!
A sailor sticks a burning pipe into his beak,
Another imitates the cripple that once flew.

The Poet in his way is like this prince of clouds
Who haunts the storm and scorns the archers' drawn strings;
Exiled on earth in the middle of jeering crowds
He cannot walk, encumbered by his giant wings.

Translated from the French by Laure-Anne Bosselaar and Kurt Brown

ISHION HUTCHINSON

The Last Circle

When the moon ownself leaps back
globed and dumb into the lime tree,
a goat–head child in a seraph frock

under my window, the sea in my head,
the vision's concentric
ache summons the undead

out of water without panic;
the child avatar gives warning,
names all the districts

death shall visit by morning,
starting with Barracks, then Duckenfield;
the scythe will harvest heads

more than the sea of cane fields;
every hill shall hear the horn
and drop under the sun's wheel;

there first the ants will darn
eyes shut so flies can minister;
worms will have what is scorned;

soldier crabs will fork their dinner
as ombudsmen john crows watch,
peeled-back heads twitching sinister

in tamarind trees, ears cocked to catch
the frequent fall of carcasses,
until the ground is covered in a swatch

of skins and faces vacant as masks,
sinewed tongues knotted in shouts,
spread across shortcuts and passes;

then the dogs will gnaw their mouths,
then the maggots will saw their eyes,
then the beetles will raise their clouts,

then their shades, water-spies,
will be called by the seabirds
to the crossing, two obols for eyes,

gone, not *into the world of light*, but shards
shining into the deep first passage;
a slave sibyl will unbind her chords

and strike a welcome song to assuage
the used-up limbs, skulls white
with horror, eyes-holes daubed

thick with the ever-frightened
look-back for the sliver glint of cane,
the salt hills in the whip-lashed

breeze, paper clouds with ink-stain
seals, the harbours chained in smoke
holding up an exhausted factory name—

Albion Sugar Estate, sending its note
to indentured Indians in soot saris,
to make sacrifice, kill a child and a goat.

MELIH CEVDET ANDAY

Silent Stones

Evening is your village where we arrive on mules
I see your salt your flour your cattle
Your heart darkened in its crackling seeds
Like a writhing caterpillar
Dreams come heavily to us like life
Gathering your visions piece by piece
You extract the provisions of your beauty one by one
And spread your skirts out at your side
Like a flight of birds dragging on the ground

I see old pictures in your eyes
Your rain your sea in the brimming dawn
I see masts in the dark and in the sea
Your protected old forests and glaciers
I've had enough leave to me the courtesy
That your gaze has filled like a river
Now I'll line your silent stones
Up to the summits of your breath-taking knees

Translated from the Turkish by Sidney Wade and Efe Murad

MEAGAN MARSHALL

Purification

When I die
put me in the bathtub,
the one with the beryl-green
beach scene curtain—

I want to watch the plastic waves,
twist on the faucet, anoint me with its drip.
In my inert glass eyes, press sand—

plum taper
on your windowsill,
melting wax into steam—

I want to breathe your bar of chamomile
soap, let it slip, cover the bellybutton drain,
allow the stains to wash themselves out—

leave me in the tub
when I die,
shroud me in vinyl palm trees.

CHARD DE NIORD

From the Curriculum of a Serpent

Search your heart for any trespass
you might have committed against
your neighbor, weighing each slight
and peccadillo on the scale of earth
beneath you, then remove the ballasts
of generous deeds from the mass of your
transgressions since they are timid birds
in the mind of your neighbor, flying off
on the wings of forgetfulness to leave
the dead weight of insult behind,
tipping the scale beyond its highest
number. Try next to guess
the number on which the sharp red
needle would settle if the numbers went
that high. Gaze down then if you can
to see how stuck is the needle
on the highest number, which is only
the partial weight of what you feared
was true about the heft of even
the smallest hurt on the scale of earth
that stretches out before you.

The Animals

They bring me tokens of myself.
—Walt Whitman

I talked back to a cow in the upper field.
Patted her brow as she lowed in the barn.
I was mesmerized also by the chickens
in the yard as they strutted and pecked the ground.
I sat at the tables of all the animals to learn
their letters: the long e of the hawk,
the broad a of the crow, the diphthong
of the moose. I grasped the goodness
in their natures, whether wild or tame.
They were the blessed, dumb angels of earth.
Why was I so moved by the mere opening
of a beak, twitch of a flank, wiggle of a tail?
They brought me tokens of myself—a cold eye here,
a Christlikeness there. I was enlarged by a bee,
enlightened by a mouse. Nothing I did
returned to them what they brought to me.
They were the geniuses of paradise still.
I watched them *half the day long* as they swam
and leapt and crawled in their *going forth*.
I called each one by name, although
they did not come, except for the dog.
I pulled them from a thicket and prayed
as they lay on a stone and bled.

Pomegranate

I didn't send you the pomegranate to write about,
but to eat.
       It is from *this* world where every seed
counts for a day of life.

Memory Is a Fire

I was shopping for an end to my travails
in the Eschaton Mall when suddenly I spied
my second wife from the Golden Age
in Lord and Taylor. I saw just then
what it was I'd lost, her Eleusinian style,
her beauty from a distance that was also near,
right there but sovereign now in the endless aisle
of millennial blouses. That bedighted.
What was I so sure of as a younger man
in charge of other men to leave her behind?
That I would forget the fire that burned
in us like an angel's dress dipped in oil?
That it would burn us clean like the camps
I torched? What did I know about the coal
inside my heart? How long it burns
like anthracite on the tragic facts.
How nothing's lost inside the dark
at the center of the flames. I needed
to burn for a hundred years to see
what I feel and feel what I see
in the country I won with so much force.

In the Brief Time We Have Left

Let the ant live that's crossing the table.
Give me a kiss.
Give me another kiss.

BERTOLT BRECHT

Thoughts on the Duration of Exile

I

Don't knock a nail in the wall
Throw the coat on the chair.
Why plan ahead for four days?
Tomorrow you will go back.

Leave the small tree without water.
Why plant a tree now?
Before it's as high as a step
You will go gladly away from here.

Pull the cap over your face when people pass.
Why leaf through a strange grammar?
The message that will call you home
is written in a language you know.

As whitewash peels from the beams
(Do nothing to stop it!)
So the fence of violence—
Erected at the border
Against justice—will rot.

II

Look at the nail you knocked in the wall:
When do you think you will go back?
Do you want to know what you believe at heart?
Day after day
You work for the freedom
Sitting in your small room you write.
What is your work?
Look at the small chestnut tree in the corner of the courtyard
To which you carried a can full of water.

Translated from the German by Monika Zobel

MIRON BIAŁOSZEWSKI

Perceived Self-Portrait

They look at me,
therefore I surely have a face.

Of all the familiar faces
I least remember my own.

Sometimes my hands
live quite separately.
Then perhaps I shouldn't count them as my own?

———

Where are my boundaries?

———

I am overgrown either
with movement or halfliving.

Always though,
either full or empty,
but existence,
crawls inside me.

I myself wear
some kind of my own
place.

When I lose it,
that means there is no me.

———

There is no me,
therefore I do not doubt.

nothing happened

———

I probably stand
everywhere
just me

how frightening

Translated from the Polish by Boris Dralyuk

MARTHA COLLINS

[white paper #12]

Five white baby dresses
Milk in glass bottles, cream on top
Sheets on beds, lines, beds
Snow window snow

His white handkerchief, our white gloves
His starched white shirt, even at home

Gray faces framed in white
Black faces in negatives

Shadows in the sidewalk's gray mirror
The Shadow knows

New coloring books, grownup books without pictures
White keys first, then the harder black
Frost on the window, breath in the air
Chalk, eraser, chalk on the board:
Black page for white words

Water filling the white tub
Layers of white lingerie
Dress train cap veil
White-ribboned candles, knife

[white paper #17]

STARK WHITE AND
COLONIAL KHAKI RULE
THE URBAN JUNGLE
        (*Elle*, April 2008)

The British brought
khaki to India, dyed
their summer whites

The American army
copied in 1898 our
first colonial war

and afterwards until
we went to the jungle
and copied trees

There is no jungle
in this our first
largely urban war

In this war our letter
stamps became flags
waving on khaki

*Why don't
you wear a flag
pin* they asked one

of our candidates
who often wears
white shirts

which look quite nice
against his khaki
American skin

[white paper #21]

red apple wagon fire-
truck haul the long over
the sea parting the waves
this letter day ribbon
stop skin we said paint
the town were you ever
scare blood on my skirt
stop we said by whatever
means to end to move
them war war no skin
so red perhaps not skin but
what spilled from inside it

Shaking the Pumpkin Revisited:
Some Poems & Ritual Events from the Indian Americas

Edited with Commentaries by Jerome Rothenberg

Pre-Face

In the aftermath of *Technicians of the Sacred* (1968) the next step I took toward the construction of an experimental ethnopoetics was an assemblage of traditional works & commentaries thereon focused entirely on one of the world's still surviving & incredibly diverse "deep cultures." The resultant work, *Shaking the Pumpkin: Traditional Poetry of the Indian North Americas*, was published by Doubleday Anchor in 1972 & in revised versions by Alfred van der Marck Editions (1986) and the University of New Mexico Press (1991). As with *Technicians* I drew from a wide range of previously published materials, supplemented in this instance by direct translations of my own & by those of later & very significant translators such as Dennis Tedlock & Howard Norman. I also continued to be freed by the opening of poetry among us to expand the range of what we saw as poetry elsewhere including sound works, visual works, and event & performance pieces on the model of contemporary happenings & performance art. My own translations – "total" & otherwise – from Seneca (with songmaker & ritual performer Richard Johnny John) & from Navajo (through the good offices of ethnomusicologist David McAllester) were also first presented here, and the commentaries, much like those in *Technicians*, provided analogues to other primal cultures & to the work of contemporary avantgardists. In the process I made no pretense about my own connection to the Indian nations in question, though for a period of a decade & more it was far from trivial, & my next ethnopoetic assemblage, *A Big Jewish Book* (later republished as *Exiled in the Word*) was in fact an exploration of ancestral sources of my own "in a world of Jewish mystics, thieves, & madmen."

After three decades in print the life of *Shaking the Pumpkin* came to a natural closure several years ago, though a revised & expanded version has remained a tempting possibility since then. The following excerpts, no longer easily accessible, will give some sense of the range of work in this & other of our ethnopoetic gatherings – part of a process of composition that I've spoken of elsewhere as "othering" & that the great Brazilian avantgardist Haroldo de Campos has aptly termed "transcreation." Such approaches, as we view them, have appeared to us not as a distortion or falsification of the original work but as the most poetic – & therefore the most honest way – to bring it forward.

Jerome Rothenberg

Uitoto Indian (Colombia)

Genesis I

1.

In the beginning the word gave origin to the father.

2.

A phantasm, nothing else existed in the beginning: the Father touched an illusion, he grasped something mysterious. Nothing existed. Through the agency of a dream our Father Nai-mu-ena kept the mirage to his body, and he pondered long and thought deeply.

Nothing existed, not even a stick to support the vision: our Father attached the illusion to the thread of a dream and kept it by the aid of his breath. He sounded to reach the bottom of the appearance, but there was nothing. Nothing existed.

Then the Father again investigated the bottom of the mystery. He tied the empty illusion to the dream thread and pressed the magical substance upon it. Then by the aid of his dream he held it like a wisp of raw cotton.

Then he seized the mirage bottom and stamped upon it repeatedly, sitting down at last on his dreamed earth.

The earth phantasm was his now, and he spat out saliva repeatedly so that the forests might grow. Then he lay down on his earth and covered it with the roof of heaven. As he was the owner of the earth he placed above it the blue and the white sky.

Thereupon Rafu-emas, the man-who-has-the-narratives, sitting at the base of the sky, pondered and he created this story so that we might listen to it here upon earth.

SOURCE: Translation from K.T. Preuss, *Die Religion und Mythologie der Uitoto* (1921), in Margot Astrov, *The Winged Serpent: An Anthology of American Indian Prose and Poetry* (1946). Republished with commentary in J. Rothenberg, *Technicians of the Sacred* (1968).

Creation by word & thought, but more particularly, the recognition of "dream" as model for the creative process: a "reality" of a different order, of new combinations of objects: "thought" running ahead of "thinker," toward the making of a "world."

"Word" & "origin" & "father" immediately suggest St. John (result of Preuss's German?) – though there the Word didn't *make*, rather *was-with* and *was*, the father. And Aristotle too had taught that the origin of the gods was in men's dreamings, "for when the soul is alone in sleep, then it takes its real nature." In Australia the mythic period of the creative-beings was called the Dream Time or the Dreaming, which also included such latterday phenomena as participated in the sacred. Siberian & North American shamans received word & song in dreams, as did the Jewish prophets & certain Christian saints & poets.

In the early twentieth century, dream (like drugs later) was turned to, to sanction the use of alternative, "non-logical" thought processes in poetry, painting, etc., until some realized that no such sanction was needed. But the dreaming remains everyone's chance for exposure to the possibilities of poetic process: of making the unknown "known."

Addenda. (1) **alcheringa** [Arunta of Australia, *alcheringa*], *n.* 1. The Eternal Dream Time, The Dreaming of a sacred heroic time long ago when man and nature came to be, a kind of narrative of things that happened. 2. A kind of charter of things that still happen. 3. A kind of *logos* or principle of order transcending everything significant. *v.* 1. The act of dreaming, as reality and symbol, by which the artist is inspired to produce a new song. 2. The act by which the mind makes contact with whatever mystery it is that connects the Dreaming and the Here-and-Now. (Adapted from W. E. H. Stanner)

(2) "From the moment when it is subjected to a methodical examination, when, by means yet to be determined, we succeed in recording the contents of dreams in their entirety ... we may hope that the mysteries which really are not will give way to the great Mystery. I believe in the future resolution of these two states, dream and reality, which are seemingly so contradictory, into a kind of absolute reality, a *surreality*, if one may so speak. It is in quest of this surreality that I am going, certain not to find it but too unmindful of my death not to calculate to some slight degree the joys of its possession." (André Breton, *The First Surrealist Manifesto*, 1924)

OMAHA

Sweat-House Ritual No. 1

listen old man listen
you rock   listen
old man   listen
listen   didn't i teach all their children
to follow me   listen
listen
listen   unmoving time-without-end   listen
you old man sitting there   listen
on the roads where all the winds come rushing
at the heart of the winds where you're sitting   listen
old man   listen
listen   there's short grasses growing all over you   listen
you're sitting there living inside them   listen
listen   i mean you're sitting there covered with birdshit   listen
head's rimmed with soft feathers of birds listen
old man   listen
you standing there next in command   listen
listen   you water   listen
you water that keeps on flowing
from time out of mind   listen
listen   the children have fed off you
no one's come on our secret
the children go mad for your touch   listen
listen standing like somebody's house   listen
just like somewhere to live   listen
you great animal   listen
listen   you making a covering over us   listen
saying   let the thoughts of those children live with me
& let them love me   listen
listen   you tent-frame   listen
you standing with back bent   you over us
stooping your shoulders   you bending over us
you really standing
you saying   thus shall my little ones speak of me
you brushing the hair back from your forehead   listen

the hair of your head
the grass growing over you
you with your hair turning white   listen
the hair growing over your head   listen
o you roads the children will be walking on   listen
all the ways they'll run to be safe   listen
they'll escape   their shoulders bending with age where they walk
walking where others have walked
their hands shading their brows
while they walk & are old   listen
because they're wanting to share in your strength   listen
the children want to be close by your side   listen
walking   listen
be very old & listen

English working by Jerome Rothenberg, from Alice Fletcher & Francis LaFlesche

SOURCE: Alice C. Fletcher & Francis LaFlesche, *The Omaha Tribe*, Bureau of American Ethnology, 27th Annual Report, 1905-1906.

The sweat-lodge in question was used as a preparatory rite by the Pebble Society (lit. "they who have the translucent pebble"), & the words of the ritual belonged to Waki'dezhinga, a former Society leader, who used them "as he entered the sweat lodge to make ready for his duties toward the sick." Membership in the society followed a dream or vision of water or of its representative, the pebble, or a dream or vision of the "water monster." Devices indicating such dream animals, etc. were painted on the bodies of participants.

    The old man of the poem is the "primal rock" of the Omaha dreamtime: an aged being sitting in the midst of water that's impossible to traverse, spoken of as having "persisted through all time since the gathering of the primal seven, to have sat at the center where the paths converge, & endured the shock of the four winds, those mighty forces which bring life & can destroy it," etc. The sacred narrative of the Pebble Society – at least in Waki'dezhinga's telling of it – places the dream-time history as follows:

    At the beginning all things were in the mind of Wakonda. All creatures, including
    man, were spirits. They moved about in space between earth and the stars. They were
    seeking a place where they could come into a bodily existence. They ascended to the

sun, but the sun was not fitted for their abode. They moved on to the moon and found that it also was not good for their home. Then they descended to earth. They saw it was covered with water. They floated through the air to the north, the east, the south, and the west, and found no dry land. They were sorely grieved. Suddenly from the midst of the water uprose a great rock. It burst into flames and the waters floated into the air in clouds. Dry land appeared; the grasses and the trees grew. The hosts of spirits descended and became flesh and blood. They fed on the seeds of the grasses and the fruits of the trees, and the land vibrated with their expressions of joy and gratitude to Wakonda, the maker of all things.

In the actual ritual (see description, below), the stones in the sweathouse represented the old man & were so addressed, while the steam was equated with the primal water, etc. The "children" of the poem are the patients about to be ministered to, & the winds are "the messengers of the life-giving force, winds of the four directions, into whose midst the child is sent, to reach the four hills of life." What we have here, in short, is a religion & poetry at a point of high & complex development.

Addenda. (1) SWEAT-HOUSE EVENT (Omaha)

A framework of slender poles is bent so as to make a small domeshaped frame; this is covered tight with skins. Stones are heated over a fire, then placed in the center of the tent. The bathers enter, carrying a vessel of water with them. The coverings of the sweat-house are then made fast, & the participants sprinkle water on the heated stones & sit in the steam while singing songs & chanting the words of the sweat-house ritual. After a sufficient sweat has been experienced, they emerge from the sweat-house & plunge into cold water, after which they rub themselves dry with artemisia or grass.

(2) The movement of the poem, in its cumulative juxtaposition of divine attributes, etc. is typical of that tribal poetry which attempts to realize a form & shape for powers that have been experienced in dream & vision before or during the event. While the poem's contents may finally be fixed, as here, there are other instances where it involves an ongoing activity, e.g. in the Crow sweat-house poem & Robert H. Lowie's description of the process by which the supplicant (= poet) articulates his sense-of-reality, etc. through language.

(3) A cross-reference of a very different kind is to the avatar of Quetzalcoatl as old-man in the Aztec myth of his transfiguration (see below):

> ...And it is said, he was monstrous.
> His face was like a huge, battered stone, a great fallen rock;
> it [was] not made like that of men. And his beard was very
> long-exceedingly long. He was heavily bearded.

Thus, Bernardino de Sahagún's informant in the 16th-century Florentine Codex, to say nothing of the Ancient-of-Days & of those primal rocks of our own tribal poetries, etc.

LUMMI (SALISH)

Animal Spirit Event

Imitate the spirit of the animal or thing inside you.

Let the one who imitates the wolf, dance squatting. Let him draw his arms up at the beginning of each measure bringing his bent wrists up below his chin with fingers pointing directly downwards. If he can, have him crack his knuckles & spurt blood.

Let the spirit of the sea, which appears half-bear & half-human & whose home is surrounded by hovering flies because there is so much food there, sing a song that goes: "O the flies in the home of the awful beast."

Let the spirit of the whistle imitate a whistle.

Let the spirit of the west wind sing: "Hey look out the west wind's going to blow."

Let the person who imitates a cedar be accompanied by five to ten other dancers. Have him warm up some cedar poles with mops of shredded cedar bark or twilled goat wool fastened at the ends, as he describes the approach of his spirit in a canoe. Let him sing the phrase, "Now the spirit is walking," then hand the poles to the other dancers who hold them vibrating from the waist. Then let him dance around the house with his own pole outstretched, the others joining him. Let him try to find food hidden in the house by prodding any bundles he sees with his pole, then toss what he finds into the center of the room, to be burnt as an offering to the dead or served to the assembled guests. Let the dance end with a great shout.

Let the spirit of the locomotive go through the locomotive's motions in his dance.

Let the man who imitates a fire swallow burning cedar bark.

SOURCE: Bernard J. Stern, *The Lummi Indians of Northwest Washington*, Columbia University Contributions to Anthropology, Volume 17, 1934, pages 63-64.

The experience of another animal's nature (or even that of an inanimate thing) was one of the major achievements of Amerindian poets & visionaries. Not a masquerade either, for when Lowie, say, writes in a passage that my eye just now lights on, of a Crow man who "could not eat a cherry without going into an ecstatic condition & acting like a bear," there is a level of experience & an utterly sane blowing-of-the-mind, so to speak, that transforms events into vision & from which the words will then emerge as song or narrative, etc.

LUCARIO CUEVISH (LUISEÑO, CALIFORNIA)

Before They Made Things Be Alive They Spoke

Earth woman lying flat her feet were to the north her head was to the South sky brother sitting on her right hand side he said Yes sister you must Tell me who you are she answered I am Tomaiyowit she asked him Who Are you? He answered I am Tukmit. Then she said:

I stretch out flat to the Horizon.
I shake I make a noise like thunder.
I am Earthquake.
I am round & roll around.
I vanish & return.

Then Tukmit said:

I arch above you like a lid.
I deck you like a hat.
I go up high & higher.
I am death I gulp it in one bite.
I grab men from the east & scatter them.
My name is Death.

Then they made things be alive.

English working by Jerome Rothenberg, after Constance G. DuBois

SOURCE: Constance Goddard DuBois, *Religion of the Luiseño Indians,* University of California Publications in American Archaeology & Ethnology, Volume 8, Number 3, 1908, page 139.

An excerpt from what DuBois labeled "Luiseno Creation - 4th Version," it was narrated by Lucario Cuevish, "an old man blind from his youth." DuBois herself pointed to the "tendency to variation in the (telling of) myths," which we can now recognize as part of the frequent *de facto* freedom of the tribal/oral poet, whose sacred "texts" are in a constant process of self-correction & transformation. The mode of the narrative (lost in the carry-over) involves the extensive use of gesture language & a "groaning style" in (especially) the dialogue; i.e. that utterances are often drawn out &/or punctuated with a groan-like sound, han–n–n–n–n—though it's not clear from her own notations that that would be the case with the lines excerpted here. At any rate the present editor has restricted himself to compressing (on basis of the apparent Luiseño text & notes for a literal reading) what seemed to be heavy paraphrases & expansions in DuBois' translation.

About the basis for such expansions & the implications of just such passages as this one, she writes: "Much of this mythology is abstraction, belonging to the domain of metaphysics." With which the present editor would likely agree, being reminded too of abstract/ concrete workings from the other India; lines, say, like these from the Brihadaranyaka Upanishad:

In the beginning there was nothing to be seen here ... but it was all concealed by death — by hunger, for death is hunger. Then Death was first & thought to have a body. Death moved about & worshipped & his worship produced water.

And what was there was froth of water, it was hardened & became the earth. Death rested on the earth & being rested he grew warm, & Agni flared up full of light

who was the sacred fire, etc. — as in the Luiseño, the union of the earth & Death (but after a detailed exploration of each other's bodies) first generates the sacred objects: nets & baskets, red paint, thorny plants, salt grass, & woman's menses. All of which would indicate, perhaps, where some of that was headed at the point of its disruption.

NAVAJO

A Song from Red Ant Way

The red young men under the ground
decorated with red wheels
& decorated with red feathers
at the center of the cone-shaped house
I gave them a beautiful red stone—
when someone does the same for me
I'll walk the earth

The black young women under the ground
decorated with black wheels
& decorated with black feathers
at the center of the flat-topped house
I gave them an abalone shell—
when someone does the same for me
I'll walk the earth

From deep under the earth they're starting off
the old men under the earth are starting off
they're decorated with red wheels & starting off
at the center of the cone-shaped house they're starting off
because I gave them a beautiful red stone they're starting off
when someone does the same for me I'll walk the earth like them &
      starting off

On the red road & on the road they're starting off
The black old women under the earth are starting off
they're decorated with black wheels & starting off
decorated with black feathers & starting off
at the center of the flat-topped house they're starting off
because I gave them an abalone shell they're starting off
when someone does the same for me I'll walk the earth like them &
      starting off
from deep under the earth they're starting off

English working by Jerome Rothenberg, after Harry Hoijer

SOURCE: Hoijer, McAllester, Wheelwright, et al., *Texts of the Navajo Creation Chants*, Peabody Museum of Harvard University, pamphlet to accompany record album, ca. 1950. The original singer was Hasteen Klah (1929).

A version of the Red Ant Way myth begins: "The fact is that the Ant People did not originate here, but their origin is traced below this earth to earth twelve, called the Dark One, on the surface of which they were the very first to come alive." And it adds: "There, you see, many of them began to live in human form ... and to kill one another by every possible means." But all of that is part of the acute sense the first poets showed not only of the animal world at its farthest morphological remove from us (the Navajos, e. g., identify 35 different types of ant by name, some say as many as 70) but of the use to which it could be put to describe the human world as well. Both in fact as part of a continuum. The Ant people (basically dangerous or "evil" but like all things never completely so) were, especially when molested (e. g., pissed upon or otherwise disrupted in their anthills), the direct cause of a variety of diseases. For these & other sicknesses related to them by an intricate network of symbol & myth, the Red Ant Way chant-event system was a cure.

Like other Navajo ceremonials, Red Ant Way contains hundreds of songs in its various versions, along with other ritual-events such as sand painting, body painting, prayerstick planting, pollen events, herb events, etc. The whole chantway system is so complicated in fact that the individual medicine man or chanter *(hatali)* literally a keeper-of-the-songs) can rarely keep-in-mind more than a single ceremony – the nine-day Night Chant, for example - sometimes only part of one. As with other "mixed media" art of this complexity (& the Navajo includes dozens of multi-layered ceremonials like Ant Way & Night Chant), translation for-the-words-alone may hit certain highlights but never the magnitude of the composite work.

LUMMI (SALISH)

A Masked Event for Comedian & Audience

1. A comedian's mask is painted red on one side, black on the other; the mouth is twisted, the hair in disarray. For a costume he wears a blanket or a strip of fur which leaves his right hand free. He dances along with the other performers. often dances out-of-time to attract attention, & repeatedly annoys the dancers by quizzically scrutinizing their masks, poking at their eyes, looking at their noses, picking their teeth, etc. Sometimes the dancers whip the comedian vigorously with cedar boughs to drive him away, keeping time with the drums as they do so. When not annoying the dancers, the comedian goes around the room pretending to take lice from the singers' hair. He sometimes goes to a very old woman or a very pretty girl to do this, using it as a pretext to caress her.

2. The audience refrains from laughing.

SOURCE: Bernhard J. Stern, *The Lummi Indians of Northwest Washington,* Columbia University Contributions to Anthropology, Volume 17, 1934, pages 57-59.

Yaqui

From *15 Flower World Variations:* Song of a Dead Man

I do not want these flowers
  moving
    but the flowers
want to move
  I do not want these flowers
    moving
but the flowers
  want to move
    I do not want these flowers
moving
  but the flowers
    want to move
out in the flower world
  the dawn
    over a road of flowers
I do not want these flowers
  moving
    but the flowers
want to move
  I do not want these flowers
    moving
but the flowers
  the flowers
    want to move

English version by Jerome Rothenberg

SOURCE: Jerome Rothenberg, *15 Flower World Variations: A Sequence of Songs from the Yaqui Deer Dance,* Membrane Press, Milwaukee, 1984. Based on literal translations in Carleton Wilder's *The Yaqui Deer Dance* (1963).

> The small nouns
> Crying faith
> In this in which the wild deer
> Startle, and stare out.
>   — *George Oppen*

"Flower world," "enchanted world" & "wilderness world" are among the English terms used to describe the other-than-human domain surrounding the settled Yaqui villages: "a region of untamed things into which man's influence does not extend" (E. Spicer). In mythic times that world *(huya aniya)* may have been *everything*, later reduced (so Edward Spicer tells us) "to a specialized part of a larger whole, rather than the whole itself. ... Not replaced, as the Jesuits would have wished, ... it became the other world, the wild world surrounding the towns" (*The Yaquis, page 65*). Within the frame of a native & independent Catholicism, it persists in the present, into which it brings the mythic figures of sacred Deer Dancer & Pascola clowns. The songs accompanying the very taut, very classical Deer Dance are, in their totality, an extraordinary example of traditional poesis: the cumulative construction by word & image of that Flower World from which the dancer comes.

Such uses of flower & deer symbology, etc., are widespread throughout Mexico – their sources deep into the native past.

Tamale Event

"For seven days all fasted. Only water tamales, soaked in water, were eaten, without chili, without salt, with neither saltpeter nor lime. And they were eaten only at midday. And he who fasted not at this time, if he were noted, he was punished. And much was this, the eating of water tamales, hallowed. And he who did not this, if he were not seen or noted, it was said – he was visited with the itch.

"And when the feast arrived, it was said: 'Ashes are put on faces,' & 'They are adorned with sea shells.' And it was when, indeed, all the gods danced. Thus it was named the dance of the gods.

"And all came forth as humming birds, butterflies, honeybees, flies, birds, giant horned beetles, black beetles – those forms men took; in these guises they came dancing. And still others were in the guise of sleep. Some had garlands of fruit tamales; birds' flesh tamales formed yet others' garlands. And before them was the maize bin, filled with fruit tamales.

"And soon also all these appeared – those who played the roles of the poor, those who sold vegetables, those who sold wood. Also appeared one in the guise of a leper. And still more took the forms of birds, large owls, screech owls. And even other birds they counterfeited."

SOURCE: Bernardino de Sahagún, *Florentine Codex,* [tr. Arthur]. O. Anderson & Charles E. Dibble, University of Utah, Part 2, page 163. The present version is unaltered from the original translation of the Nahuatl.

NAVAJO

Mud Events

1. The organizers of the event strip down & smear themselves & each other with mud & water from head to foot. They dip their headbands in mud before tying back their hair.

2. The participants run & dance about, then ask others to join them, lifting the newcomers high in the air, tossing them up & catching them again, or throwing them up & down in a blanket.

3. A small piece of sheepskin with a red blotch in the center (of fresh menstrual blood, excretion from the sore of a horse, etc.) is rubbed on the heads & backs of participants; some are made to sit on it.

4. Participants run into the audience & pull horsemen off their horses: then they oblige them to undress & join the mud event. The horsemen are smeared from foot to head, especially the back, face & hair. The original participants blow upon them, spit on them, & put mud into their mouths. Horses are also caught & bathed with mud.

5. At the end of the event the organizers lie down flat on their stomachs one in line behind the other & so close that the head of each one touches the feet of the one in front of him. The last one gets up, walks along the trail of bodies & lies down; the next one does the same in leapfrog style until each participant has walked the length of the entire line. Some actually step on the prostrate bodies, while others place their feet on the ground close by the men. When this is over, all the participants stand up, form a snakeline & run over to a spring of water, where they sprinkle cornmeal on themselves & wash.

SOURCE: Gladys Reichard, *Social Life of the Navajo Indians,* Columbia University Contributions to Anthropology, Volume 7, 1928, pages 132-133.

For other acts of earth- & body-rootedness the reader may compare contemporary performance works that involve daubings, etc., as in Allan Kaprow's *Soap*; instructions for the 2nd evening:

bodies dirtied with jam
bodies buried in mounds
at the sea edge
bodies cleaned by the tide

— but remember too the generations of experience that gave these Navajo events their context.

TULE/CUNA

Spyglass Conversations

(A girl looking through a spyglass says)
You cannot see mountains and valleys in the clouds,
I see the clouds as big as trees.
When I look far away I see the clouds like cliffs of high, gray rocks.
I see a cloud that looks like a coconut tree.
The clouds come up and come up in different shapes.
There are clouds that look like breakers,
You don't see the colors and shapes of the clouds,
I see them like people moving and bending, they come up just like people.
There are clouds like many people walking.
I see them every time I look out to sea with the glass.
Sometimes a cloud comes up like a ghost, and sometimes like a ship.
I look far off through the glass and see everything.
I see a cloud that looks like a sea horse, a wild sea horse that lives in the
    water
I see a cloud like a deer with branching horns.

(The boy beside her says)
You don't see that at all.

(But the girl says)
From the time I was a child I didn't think I would see such things as
    these.
If I don't look through the glass I can't see them.
Now I find out the different things the clouds make.
Do you want to see them too?

(The boy says)
All right. I want to see them too. *(He looks through the glass.)*
Now I see funny things.

(The girl says)
Now you see all those funny things.

(Then the boy says to a younger girl)
You want to see them too?

(But she says)
I'm too young.

(The boy says to the older girl)
Look down into the water with the glass.

(The older girl says)
Now I see strange things under the water.
I see things moving around as though they were live animals.
I see things there that look like little bugs – many strange animals under the
sea.

Translated by Frances Densmore

SOURCE: Frances Densmore, *Music of the Tule Indians of Panama*, Smithsonian Miscellaneous Collections, Volume 77, Number 11, 1926, page 31.

    (1) "The boy and the older girl are 'doctors' (possessors of mysterious powers) .... The Tule had seen spyglasses but did not own one." Other Tule (Cuna) journeys were, however, carried on into earth, air & sea, as in the trip of Nele Pailibe or that along Muu's way. The spyglass, then, is confirmation of powers attested to in other songs; thus:

> Go to sleep & dream of many animals - mountain lions & ocean lions.
> You will talk to them & understand what they say
> & when you awake you will be a shaman like me.
> (Densmore, *Tule*, page 18)

    (2) Densmore's recordings were made during a Washington visit by eight Tule Indians in 1924. The typical Tule song (she tells us) is in the form of a "simple, continuous narrative" with hardly any repetitions, etc. – often acting as a kind of scenario for the actions it accompanies. The way the words are sung "suggests melodic speech" (rather than chants) "in which the rhythm is determined by the accents and lengths of the words." It's also common to improvise, i.e. "the substance of the words and the general character of each song is 'learned,' but ... each performance of the song is an improvisation. ... The Tule said they did not intend to 'sing a song always the same.'"

NAVAJO

Language Event II

Hold a conversation in which everything refers to water.
If someone comes in the room, say: "Someone's floating in."
If someone sits down, say: "It looks like someone just stopped floating."

SOURCE: Gladys A. Reichard, *Navajo Religion: A Study of Symbolism*, Bollingen Series, XVIII, Pantheon, 1959, 1963, page 270.

Navajo Animal Songs

1.

Chipmunk can't drag it along
can't drag it along

Chipmunk holds back his ears

2.

Chipmunk was standing
jerking his feet
with stripes
he's a very short chipmunk

3.

Mole makes his pole redhot
Says: I'll shove it up your ass
Says: feel how it shakes your belly

4.

Wildcat was walking
He ran down here
He got his feet in the water
He farted
Wow, wow! says Wildcat

5.

A turkey is dancing near the rocks
shoves out his pelvis
woops–a–daisy we all go crazy

6.

Big Rabbit goes to see his baby
pisses
pissing all around him

7.

Pinionjay shits pebbles
now he's empty

English versions by Jerome Rothenberg, after David McAllester

SOURCE: David P. McAllester, *Enemy Way Music,* Papers of the Peabody Museum of American Archaeology & Ethnology, Harvard University, Volume 41, Number 3, page 80.

A group of moccasin game songs, as given by Son of Bead Chant Singer. When he recorded "wildcat," McAllester writes, "he was so amused he had difficulty finishing the song, and his daughter laughed so loud she had to sit down on the ground. The first line of the song was enough to set the audience laughing in anticipation of what was to come." Writes Reichard of moccasin game songs in general: "Matthews, in an early work, 'Navajo Gambling Songs,' refers to the large number of songs concerned with the moccasin game. One old man said there were four thousand, and another that there was no creature that walked, flew or crawled in all the world known to the Navajo that had not at least one song in the game and that many had more. The reason is almost certainly that the game originated as a contest for day and night in which all living things participated" (Reichard, *Navajo Religion,* page 287). The reader should remember too (especially if he still tends to equate sacred & sober, etc.) that laughter is itself an old form of religious language, if a dangerous one. Says McAllester about the thin line walked here: "It is interesting that the moccasin game songs which contain laughable remarks about various animals and birds are sung only after the first killing frost when it is safe. There is a minimum of danger from retaliatory lightning, snake bite or damage to crops after this time of year."

Crazy Dog Events

1. Act like a crazy dog. Wear sashes & other fine clothes, carry a rattle, & dance along the roads singing crazy dog songs after everybody else has gone to bed.

2. Talk crosswise: say the opposite of what you mean & make others say the opposite of what they mean in return.

3. Fight like a fool by rushing up to an enemy & offering to be killed. Dig a hole near an enemy, & when the enemy surrounds it, leap out at them & drive them back.

4. Paint yourself white, mount a white horse, cover its eyes & make it jump down a steep & rocky bank, until both of you are crushed.

SOURCE: Robert H. Lowie, The Crow Indians, Holt, Rinehart & Winston, 1935,1956, pages 330–331.

The events resemble Dada activities, say, & also the political gestures of the provos & crazies, etc. of the late 1960s. But the phenomenon (contraries, warrior clowns) was by contrast a deep-seated aspect of Plains Indian life, not unlike traditions of the Japanese & others. Ran the Crazy Dog prayer: "I do not want to live long; were I to live long, my sorrows would be overabundant. I do not want it!"

Aztec (Nahuatl)

The Flight of Quetzalcoatl

*

Then the time came for Quetzalcoatl too, when he felt the darkness twist in
    him like a river, as though it meant to weigh him down, & he thought
    to go then, to leave the city as he had found it & go to go, forgetting
    there ever was a Tula

Which was what he later did, as people tell it who still speak about the Fire:
    how he first ignited the gold & silver houses, their walls speckled with
    red shells, & the other Toltec arts, the creations of man's hands & the
    imagination of his heart

& hid the best of them in secret places, deep in the earth, in mountains or
    down gullies, buried them, took the cacao trees & changed them into
    thorned acacias

& the birds he'd brought there years before, that had the richly colored
    feathers & whose breasts were like a living fire, he sent ahead of him to
    trace the highway he would follow toward the seacoast

When that was over he started down the road

*

A whole day's journey, reached
THE JUNCTURE OF THE TREE
(so-called)

                fat prominence of bark
                sky branches

I sat beneath it
saw my face/cracked
mirror

an old man

                  & named it
                  TREE OF OLD AGE

thus to name
it to raise stones
to wound the bark
with stones

to batter it with
stones the stones to
cut the bark to fester
in the bark

                  TREE OF OLD AGE

stone patterns: starting
from the roots they
reach the highest leaves

★

The next day gone with walking
Flutes were sounding in his ears
                  Companions' voices
He squatted on a rock to rest
he leaned his hands against the rock
                  Tula shining in the distance
: which he saw he
saw it & began to cry

he cried the cold sobs cut his throat

      A double thread of tears, a hailstorm
      beating down his face, the drops

burn through the rock
The drops of sorrow fall against the stone
& pierce its heart

& where his hands had rested
shadows lingered on the rock: as if
his hands had pressed soft clay
As if the rock were clay

The mark too of his buttocks in the rock,
embedded there forever

The hollow of his hands preserved forever

A place named TEMACPALCO

★

To Stone Bridge next

water swirling in the riverbed
a spreading turbulence of water

: where he dug a stone up
made a bridge across
                    & crossed it

★

: who kept moving until he reached the Lake of Serpents, the elders waiting
        for him there, to tell him he would have to turn around, he would have
        to leave their country & go home

: who heard them ask where he was bound for, cut off from all a man
        remembers, his city's rites long fallen into disregard

: who said it was too late to turn around, his need still driving him, & when
    they asked again where he was bound, spoke about a country of red
    daylight & finding wisdom, who had been called there, whom the sun
    was calling

: who waited then until they told him he could go, could leave his Toltec
things & go (& so he left those arts behind, the creations of man's hands & the
imagination of his heart; the crafts of gold & silver, of working precious
stones, of carpentry & sculpture & mural painting & book illumination &
featherweaving)

: who, delivering that knowledge, threw his jeweled necklace in the lake, which
vanished in those depths, & from then on that place was called The Lake of
Jewels.

★

Another stop along the line

        This time
        THE CITY OF THE SLEEPERS

And runs into a shaman

Says, you bound for somewhere honey

Says, the country of Red Daylight know it? expect to land there probe a little
wisdom maybe

Says, no fooling try a bit of pulque brewed it just for you

Says, most kind but awfully sorry scarcely touch a drop you know

Says, perhaps you've got no choice perhaps I might not let you go now you
didn't drink perhaps I'm forcing you against your will might even get you
drunk come on honey drink it up

Drinks it with a straw

> So drunk he falls down fainting
> on the road & dreams &
> snores his snoring echoes very far

& when he wakes finds silence
& an empty town, his face
reflected & the hair shaved off

> Then calls it
> CITY OF THE SLEEPERS

★

There is a peak between Old Smokey
& The White Woman

Snow is falling
& fell upon him in those days
> & on his companions
> who were with him, on
> his dwarfs, his clowns
> his gimps

> It fell

till they were frozen
lost among the dead

The weight oppressed him
& he wept for them

He sang

The tears are endless
& the long sighs
issue from my chest

further out
THE HILL OF MANY COLORS

which he sought

Portents everywhere, those
dark reminders
of the road he walks

*

It ended on the beach
It ended with a hulk of serpents formed into a boat
& when he'd made it, sat in it & sailed away
A boat that glided on those burning waters, no one knowing when he
          reached the country of Red Daylight
It ended on the rim of some great sea
It ended with his face reflected in the mirror of its waves
The beauty of his face returned to him
& he was dressed in garments like the sun
It ended with a bonfire on the beach where he would hurl himself
& burn, his ashes rising & the cries of birds
It ended with the linnet, with the birds of turquoise color, birds the color of
          wild sunflowers, red & blue birds
It ended with the birds of yellow feathers in a riot of bright gold
Circling till the fire had died out
Circling while his heart rose through the sky
It ended with his heart transformed into a star
It ended with the morning star with dawn & evening
It ended with his journey to Death's Kingdom with seven days of darkness
With his body changed to light
A star that burns forever in the sky

SOURCE: Translated by J.R. from Spanish prose translation by Angel María Garibay K, *Epica Nahuatl* (Biblioteca del Estudiante Universitario, Mexico, 1945), pp. 59-63.

COMMENTARY [from *Technicians of the Sacred*].

Archaic thought is coherent & directed, but the coherence isn't based on consistency of event so much as covering the widest range of possible situations. Like a shotgun blast, say, or a saturation bombing – effective against known targets & some unknown ones as well. So, the "greatest variation in legends and interpretations of the disappearance of Quetzalcoatl" may simply be noted & would have caused the Nahua makers no special discomfort. The important thing was for any account to hit home – to present the god's doings as image of how-it-really-is.

The present version comes from Bernardino de Sahagún's sixteenth-century *Historia,* with the ending from the *Anales de Quauhtitlan,* & begins after whatever-had-happened to get him on the road. ...The *Anales* in this case are the more articulate. In brief the gods Tezcatlipoca, Ilhuimecatl, & Toltecatl decided to force Quetzalcoatl out of his city "where we intend to live." Tezcatlipoca thought to bring it off by "giving him his body," so showed him "a double mirror the size of a hand's span" & "Quetzalcoatl saw himself, and was filled with fear, and said: 'If my subjects see me, they will run away!' For his eyelids were badly inflamed, his eyes sunken in their sockets, and his face covered all over with wrinkles. His face was not human at all!" (I. Nicholson, *Firefly in the Night,* p. 69) ...

The force of the myth is in the image in the mirror: the journey a dark night before his re-emergence through fire & transfiguration. As plumed serpent Quetzalcoatl "belonged equally to the dark abyss and the celestial splendor," writes Laurette Sejourné. And further: "Quetzalcoatl taught that human greatness grows out of the awareness of a spiritual order; his image must therefore be the symbol of this truth. The serpent plumes must be speaking to us of the spirit that makes it possible for man – even while his body, like the reptile's, is dragged in the dust – to know the superhuman joy of creation."

His identification with the planet Venus says this also.

SYMPOSIUM ON TRANSLATION

FADY JOUDAH

Lily of the Valley

All poetry is translation. And all translation is a variation on the theme of mimesis, thievery, or mutation. Yet to translate a poetic text is seldom equal to authoring an "original" text; an often valid claim frequently corrupted with standard "valuations" whose frontier is the patchwork of word and syntax choice, and the insoluble schools of fidelity and infidelity. Then there is the guest vs. host language (or perhaps donor vs. host, as in organ transplantation, with the potential threat of corporeal rejection). What one poet or critic finds "foreign" or "awkward" (and subsequently worse) in a particular stanza or line would likely render other aspects of the poem "inferior," or entirely "different," at least, if the same "corrective" palate were applied to the remainder of the translation. This domino-effect is intrinsic to the "unity" within a creative work; a cohesion that more than likely reflects the translator's (or critic's) private affinity to lexicon, rhythm, and poetics, and cannot be simply utilized, with much significance, as critical proof of another's work. What is "awkward" for one becomes "dexterous" for another; an oscillation between the particular and the universal in the mind's tongue. That translation is bound to the guidelines of the "original" text and those of the host language is a paradox that can become a pretext for dogma, where in fact it is valence for plurality. Translation is often a sublimated psychosis about, or a whirling around, the "original" work and the host language; the illusion or delusion of knowing and unknowing what *is*.

Let's say the "original" work is a raceme. What then becomes of "the nature of things?" The work is a mixture of its components: a variable total of possible translations and readings a work holds within itself. These components or possibilities are arranged into an equal number of clockwise and counterclockwise rotations, encompassing the essence and "spirit" of the work. In a "pure" state the mixture, the whole of the work, reflects no *polarized* light, because the rotations and possibilities, amassed together, cancel each other's reflections. However, subjectivity renders perception of such a state impossible (even for the "original" author). Thus, taken separately, each component, each artful rotation, to the left or right, (con)-textual or otherwise, is indivisible, and gives off its own radiance.

Or maybe translation is chiral: the mirror image that is impossible to superimpose on the "original" subject; a stereoisomer: containing the same building blocks of the "original" compound, but differing in spatial arrangement; made new, "natural" in its own right (or left), dexterous in its own light.

PIERRE JORIS

Seven Minutes on Translation

The text that opens my recent volume of poems, *Aljibar II*, starts with a line that came to me unbidden, out of the blue. It reads: "My father was a healer and a hunter; is it any surprise that I became a poet and translator?"

The algebraic *ratio* the sentence proposes would equate **healer** with **poet** and **hunter** with **translator**. This may seem a bit too pat, too linear, and maybe it is more useful to imagine the terms as occupying the four corners of an X, crossed sticks, a chiasmatic figure that creates movement and connections between all four terms.

And indeed, I can easily see the poet as both healer and hunter, and the translator as both hunter and healer. But the details of that discussion will have to wait for another time—today I want to briefly address the question of translation. Let me try to do it in a kind of list, i.e. a kind of list poem, perhaps.

Why do I translate?

Because it pleases me.

Because it beats watching television, except when the Mets are on, but they play so lousily much of the time that I avert my eyes & continue to translate, looking up only to check the score.

Because, to be frank, I want to know what the poets in Ghana are up to.

Because I am foolish enough to believe the 16th century philosopher & poet Giordano Bruno, who said that all science has its origin in translation. He was burned at the stake for that sentiment, as well as for a few other peccadilloes, in 1600 on the Campo Fioro in Rome. Bruno is of course the patron saint of translators.

Because by accident of birth I was blessed or damned with a batch of different languages & a perverse pleasure of pitting them and their different musics against each other.

Because I can.

Because I love doing it.

Because I have to. Because if we don't translate the world, it will be a way shittier place than it already is.

Because when I can't write poems I can still do so by translating other poets' poems.

Because once upon a time in a far away country in this galaxy, I was foolish enough to believe that I, an impecunious young poet, could pay the rent with translation gigs (which never worked because I found out I hated translating the books—novels, non-fiction treatises, how-to-do manuals etc.—that would have generated enough money to pay the rent).

Because I speak with a many-forked tongue & always wanted to be a Mescalero Apache healer.

Because the congealed mass of anglo-'merican ugliness, greed, & basic Christian fascism will continue to blow up the people & libraries & homes & museums of a hundred Baghdads unless we can make enough American citizens realize the beauty of the other, of the poetry of the other, of the speech of all the others.

Because I have never been able to convince my department (at the university, that is, not the store where most everything is indeed made in China, Mexico, Korea & elsewhere) to impose the learning of (at least) two foreign languages, one of which should be a non-Indo-European language, on the graduate program as a *conditio sine qua non* (translate that) for being admitted to a Ph.D. in literature.

Because outside of writing & cooking, it is the only practical thing I have the skills and knowhow to do.

Because I love to steal lines & images & sounds from all the foreign poets I read & incorporate them into my own poems (that's the poet-as-hunter).

Because it is the best excuse I've found to buy many books & travel to many countries to hang out with poets & other alien deviants.

Because the best way to learn how to read poems is to translate them.

Because the best way to learn how to write poems is to translate other poets' great works.

Because in order to think new thoughts, we have to renew the language & the best way I've found to do that is to spindle, mutilate & mutate it by writing with the language of the foreign poet in English (cf. Hölderlin's working of Greek language into German).

Because it permits you to have intense love affairs with people far away or long dead.

Because I have this weird ethical sense that because I can do it, I have to do it so as to help out my linguistically challenged *concitoyens* (untranslatable due to inevitable loss of pun).

Because translation & its social counterpart, miscegenation, are the only things that can possibly make this world a safer & more viable place.

Because, although I gave up translating into French a number of years ago, last year I could not resist saying yes to translating twenty-five pages of Allen Ginsberg poems for a French version of Philip Glass' opera *Hydrogen Jukebox*, because the last time I saw Allen in Paris he had asked me to be involved with translating his work, something I had neglected until now when the occasion to pay back my dues to him presented itself out of the blue.

Because forty years later I still have not translated all of Paul Celan's work & for some crazy un-reason I feel that I should do so.

Because most of my US poet friends are on good terms with their franco-French *compadres* & translate each other with fierce intensity which gives me the space to concentrate on translating the North African poets who would otherwise go untranslated in the main; thus are the books forthcoming by Habib Tengour, Abdallah Zrika & Mohammed Al Amraoui.

Because the Mets are losing again.

⋆ This speech was delivered, with abbreviations, at the 2004 ALTA Conference in Las Vegas.

Mary Ann Caws

Thinking about Translation

Here's a big caveat to begin with—my real translating excitement doesn't come in translating narrative or explanatory prose. The times my heart beats more quickly all have to do with that other thing Monsieur Jourdain wasn't doing and that, I venture to think, none of us ever feels we do well enough—that is, the trying to render a poetic text, albeit a poetic prose text, into something that we can, perhaps others can, live with.

So it's like this: I can't imagine anything more exciting than the moment I sit down to start a new translation, or then the moments that follow that one. Let me point out, though, that, unlike my beloved frequent co-translator Patricia Terry, who can miraculously render poems into rhymed and rhythmic equivalents of themselves, I don't do the rhyme thing. What I want to do and mean to do has the wish to bring over the something or other inside the poem into the sort of English that makes interior sense.

New things all the time in translation. A few years ago, I heard Clive Scott, Mr. Poetics in the U K, as we think of him, speak on the livingness of translations, on the Bergsonian view of the motion they must keep in their intention and being, and on his recent conversion away from the linear to the tabular typographic. This shift in the translational mind set he described as related to metatypography of the Meschonnic sort, with a "renewed self-consciousness" at every deviation of font, like differing architectures or "sculpturing mechanisms." "A tabular text," he points out, "cannot be quoted—it can only perform itself or be performed—or shifted to a support with a different format." It's always in draft form. But in its invitation to infinite reconstructions, redispositions, and potentialities, he claims that it makes available choice and chance. His excitement about it was palpable, demonstrable, and incredibly complicated for listeners like me. That isn't where I'm going, but the livingness of it got right across. The point of all our continuing stress on translational possibilities is just that: the excitement of the thing.

Now the translational field that I most work in is that of art and text: the translation of former art into present art, and of the written or spoken language into the visual one. That said, though, I had more actual fun writing the very diverse chapters of a book of just plain literary translation, *Surprised in Translation*, than I could possibly have imagined. To look at the ways Roger Fry and others, Bloomsburyians and not, deal with Mallarmé, or Mallarmé dealt with Whistler's "Ten O'Clock," or the ways Beckett deals with Beckett, or the way Pound chops up Rimbaud and makes the new half-size poems work, or Bonnefoy stretches out Yeats and the sonnets of Shakespeare is right up there with the delights of being. And I got to express my anger about the slaughter of Virginia Woolf in French--what could be more relieving to an impassioned reader betrayed? But of course the real joy was finally saying something about what it was like to work for so long with such commitment to the poems of René Char, to work by his side and near his lavender field. I've no idea if that part comes across with anything like the radiance I bathed in so many years, but I can only hope so.

The thing I like the most about making new translations is the reading aloud of both texts, the original and the one you just gave birth to, so you can change the language and the perception of the document. Something about shaping it afresh gives you a fresh delight every time. What gives you hope as a translator is often the new openings there seem to be. There are, everywhere springing up, all sorts of new ventures, such as, on the poetry translation front, the new venture of Black Widow Press, which is soaring through a series of French-language poets—Tzara, Eluard, Breton, Guillevic, Desnos, Laforgue, soon to be Char, Reverdy, and others. New openings now.

Those are the two clues I would take to my present optimism about the work of translation. First, openness, which seems to me to be present in much that has to do with poetry and indeed with translation. It is about revivifying works old, medium-old, and new, things we had forgotten about, taken for granted or left aside.

And the final clue is the nowness of it, like the recent notice taken, in the New York Times, of small poetry magazines, such as *Circumference*, for which I translated Bernard Noel's latest poem, called "Le Jardin d'encre" —that garden of ink is the one all of us as translators inhabit for a good part of our lives.

This poem seemed to me straightaway to be consoling in its presentness and— to develop a notion from the first line—a kind of "despiteness":

> et maintenant c'est encore maintenant
> bien que tout glisse

> and now it's still now despite everything
> sliding

Everything slides, yes, but arrives somewhere positive, at the final limit, at the concluding lines of this long poem:

et maintenant allons main dans la main au jardin d'encre
l'arbre qu'a planté le pinceau est aussi un arbre de mémoire
et renaissante la lecture est là qui bruit parmi les feuilles

and now we go hand in hand to the garden of ink
the tree that the brush planted is also of memory
and the reading reborn rustles there among the leaves

From my point of view, chief among the important things about this poem is that from the initial sliding down to the final tree of memory and the reading among the leaves in this garden of ink so entitled in both senses, all the expressions work in the present. The final optimistic merging of text and nature, of rebirth inside and out, of what is thought and written and what is experienced collectively and greenly, seems to me to awaken that great surrealist saying: "Always for the first time." This garden matters greatly to all of us here and to all of us, who care about translation and poetry.

Nikolai Popov

Difficulty

"I translate because it is difficult," the late Willard Trask once said. (If this sounds like Tertulian's "I believe because it is absurd," both syntactically and theologically, it's no accident: acts of translation require faith in the possibility of clearing ontological barriers.) Brazilian *transcreator* Haroldo de Campos concurs: "Unless the something is too difficult to translate, it's not worth translating." [1] This *is* the fascination of what's difficult (Yeats) in our line of work: it *is* difficult to translate, not in the sense that such-and-such a text or language confronts us with such-and-such severe difficulties of reference, idiomaticity, etc.: those are problems and problems *can* be solved, one way or another—even evaded, if you will. Translation *as such* is difficult: it's against the grain of our voice; it's *au rebours* (against) everything that goes without saying, everything that "comes natural." Under the double dispensation of Adam's curse and Babel's, we must labor to translate. We must labor for the poem to be beautiful and difficult.

Talking about difficulty to translators is carrying coals to Newcastle, live coals, if you will. Difficulty is our enemy and element. Not only do we, as translators, know difficulty more intimately than other seekers of the *mot juste*; not only do we try to negotiate, finesse, or sweep it under the rug, so to speak, but we also grow it. Insofar as translation involves—and is even aimed at— restoration and re-creation, difficulty is not simply a matter of clearing obstacles. In literature where difficulty is a special value (for not only *modern* beauty is difficult), the act of translation is a restitution of difficulty. We morph, if you will, from masochists who suffer the text, to sadists who inflict it on gluttons for esthetic punishment.

We re-spell difficulty. Translation and hermeneutics start at the same place (that which is "not at once intelligible"[2]), but once the difficult or unclear moment is clarified and explained the hermeneut's job is done, whereas we must re-invent the difficulty. (A writer once told me that the foreign writers he read in translation as a boy in Iowa always seemed to him to write more clearly than English writers. His enthusiasm was genuine but praising the *clarity* of the foreign-in-translation hides an essential ambiguity: Garnett's superb and still popular translations *are* clearer or less difficult, if you will, than Dostoevsky's (messy) originals—but is that a good thing?)

---

[1] Quoted by Charles Middleton (*The Poet's Other Voice*, p. 191).
[2] Steiner, George, "On Difficulty,", in *On Difficulty, and Other Essays*, p. 19.

I mention hermeneutics because I'll sketch, very briefly, a hermeneutic framework based on George Steiner's essay "On Difficulty," and then move on to issues that are logically *post*-hermeneutic, i.e. what to do AFTER we have understood--or not understood.[3]

But first, the *word* difficulty. Difficulty refers to that which is not easy (dis+facilis), my dictionary tells me, and that is perhaps the first difficulty with difficulty.[4] Difficult is a recalcitrant word: originated by back-formation, from an abstraction, negative, dif-facile. It is not, according to my concordance, to be found in KJV. Abraham, Jonah, Peter—they are all eloquent reticents; but they are full of trouble, not (in) difficulty. (They do not face challenges: notice how the cliché discounts difficulty.) In languages *other* than English, the notion of difficulty has more body and is associated with tangible qualities: there one senses the physicality or gravity of difficulty, e.g. in German difficulty evokes weight; in Russian, labor. The English word's lack of physicality makes it difficult to quantify: it is an abstract, therefore elusive, perhaps even uncanny/ghostly notion, the way negative categories are. Hence the temptation to turn it into a problem, a mere problem, something that can be solved, intellectually or otherwise, without remainder. (This is a characteristically American, pragmatic attitude, I might add; as such, it differs from the preoccupation with difficulty in recent "theory" where difficulty and theory became synonymous; but it also differs from the pragmatism of art where form, not (truth) content is at stake.)

Steiner's essay "On Difficulty" is a good point of departure precisely insofar as hermeneutics is not just the science/art of interpretation but the discipline of interpreting difficult texts. (A transparent text, if such a thing existed, would not need a special interpretive discipline; hermeneutics is interested in texts where meaning is always difficult, always in question.) Steiner's taxonomy is immediately relevant to translation—which is not surprising, considering that Steiner subsumes translation under hermeneutics. But insofar as the translator's work goes beyond interpretation/understanding and involves re-creation (or post-creation), we need to extend—perhaps double—his categories.

---

[3] Translating without understanding results in anecdotal incompetence; in certain cases of literal translation, however, there is nothing to understand, no meaning in the hermaneutic sense. See my remarks on the "English" versions of Morgenstern's "Night Song," in "The Literal and The Literary," The Iowa Review, XXXII:3, 2002.

[4] I have stolen this phrase from Hazard Adams's discussion of the esthetic and theological provenance of difficulty in "The Difficulty of Difficulty" but where his interests are theoretical, historical and interpretive, I'm concerned with language, form, and art insofar as translation is an art and creates new things. See *The Idea of Difficulty in Literature*, pp. 23–50, and other essays in that volume exploring the issue of difficulty in recent "critical theory."

Here are Steiner's categories (applied to the poetry of Paul Celan):

1: CONTINGENT (or epiphenomenal) DIFFICULTIES (e.g., obscurity of reference as a result of archaic, dialectal, arcane, technical vocabulary; neologisms; argot, slang: "writers are passionate recitators of buried or spectral words" [20]): consider Celan's vocabulary of glacial geology, cranial neurology, mining technology, etc. Contingent difficulties need not detain us: they have little to do with form and can be overcome by looking up unknown meanings.

2: MODAL DIFFICULTIES are rooted in cultural assumptions and "orders of apprehension that are no longer natural to us." (33) They can be overcome through scholarship (i.e., we can learn to recognize and "understand" a remote idiom) but "we cannot coerce our own sensibility into the relevant frame of perception." Steiner sees modal difficulties in Lovelace's "La Bella Bona Roba" (a poem in praise of fat carnal quarries, from venery to kenosis [kenosis is not an STD although theologically speaking the case is less than clear]), and, generally speaking, derives modal difficulties from the "syllabus of sentiment and allusion" in the Renaissance epics of Boiardo, Ariosto, and Tasso. (33) An example closer to my concern here would be the syllabus of feeling and belief in the *Book of Psalms* (and its impact upon poetry from Luther on): a reader divorced from that syllabus would have insuperable difficulties in responding to Celan's Psalms. (Some modal difficulties will never yield to scholarly and/or imaginative recuperation. The case goes beyond translation of literature as Quine's brilliant argument regarding "inscrutability of reference" and "indeterminacy of translation" demonstrates.)

3: TACTICAL DIFFICULTIES arise from the writer's will (e.g., the obscure/Aesopian language of Eastern European writers designed to baffle the Marxist censor; the "night" language of *Finnegans Wake*); or from "the failure of adequacy between [the poet's] intention and his performative means." Hermetic poetry, from Gongora to Mallarme to Khlebnikov teases us out of thought in order to dislocate the habits of ordinary language. Here we confront explicitly *esthetic* difficulty, i.e., difficulty as a positive esthetic category; occasionally as the key esthetic category, the *difficile beaute* of post-symbolist esthetics (Bosanquet et al.), and the notion of "difficult form" (*erschwerte, zatrudnennaya*) in formalist poetics. Celan's so-called hermeticism belongs here, a hermeticism partially derived from—but ultimately irreducible to—Mallarméan poetics (see his Büchner-prize speech; I'll have more to say later about a hermeticism that mistrusts hermeneutics and especially the facility of "to understand is to forgive").

4: ONTOLOGICAL DIFFICULTIES, like Rilke's angels, raise their terrifying/beautiful heads when the poet is not a persona but an openness/listener to language. Unlike tactical difficulties, these are so to speak *post*humous.

This is Steiner speaking the language of Heideggerean hermeneutics; Steiner's ultimate illustration, however, is a poem of Paul Celan's, "Largo." That is no accident. "Largo" opens with the line "*Gleichsinnige du, heidegängerische Nähe*" (a pun on Heidegger's famous wood- and bog-paths), and a few lines later evokes an *Amselpaar* (an anagram of Celan's name and a translingual pun/?/ on Kafka's Czech name (blackbird), and mother's name, the same as Celan's mother's name, Antschel.)

Of these sorts of difficulty, 1 and 2 are centrifugal: they lead out of/away from the language of the poem and in the direction of reference and/or the reader; 3 and 4 are centripetal: they conduct a rhetorical *Engführung* leading into the heart of language; in a sense, 4 subsumes all four.[5]

A translator, of course, is an openness/listener to two languages--which makes translation and difficulty ontologically synonymous. (Quite frankly, to a translator, the difficulties of the hermeneut seem mere problems: they can be solved; but ironically, we are the ones who confront the problem of difficulty as constitutional, and must treat it as practitioners: we always have a practical task not just a speculative agenda.) That's why we are the hosts of difficulty—in every sense of the term, guest and host, enemy and friend.

I mentioned a moment ago the notion of "difficult form" which is a not-quite-adequate translation of the formalist notion of *zatrudennaya forma*: form *made* difficult or *more* difficult, where the degree of poetic difficulty is directly proportionate to the esthetic value of the poem. Hermeneutics does not care about form (to say the least). We do. In my practical work I remove entire layers of difficulty associated with the materiality of the source language and the rhetoric of the original author who took advantage of his medium: I must, eventually, do something to restore and re-create the difficulty I encountered (and admired) because it has esthetic value.

With regard to form and medium in Celan, yet another factor invites consideration: his notorious personal difficulties with the German language and with certain formal traditions that go back to sacred Jewish and Christian—genres. Much has been written about his mother language being the language of murder—in a poetologically non-trivial sense: namely, the poetologically significant fact is not that the Germans

---

[5] By recapitulating Steiner's hermeneutic language with the help of Celan's *Engführung*, I'm taking the discussion on an un-Heideggerean path (this is not the place to discuss Celan's very complex relationship with Heidegger). *Engführung*, the title of Celan's longest poem, has been translated variously as "Stretto," "Straightening," etc., and has a host of implications, ranging from the esthetic to the industrial.

murdered 6 million Jews (that by itself won't produce a good poem), but that the German language was implicated in the murder as intimately as it was shared by mother and son. It was their house of being, in life, in death. Some of the difficulties one encounters in Celan come from the way he breaks the German language (I mean "break" both prosodically—language is broken into lines of verse--and literally, language is wrecked).[6] It is debatable whether that wreck is the ultimate poetic destination and, hence, the embodiment of Celan's tragedy as a poet, or whether it is the enabling condition of his poetry and as such that which made possible his triumph as a poet (aside from his personal tragedy as a human being). And let us not forget that translators always face the mother's tongue as an adversity (*Aber-du?*), insofar as the mother of the translation is the poem—and to be a poet at all one has to force one's tongue to say things it has never said before and may, in fact, never want to say. For lack of time, I put aside difficulties related to Celan's somatic and psychosomatic troubles—difficulties that he sought to resolve, among other ways, through translation. An entire reading of Celan could be produced as an allegory of difficulty, *la difficulte d'etre—et de mourir*. My focus here is not on thematized difficulty (psychological, existential, etc.) but difficulty embodied, languaged, if you will. This difficulty is manifest in the forms of deformation one encounters in Celan—and to that form a translation must respond if it aspires to be something more than mere paraphrase.[7]

The translator of Celan encounters Celanian difficulty as a paradox of sorts: an enabling *and* disabling condition. And insofar as the paradox has an esthetic dimension, it seems to invite a translatorial rhetoric predicated upon paradox as well. Difficulty all too easily leads to paralysis but it needn't; if there is a changing key" that can unlock his house of difficulty (see "You hold a changing") it involves treating difficulty as a species of poetic license.

What is true of Celan is true of translation as such. The paradox that something can be an enabling AND disabling factor is generally characteristic of translation. Consider so-called untranslatability. I always begin my classes by saying that translation is impossible, and that everything that's interesting about it follows from this admission. This attitude is not posturing but the only positive attitude, I think: puns, for example, are untranslatable, so logically one should

---

[6] See "MIT ERDWÄRTS GESUNGENEN MASTEN," a poem *of* wreckage, flotsam and jetsam, broken images: I discuss Celan's poetics of catachresis (in German *Bildbruch*) as ontological *Bildbruch* elsewhere.

[7] Paraphrase, in translation theory and elsewhere, is something of a fiction insofar as it presupposes absolutely transparent form. A Celan trot must contain mini-treatises on grammar, poetics, and all sorts of other matters.

not try to "translate" them; more generally, the translated text is never—*and can never be*—"the same" (many of you have heard this reservation followed by the proscription "therefore you shouldn't translate"). My view of the matter is that difficulty is also a species of poetic license; the greater the difficulty, the greater the license. A dangerous, very dangerous license, but it is the very thing that makes translation worth doing.

Poets dream of (and dread) being translated because immortal as their work may be its afterlife is in (our) mortal hands. Poetry as you know has been defined as that which is *lost* in translation (conversely, translation is that which loses poetry). The adage is attributed to Robert Frost but it predates him by a long stretch: it antedates even the Romantic view of poetic language it evokes, i.e., an indissoluble, organic, indeed sacred and mysterious bond between the matter (or letter) of a given language and the spirit of its poetry. Ultimately, the spirit of this adage goes back to the Church fathers (read St. Jerome, patron of translators), and the notion of a "sacred text."

The post-Romantic/modernist view which estheticizes (and re-sacralizes) the sacred comes down to the following crux or difficulty: If the literary is coterminous with an intentional focus on language (as Mallarmé, Benjamin, Jakobson have claimed, in various ways), then the literary and the literal are one and the same. If the "literary" (i.e., the poetry of the poetry) is identified with the spirit (or any spirit-oriented term: vision, intent, moral), then the poetry of poetry is more or less *trans*latable. If, on the other hand, the literary is indissolubly bound up with the letter (matter), then the literary is more or less *un*translatable. A strange corollary of this state of affairs is that not literary but *literal translation is the impossible one.*[8]

As a translator I'd be the first to acknowledge that poetry (or any verbal artifact perceived to have aesthetic qualities) is untranslatable and therefore that translation of poetry begins with a loss, but I'm not going to beat the drum of loss to death—in the name of difference (as though anything in translation could be the "same"). I emphasize that translation *begins* with a loss because for me this is the obvious, and not trivial, point; everything that's interesting and makes translation worthwhile (for both practitioner and reader) follows from this challenge. What can be found in translation--*and nowhere else*--is therefore a far more interesting question.

---

[8] Derrida who had a bloodhound's nose for aporias exemplified the aporia of untranslatability with cases where you'd have to translate into English an English word embedded in, say, French: you can't. You can't translate it (along with the rest of the translated text)—and you cannot not translate it.

The license a translation claims (and must claim) is essentially different from the license of the poet: Dryden observes that to translate a poem well is harder than to write a new poem, in which one is always free to change direction. Translation becomes a powerful agent of change precisely when writing one's own poem becomes too easy. That was a Russian formalist article of faith. Jakobson, whose view of literary language is my guide, places at the heart of the literary the figure of paronomasia, or paronomy. Paronymic attractions *occur* at level of the literal which is the arena where phonetics clashes with orthography, slowing down or sometimes even arresting the comforting progress of comprehension, and refocusing attention from meaning to means. If paronymy is not just one of many rhetorical means but *the* rhetorical dominant of a poem (or a style or an entire oeuvre), the principle of literal fidelity ought to become a principle of rhetorical fidelity—fidelity to paronymy, that is. In cases where paronymy is the dominant of a poem/style, the phonographic fundamentals of the *translated* poem *must* be governed by paronymy, or else the translation will have lost (or lied about) what's most important, and no literalist fidelity to "content" (paraphrasable content) can compensate for that loss. What you have then is not translation but gloss—a bigger loss. Translation must respond to the discipline of difficult texts with a creative discipline of its own.

Let me now cut to the chase: here is a poem of Paul Celan's which quite literally arose out of calumny and went on to challenge translation in principle (as it happens, it is one of a dozen or so "trial" poems which Heather McHugh and I did in order to test our assumptions and method):

[GERMAN OVERHEAD]

1, 213

With wine and being lost, with
less and less of both:

I rode through the snow, do you read me,
I rode God far – I rode God
near, he sang,
it was
our last ride over
the hurdled humans.

They cowered when
they heard us
overhead, they
wrote, they
lied over our neighing
into one of their
image-ridden languages.

    This haunting, elusive poem was Celan's response to a newspaper review of his work which contained inaccuracies: that was the occasion. But poets don't write poems about God, let alone riding God, in response to newspaper reviews. There was a deeper occasion or source: a false accusation of plagiarism leveled at Celan by the widow of the poet Ivan Goll and other people who took her side driven by a range of motivations, from personal envy to, no doubt, anti-semitism. (Celan became Kafka's character: he woke up one morning to find out that someone had been telling lies about him.) The accusation called into question Celan's very being *as* a poet, that is, his life or afterlife. The insidious thing about calumny is that it's very difficult to respond to in terms other than negative. To a poet of Celan's disposition, the accusation must have seemed particularly perplexing: he was a poet and a translator; he had translated Goll (as well as arguably stronger poets than Goll: Shakespeare, Dickinson, Mandelstam); his whole work is extremely conscious of the poetic histories of German words, going all the way back to Luther and beyond, and of the different strands, German and foreign, German and Jewish, woven into those histories--and destinies. No one who's read Celan with any care would fail to notice that his poems are strikingly—often forbiddingly—original; no one who's read Celan with proper care would fail to notice that his poems are also about and of other poems, about and of and often against the German language.

    The poem at hand sounds a cautionary note (or yell, of you will) against any interpretive or translative reduction (don't expect me to tell you what it means). It turns calumny—lies, false reports—on their head: not in personal terms, painful as those might have been, but in principle. It is "about" its own difficulties—the difficulty of writing poetry, the difficulty of translating poetry—and it calls into question any act of translation, transcription, transmission—any trans at all—including its own. Like other later poetological studies of Celan's, it is informed by the tension between voice (the traditional medium of the lyric) and inscription (the *first* translation). Voice, *human* voice, by definition, is single and always already articulated in a specific tongue; a grapheme, on the other hand, can be shared by several writing conventions. Celan's own linguistic predicament gives this commonplace a twist: all the languages he used were, in some sense, foreign[9]; none could provide the security of an indubitably voiced lyric subjectivity. Hence, many poems contain what one might call *translingual effects*. For example, in the poem at hand, the word *Neige* means "remainder," "end," or "dregs" in German; the "same" grapheme in French spells the word "snow." The phrase is hardly over when snow "literally" befalls the poem in line 3. To the English eye, *neige* also moves in the nearness of "neigh" (which in this poem will turn out to be God's "song"!) and its homonym, the negative "nay." The latter, retranslated into a German verb (*negieren*), brings us back, with a difference, almost to the place where the translingual steeple-chase started.

A corresponding tension obtains between presentation and representation. The representers, i.e., those who busily and fearfully make sense out of the sheer music of sound (whether animal or divine) are exposed as liars. One of the poem's drafts suggests the proximity, for Celan, of things understandable (*verständliche*) and things imaged or illustrated (*bebilderte*). Against the attempt to contain this music in understandable transcription or visual images, the poem advertises its iconoclastic resistance to comprehension and pours Nietzschean scorn on the attempt to trap art—or divinity—in images. Translators, among others, thus encounter a troubling image of their enterprise; hence our commitment, here and elsewhere, as much to a translatorial *reconstruction* of meaning as to the phono-graphic complexity of Celan's poems, i.e., to the dominant figure of paronymy which explores the tension between sound and sight (or letter), reading and hearing, singing and writing. The music of the poem (and this is no ordinary music—make no mistake) transcends any facile understanding of the harmony of sound and sense. (What *is* the music of art? Is it grief-stricken lament or horse laughter or intoxicated exultation or the sheer sound of the inhuman? In another poem of the same period Celan says "there are songs to sing beyond humanity.") The poem's phonographic fundamentals are governed by paronymy, and the thing about paronymy is that it is not a "reasonable" figure: ride, rid, and read; heard, hurdle, and head foreground an intransigent materiality, to translate which (into an image-ridden language) would be to belie it. The poem sings of untranslatable--and exultant--grief: it is a counterstatement to what, in the aftermath of the Holocaust, is equally suspect as a principle of ethics *or* art: that to understand is to forgive. *Do you read me?*

---

[9] As Lacoue-Labarthe suggests in *La poésie comme expérience* (1986).

Where some would sing, on a wing and a prayer, Celan rides, on a hoof and a curse—and someone, no-one, is invited to read the unreadable. (In German, the poem's linguistic drama is configured differently, of course: there are different trails of sound and paronymy, e.g., the reverberation of the opening ai-sound: b**EI** w**EI**n und verlorenh**EI**t b**EI** b**EI**der n**EI**ge, etc. German *Wein*, wine, is paronymically very near to *weinen*, cry, weep (remember Joel 1.5: Awake, ye drunkards and weep; and howl, all ye drinkers of wine, because of the new wine; for it is cut off from your mouth); also, the series *hörst du* – *hürden* -- *hörten*; also, the quasi-rhyme *Ritt-Gott*. It's also noteworthy that Celan's poem quotes from (alludes to) the translation which institutes modern German, Luther's Bible; namely, Luther's H*ürden* (Jeremiah 25). And here translation runs into an aporistic difficulty: to translate a translation is not to translate precisely the *fact* that it is a translation.)

As we say in our introduction to *Glottal Stop*, no language other than German can reproduce Celan's tragic relation to the language which was his instrument and his life, a language that had remained silent through the horror. Like Buechner's, his words come to us framed by those invisible quotation marks that always listen "not without fear, for something beyond themselves, beyond words." The beauty, the daring, the tragedy of Celan's poetry cannot be comprehended merely in terms of reference. (What is "reference" in Celan? What is reference if it refers to nothing, e.g., as in the famous line "we are nothing's [no-one's] rose"?) As translators, McHugh and I sought, cautiously, to create poems that follow Celan's intentional mode (Benjamin's *Art des Meinens*), and the intensity of his listening to language itself. [Let me make this clearer: if your German-language poem engages, enacts a breakdown of its own language because that language was speechless/struck dumb in the face of horror, this situation both changes and does not change in the realm of another language: it changes insofar as that other language did not have the same encounter with horror; and, were it to break down, its own fault lines would be different; yet it doesn't change insofar as Celan operates on the verge of language as such, and it remains a legitimate question whether poetry as such, not just poetry in the German language, can respond to any horror which calls it into question.] Given the fundamentals of Celan's poetics (phono-graphic, grammatical, and rhetorical) any attempt to isolate a "literal" meaning apart from those fundamentals would seriously impoverish and distort the effect of his poems, both individually and as a whole.

Everything in a poem is literal, that is, made of letters, blanks, and their interrelationships on the page, and the literal is everything. Precisely this omnipresence of the letter, the depth of Celan's probing into the matrix of his "original" language, prohibits naive replications of line or meaning. Celan's word order in German is quite natural, but the same linear order in English can sometimes misleadingly suggest experiments in syntax where there are none, and so on. As a translator, Celan often breaks down the poetic syntax of the poet he translates, be it Valéry (whose estheticism makes him impatient) or Mandelstam (who is his hero): the German syntax of Celan's translations, however, does not deviate from the grammatical norms of German: which is to say that "break down" does not mean "destroy" but rather "analyze": the poetic syntax of the translation reflects upon and analyzes the poetic syntax of the original and thereby prevents a straight emotional or aesthetic response: the translation challenges you to pay attention to how language works. And that, in short, was our chief challenge in translating Celan: we often sought higher levels of fidelity than those of the word, the line, or the individual poem in order to re-create, where possible in English, effects that seemed characteristic of his art as a whole.

The methodical search for higher levels of fidelity suggests what one might call a staggered recuperation of difficulty, via the shift to a higher level of language (Jakobson: languages differ not in what they can—but in what they must—express); to a wider body of work; to a broader frame of comprehension (hermeneutics). It also mandates a self-reflexive mode, i.e., a translation which reflects its own rhetoric. In the case of a poetry as self-reflexive as Celan's this would mean *doubling* Celan's own rhetoric. Such an escalation of difficulty, of the music of difficulty, if you will, is what Celan himself proposes in "Cello Einsatz," a poem controlled by translingual paronymy of cello : ciel [Fr] :: Celan.[10]

In practical terms, such a method of escalation, self-reflection, and doubling implies deformations on the level of (i) phonography, (ii) morphology, and (iii) syntax. "WITH WINE" (see above) can serve as an example of the first

---

[10] Here are the opening and closing lines, in Hamburger's version:

CELLO ENTRY
from behind pain:

the powers, graded
towards counter-heavens,
roll out indecipherable things
in front of arrival runway and drive [...]
all things are less than
they are,
all are more.

class of deformations. I say deformations because, obviously, the reinscription of sonic and graphic paronymy must involve different sounds/letters and works against a different backdrop of visual, aural and articulatory habits. I'll address morphology and syntax through the poem "LICHTENBERGS ZWÖLF"— but first a few more general considerations.

Morphology. Compounds in German are *not* unusual but (many of) Celan's *are*: he breaks the standard compounding patterns. Compounds in English are not usual. Worse: when they occur they come laden with poeticalness (consider, for example, the minor fashion of compounding around the turn of the twentieth century inspired, in part, by continental symbolism). The big exception in English is Hopkins—but you can't apply "The Wreck of the Deutschland" to Celan directly without creating very misleading associations. A provisional way out of this predicament would be to break English morphology in a way that calls attention to itself without dragging in misleading poetical associations.

Syntax: Celan's syntax may seem difficult to a non-native reader but as *German* syntax it's not particularly difficult. Therefore, do not reproduce German syntax: it would make the form of the English difficult but misleadingly difficult. Ah but: poets use grammar in non-trivial ways. If you write poetry in German you take advantage of what German syntax compels you to do. Therefore, do reproduce the poetically significant syntax. The situation is not just difficult but aporistically difficult.

2.91 [German overhead]
LICHTENBERG's *heir-*
loom: twelve
nap-
kins and a tablecloth:
a Saturnine salute
to the ring
of fast
fading language
towers
inside the sign
zone.

All

—there's no heaven, no
earth, and the memory of
both's blotted out
down to one blue *nut-*
hatch trusting in the ash tree—

he had:
a white comet
picked up from the city *ram-*
parts.

A glottis, a voicecrack,
keeps it
in the *uni-*
verse.

Red: the loss
of thought thread. The wailings
over it, the wailing
under it—whose voice is it?

In other words—don't ask
where—
I almost—
don't say where or when, again.[11]

    Celan's poem is "about" a great deal at once. It is about a thing. It is about a thing made of words (a piece of language in a letter). It is about a human relationship—of filiation and memory, love and loss—mediated by the thing, the heirloom with its poignant ambiguity, as a remainder of the missing person, i.e., a reminder of the loss—which makes the inheriting subject the inheritor of nothing—of death. It is about the analogous (human!—and transhuman) relationship of filiation in the medium of language and literature: Benjamin, who included the Lichtenberg passages Celan cites in his epistolary anthology *German Men*, stands in the same relation of linguistic and spiritual filiation to

---

[11] I have used italics, for the purpose of this talk, to indicate reinscriptions of morphological difficulty. The version cited here is slightly different from the one published in *Glottal Stop* (a translator's work is never done).

Lichtenberg as Celan does to Benjamin when he he quotes from the latter's forgotten collection with its title made poignantly ironic by history. And it is about the filiation, inheritance and bereavement across time (and space) in and of language. What Celan saw in the Lichtenberg image collected by Benjamin was not simply the sentimental story of the son brought to tears by an heirloom, a thing which carries the human bond of memory—and loss (this story is not unimportant but it's not what shapes the poem); Celan the poetologist, if I may say so, saw that napkins are blank letters. That is, nothing. A thing of sentimental value—and a nothing, mute, silenced by and to death. The wireless transmission of language from one towering figure to another (Lichtenberg, Benjamin, Celan) is silenced by and to death. It fades, failing to transmit the inmost message; at best, it garbles it. (For Europeans who lived through radio Wars II and III— hearing the mad and murderous speeches and propaganda beamed from Berlin and Moscow, and later when the jamming radio towers strove to drown the voice of Radio Free Europe, the VOA, and the BBC, skull-splitting noises I grew up on—radio as a medium of language has far more powerful resonances than it ever did in this country.)

Now, insofar as mediation is concerned, translation and transmission are interchangeable, and the translator of this poem gets caught in the translatorial effects of Celan's poem by the very act of signing on. We're on the same wavelength (and not the same). And just as Celan's use of Benjamin's use of Lichtenberg heightens the self-reflexive dimension of "LICHTENBERGS ZWÖLF," so is the translator, I think, duty-bound to work reflectively.
Hence our very deliberate (but, also, facilitated by the resources of the English language) reinscription of the filiating link in "*heir*-loom" (the line break highlights both the brokenness and the fictiveness of the relation, if you will) and nap*kins*.

Lichtenberg's zwölf mit dem Tischtuch
Ererbte Mundtücher—ein

Lichtenberg's *heir*-
loom [...]
nap*kins*

The latter, you will notice, is not a proper—morphemic—filiation; but so much the better, insofar as translation is concerned, because by translating we are necessarily jumping across grammatical borders. And speaking as the reader (not as one of the makers of the English poem), I should say that the effect of reflexive filiation depends on the (fictive) iteration and breakage of heir–loom: napkins alone would not suffice: you need another wave to make its mute core (kin) resonant.

[N]ut-/hatch, ram-parts, uni-verse are designed/broken for the same morphological effects; "voicecrack" is reinscribed/doubles the single word in the German which in German is *conceptually* transparent (the anatomical term "glottis") but morphologically resonant, especially in *this* poem of doublings and splittings, wholes and cracks, ones and parts. The language of the poem uses others' words and others them; and so does the translation. That's why Celan's German "damit" becomes "in other words" at the end of our poem.

As for syntax, when I *look* at the syntax of "LICHTENBERGS ZWÖLF" I see

    1. Attributive syntax, Germanly ponderous;

    2. appositives (indicating an effort to specify, a failed effort, I might add)

    3. Breakages/breakdowns ranging

    3.1. from line breaks disrupting the bonds of natural following such as proclitics

(ein / Planetenruss; an / die Sprachtürme;

    3.2. to the huge interruption "sein […] vom Stadtwand";

    3.3. to the broken (unfinished) sentence(s) at the end.

I see, in short, that the poetological significance of Celan's attributive syntax is outweighed by other kinds of syntactic deformation. Normally, one might be tempted to tinker with German attributive-like syntax but in this case one would do better, I think, to normalize it deliberately because we need a normal/normalized syntactic backdrop *against* which other syntactic deformations stand out, stark. Normalizing the attributive syntax doesn't make the poem less difficult but is a means towards making the English version commensurately difficult.

I'll conclude with a poem which contains difficulty-recuperating deformations and reinscriptions of all sorts:
2, 122 [GERMAN OVERHEAD]

Spasms, I love you, psalms,

O semensmeared one, feelwalls
deep in the gulch of you exult,

You, eternal, uneternaled,
eternaled, uneternal you,

selah,

into you, into you
I sing the scarscore of the bone-staff,

O red of reds, strummed far behind
the pubic hair, in caves,

out there, round and round
the infinite non of the canon,

you throw at me the nine-times
twined
and dripping wreath
of trophy teeth.

     "Spasms" extends the series of unholy psalms Celan wrote as far as it could go: it is an extreme example of blasphemous but nonetheless sacral revisionism in that the religious bond of the psalmist and god is framed as sexual intercourse. For Celan, this act of oral sexual intercourse is nothing other than a fundamental *ars poetica*-- just as it was for David (remember that in Latin *sacer* means both sacred and accursed or, closer to Celan and the Hebrew tradition, that the sexual charge of the psalmist's exultations whose sexual member bears the mark of God). Celan conjoins the second-person pronoun with the image of a narrow chasm (*Du-Schlucht*: note the cavernous assonance [if you're inclined to pun on God's cavities and orifices, in English, Celan's coupling of pronoun and generative empty space results in *youterus*]) in a figure which can be said to represent the ultimate *Engführung* (stretto, straightening, -- see the eponymous poem) of language, from speaker to collocutor, from human throat to divine abyss. The pressure exerted upon language in this narrow and perilous passage produces the poetics of paronymy exemplified here in what may be the quintessential pair of paronyms, psalm-spasm. Every item of the original poem has been subjected to this pressure which drives language beyond language.

KHALED MATTAWA

Translation and Identity

Back in 1986, a few months after Reagan's bombing of Libya, my parents and I, in Greece at the time, went to the American embassy to apply for a visa so they could come and visit me. I had arranged for the appointment a few weeks earlier, and we showed up an hour before time. When the interview time came, I walked up with my father to the bureaucrat behind the bulletproof glass. Recognizing somehow that my father spoke no English, she asked if we had a translator. I said, "I'll translate for him." Then after shuffling through the application forms for sometime, she asked my father, "Why do you want to come to America?" My father said "Siyaha," (the word meaning tourism). I, translating on his behalf, said, "He wants to visit me and my brother, spend some time with us, see the country a little bit." At that point the consulate official said, "Okay, stop! He said one word, and you're going on and on. That's why we don't like family members translating for applicants. This interview is over." And she collected the papers and went back inside.

To absolve myself of inciting melodrama, let me clarify that we were not refugees, but members of a comfortable middle class family. If my parents were to come and visit, it really was to see us. But there were factors to consider: in those days any Libyan living in the U.S., not registered with the People's Bureau, was suspect. Several returnees from the U.S. were arrested upon arrival and spent years in prison, and, as usual, without charges. So while not refugees, and not impoverished, we were not protected from the capriciousness of Qaddafi's regime.

My reaction to the consulate official's quick dismissal of us was to stand dumbfounded, if not ashamed. Having been a kind of exile of some years, I thought I was adept at "translating" myself, my background, etc. My encounter at the American embassy was the first attempt to translate the U.S., if you will, to my background, to my family. And when my father asked me what would come of our interview, I lied, and for the life of me, I can't remember the lie I told him.

There's an obsequiousness in this kind of translation, and maybe in all translation, an attempt to smooth out the kinks of difference. In cases like what I've been reporting, an attempt to make the powerful less powerful, and the powerless less powerless. That's how I interpret my effusiveness in translating my father's one-word answer. I thought he needed help, and that the American consular needed help understanding us. But I had forgotten that my father's cryptic answer was how he had operated for years before authorities. I am certain that when he faced the Libyan Internal Security officer at the Benghazi airport, his answer was also the passive-aggressive word, "tourism." His tone was neither defiant nor solicitous, but lugubriously nonchalant with no admission of need and imbued with the confidence that this moment will pass. People in authority distrust being loved and love being hated, but are generally impotent before apathy. They can't stand the refusal of being translated.

Somewhere in my work as a translator this thought still offers considerable guidance: translation occurs between parties of equal power. Between Norwegian and Italian, for example. But much of what I do as a translator does not take place in a cultural détente. This is the legacy of centuries of European dominance in the world, the legacy of the last six decades of American Imperialism, Orientalism, the Crusades, and fear of non-whiteness. And in a state of being—the one who has lived as a translator, the one who is intent on measuring unbridgeable distances, and who begins to imagine how these distances can be crossed—I, in the American consulate in Athens, wanted to become a kind a ferry, more than willing to bring the Other to my shore. What I've learned since then is that when we commit acts of generosity borne out of weakness, we set ourselves up for rejection, and that solicitude is not a viable way to cross distances. What would have happened, had I simply said "tourism" while representing my father? I am certain there would have been follow-up questions.

A literary case in point: here's how Rabindranath Tagore, the great Indian poet, approached translating his own poems. By the time he was awarded the Nobel Prize in 1913, Tagore had helped transform Bengali, and indeed, Indian literature. His poetry was dense in imagery, conceptual thought, and allusion steeped in the cultural heritage of India. Rendering his poems into English, he felt:

> English readers have very little patience for scenes and sentiments which are foreign to them; they feel a sort of grievance for what they do not understand—and they care not to understand whatever is different from their familiar world.

And so Tagore chose poems that English readers would find palatable. In his native Bengali, he had written mostly about secular matters. In English, however, he presented only his devotional poems because English audiences were familiar with the stereotypical guru-persona. He made his poems much more simplistic "by circumventing areas that offer resistance." Tagore's attitude cannot be reduced to an inferiority complex. There was a power imbalance that he thought could be shifted by appealing to a sense of shared humanity. It's also important to recognize that as far as his culture was concerned, the British intelligentsia had already perceived him. This stacked deck is what Sangupta calls the "'symbolic order' of the English language where meaning and signification are already fixed according to the differential network of relations." This system "patterns and regulates all thought and action within a given discursive field." A colonized subject like Tagore "seems to have had no option but to deploy the symbolic order of the English language which already has an existent repertory of discourse defining the alterity of the East."

In other words, the Other has already translated you, has fixed you within given parameters. This happens among all different groups, even among Norwegians and Italians where no obvious power struggle exists. But it's more evident when a power struggle does exist, and within that, there are options for the work to be translated. We expect a kind of one dimensionality in the work of a writer from a problematic region: there's the rebel exile who has resorted to us for protection, and who confirms to us how awful his home country was. There are plenty of these; some have won Nobel Prizes. Then there's the esthete who just wants the freedom to perform and examine the perennial concerns of art, not politics. Then there's the melancholic exile who bemoans his displacement, and whose work is to remind us of the charms of the Old World, a lost innocence that we find utterly charming. Deviate from these, show ambivalence, or, God forbid, critique your 'hosts,' and you're pushed into margins you did not know existed.

Clearly I am here conflating the author and the translator; to explain that, let me go back to another originary moment. In December 1988, I'd gone to New York and taken a translation of Lorca's *Poet in New York* with me. I don't think I was that narcissistic then, but it just so happened I'd taken it with me. In Brooklyn in one of the Arab grocery stores on Atlantic Avenue, I found some books of Mahmoud Darwish. I had been writing for a few years, but it had been only a few months since I allowed myself into poetry. At night, I'd go back to my room where I would read a little bit of Lorca and put that aside and read some Darwish and translate it into English and then go back to Lorca. Between reading from both, I wrote my own words. I had two floods of translation coming at me, and I don't know if my poetry joined them or split off from them. In translating Darwish, I was creating English equivalents for ideals I wanted to express, experiences I did not know how to make a place for in English. What was really interesting for me at the time about Lorca was the anger—the anger he felt about "the machine." And how that rage suggested a way of being and an unequivocal way of saying things. But I think what was most astounding about

Poet in New York was the innate joy and ever-ready leaps into ecstasy, even in the middle of what he perceived as infernal. That anger and that rich mythological or pseudo-mythological language.

I will note to you that I came to the United States fully-grown—or at least very aware of who I am in a cultural sense. Obviously I am from another place. And that feeling was there with me at this moment of writing in New York. I was a foreigner, engaged in a constant project of translation, and there was no way of passing for a native. And that lack of unfettered passing forces one's eyes and conscience to contemplate ways of breaking through the system while insisting on dignity. And so, I agree with Derrida that a translation contaminates the original text with meanings it did not have—and as such a text in translation trails more than one language behind. And inversely—by that I do not mean any over-optimistic view of hybridity, or a high estimate of the cultural middleman—inversely, it is also possible that a translation can contaminate the host language. If we allow the sign at-play to move all over the air-hockey table of signification, translation can contaminate both currents.

Having Darwish and Lorca through translation before me provided a way to smuggle goods into the language. At that moment, I hadn't decided whether to smuggle myself into the culture; the question was how and under what condition, essentially what persona to adopt, what identity to don. I did not think of it in terms of contamination then, nor did I recall on those nights in Brooklyn my father's taciturnity or untranslatability. But I was definitely aware that my encounter with writing, and even in a field as marginal as poetry, was an encounter with power, with a symbolic order that has a discriminating taste for which truffles to pick from the ground. Essentially translation, as far as my writing was concerned, as far as I was concerned as a person, provided a sense of how to resist being consumed, and if swallowed, to be a cause of great discomfort.

PETER CONSTANTINE

Vanishing Balkan Worlds: The Translator as Language Preserver

The Greek side of my family is from Corinth, from the Arvanitic villages established in the Middle Ages by migrating Albanian tribes. The language of these villages—Arvanitika, or Arbëríshtë as we call it—is a medieval form of south Albanian (Tosk) that developed independently of modern Albanian, creating a separate language that is to Albanian as perhaps German is to Dutch. (The first written reference to the Arvanites is in 1079 by the Byzantine historian Michael Attaleiates.) I grew up in Greece in the 1970s, and everyone over forty in our world seemed to speak Arvanitika well, though never in front of non-Arvanites. The elders would speak Arvanitika to us, and we, as a young modern city generation, would reply in Greek. My uncles would speak the language to grandmother, whose Greek was not fluent, but among themselves they spoke Greek most of the time, sprinkled with a few phrases of Arvanitika. Jokes, puns, and word games were always in Arvanitika. It was the code-switching that speakers of dying languages do, but we were not aware of that at the time.

Today there is a growing concern for the world's linguistic diversity, as many lesser-spoken languages are marginalized and dying out, replaced by national tongues. These too are felt to be under threat by the globalizing force of English. Albanian, Greek, Bulgarian, and other mainstream Balkan languages struggle to absorb a steady flow of new technical vocabulary, either importing it directly or creating vibrant neologisms. The marginal sister languages of these national tongues, however, oral languages spoken by dwindling populations in remote villages, are being abandoned by a younger generation that looks to Tirana, Skopje, or Athens for its speech models. These marginal languages, like dying native tongues worldwide, live within their own cultural reality. In Albania alone there are villages where there are speakers of local Slavic forms of Montenegrin, Macedonian, and Bulgarian, the Latinate Aromanian and Vlach, and probably a handful of elderly speakers of Adhyghe, a Caucasian Circassian language that has survived since Ottoman times. These are rich and expressive languages within the strictures of their local worlds, but their local worlds are becoming marginalized and in many cases no longer exist. The Albanian Montenegrin, spoken in villages north of Shkodër, has no words for machinery, electronics, or modern commodities, but does have an intricate vocabulary for botanics and agriculture. *Ujem* and *korrike*, for instance, are words for the amount of grain a farmer pays a miller to grind his harvest, while *polonitse*, *babuna*, *mashterk*, and *koshik* are the names of different weights of grain ranging from ten to a hundred pounds. There are different kinds of ploughs—*pluzhitse, jarm*, and the two-handled *demalug*—and there is a word for every inch of a plough. But for the simplest modern household items—*llampë* (lamp), *frigorifer* (refrigerator), *prizë* (electrical outlet)—there are only Albanian words. The Greek Epirotic dialects of southern Albania, which are almost unintelligible to Athenian Greeks, also have extremely focused vocabularies. Villages that used to thrive on tin work, for instance, have dozens of words for leather strips and animal skins of different sizes that are used for polishing the metal at various stages of plating—τσουβρίμ (*tsouvrím*), τσαρμπίμ (*tsarbím*), σιουλοσκούτι (*siouloskoúti*).

Whole microcosms of Balkan languages have become critically endangered in the past quarter century, as new worlds have become established. Language communities that miraculously prevailed throughout the harsh and homogenizing years of Albania's Enver Hoxha dictatorship are now facing extinction as Albania forges ahead in its effort to modernize.

Greece's minority languages are also facing extinction, as younger speakers of Arvanitika, Vlach, Pomok, Po-Nash, Romany, and Tsakonika neglect their languages for the opportunities mainstream Greek offers.

As an American literary translator, I felt that Arvanitika, a purely oral language, was outside my field. Whenever I asked my family about our oral poetry, village narratives, or songs, the answer was always that life in the old days was too hard for such indulgences as gathering around the hearth to tell tales or sing. Every minute of the day or night had been a struggle for survival. *Nde més të nátësë shkarísinjëm dhítë për të klósinjë, edhé i përjërën menate nde shtrúngë për t'i mjëlëm*—"In the middle of the night we'd take the goats out to graze, and in the morning we'd bring them back to the sheepfold to milk them." *Chë kur njóxa vete hënë time, ngindem me nje kopé dhí*—"Since I can remember, I found myself herding a flock of goats."

By the year 2000 there were no fluent speakers of Arvanitika under seventy left in our village. There were many deaths in our family, and during an Easter trip back to Greece in 2004, I realized that my seventy-five-year-old uncle was the last fluent speaker I knew. Should he fall silent, there would only be what linguists ominously call "terminal speakers" left, speakers like myself who can understand what is being said in Arvanitika but were never expected to be able to carry on a sustained conversation. I realized that ours was indeed a vanishing world, and that this was the last chance to capture as much of its language as possible.

In Greece there is no concerted effort to document and record our language. In the 1990s the European Bureau of Lesser Used Languages had sent linguists to our villages for an initial survey of the state of Arvanitika and the number of speakers, but they left after they were attacked with sticks by villagers wary of outside interest. There have been extremely valuable linguistic studies of Arvanitika, but they are mainly specialized books and articles written by linguists for linguists in German and English. However, the titles of these works are unfortunately offensive to our community, as they identify Arvanitika as at best a marginal Albanian dialect, and at worst as a degenerated form of Albanian. (The title of the single most comprehensive and expert linguistic description actually refers to our language as "*Albanian language remnants*".)

My work as transcriber began with many hours of one-on-one Arvanitika sessions with my uncle; passive knowledge of a language, however deep, usually means that one has little sense of the structure of the language. One has to relearn it from the beginning. *Punónj, punón, punón*—I till the fields, you till the fields, he tills the fields. *Kam punúare, ke punúare, ka punúare*—I have tilled the fields, you have tilled the fields, he has tilled the fields.

We discussed things such as greeting rituals. You don't just ask *Ch'bënëtë?*—"What's up?" If you meet an acquaintance from another village on a mountain path, your greeting must begin with *Si yanë uiñtë?*—"How are your olives?" *Ch'bënëtë stani?*—"How's the sheep pen doing?" *Si ishtë grurtë?*—"How's the wheat?" One might then also ask about the wife and children.

After weeks of verbs, nouns, adjectives, and adverbs, my uncle began to describe the old village life in intricate narratives. I started making sound recordings with the idea of setting up an Arvanitika language website and archive that might serve as a forum for current and future generations interested in relearning the language. As often happens with critically endangered languages worldwide, a community's interest in its neglected and dying language seems to resurge once it is irrevocably lost.

SHON ARIEH-LERER

Arvanitika Proverbs from Corinth

Mali i ljartë nuku úljatë për t' i prézmë luljëtë.

The high mountain will not bend down for you so that you can pluck its flowers.

Kózmi dígjetë edhé bljáka kríkhëtë.

The world is on fire and the old woman is combing her hair.

Kasidhjári kur zu lesh, e vu ksúlene nde vésh.

When a bald man grows hair he carries his cap in his hand.
(Literally, "he wears his cap on his ear.")

Milingóna chë dó të báretë bën krykhë.

If an ant wants to get lost, it should sprout wings.
(Don't try to be different, it will get you into trouble.)

Gljúkha kokálj nuku ka, edhé kokálj chan.

The tongue has no bones, but will break bones.

Rredh bíshti i ghaidhúrit nde pus!

The donkey's tail is dripping into the well!
(After a donkey has fallen into the drinking well and been pulled out, the least of one's worries should be that dirty water from its tail is still dripping into the well. The proverb suggests that one focus on the real problem at hand.)

"Na úljku!"—"Ku'shtë gjúrma?"

"Here's the wolf!"—"Where are his tracks?"
(When a wolf is attacking you, don't worry about where his tracks are. There
are more immediate issues.)

CHANA BLOCH

The Assignment

A taste for language was my inheritance as the child of immigrants. My father, who had learned English in night school, recalled one homework assignment with relish: a letter of condolence to President Coolidge on the death of his son. "Dear Mr. President, I share your *bereavement*," he began. The teacher asked him to copy his letter onto the blackboard for everyone to read—the first published work in our family. "I really went fishing for that word," he confided to me in his heavily-accented English.

My parents came to this country from small towns in the Ukraine. At home they spoke English, not Yiddish—they wanted to be "American," whatever that meant—though they sent me to a Yiddish *folkshule* every day after school. Not a Hebrew school: Hebrew belonged to the men and the boys. We lived in the South Bronx, in the shadow of the Jerome Avenue El, a neighborhood soon to become loud with gang wars, but at that time almost too quiet: my friends and I referred to it with disdain as the Bronx Bourgeoizoo. My parents had settled into a life of placid routine, and who could blame them? They'd already endured their quota of violent uprootings. The safety they plotted for me I experienced mostly as a constraint. My innocence about life, like my virginity, was an embarrassment, and I was impatient to lose it.

Yiddish and Hebrew literature offered tastes, smells, pungencies of experience I could only imagine. In Yiddish poems by Jacob Glatstein and stories by Isaac Bashevis Singer, I sought the life of Eastern Europe that my parents had escaped. The life in Palestine and Israel that they hadn't chosen I discovered in Yiddish poems by Abraham Sutzkever, and later in Hebrew poems by Dahlia Ravikovitch and Yehuda Amichai. Reading can bring you close to the very threshold, but the act of translation brings you inside. I began translating these Yiddish and Hebrew writers in much the same spirit that I went to Budapest, Prague, East Berlin, Warsaw and Auschwitz one summer to see and hear what remained of Jewish life in Eastern Europe.

For their part, the Yiddish and Hebrew writers shared an urgency to be heard that was different from anything I'd encountered among writers of English. For those who wrote in Yiddish, especially, translation was a necessary condition of survival. Who, after all, was reading them in Yiddish? Or who would be, in a couple of years? As Irving Howe put it, "the potential readers of Glatstein became the actual readers of Eliot." In America, Yiddish is preserved mostly in a debased form, in the jokes of stand-up comics and the handful of words that have made it into Webster's: *schlep, schmooze, schlock, schmear, shtick* (this is celebrated in some quarters as a cultural achievement). Cynthia Ozick has a painful story called "Envy; or, Yiddish in America" about Ostrover, the fiction writer (a shrewd portrait of Singer) and Edelshtein, the poet (who in some respects resembles Glatstein), the first reaching a large audience through his translators, the second desperate because he has none. Behind both of them stands the destruction of Jewish life in Europe, the death of Yiddish: "Of what other language can it be said that it died a sudden and definite death, in a given decade, on a given piece of soil?"

It was not by chance that the first poem I translated was Glatstein's "Smoke," a Yiddish poem about the Holocaust:

> *Durkhn krematorye koymen*
> *Kroyzt aroyf a yid tsum asik yoymin.*
> *Un vi nor der roykh farshvindt,*
> *Knoyln aroyf zayn vayb un kind.*
>
> *Un oybn, in di himlishe hoykhn,*
> *Veynen, benken heylike roykhn.*
> *Got, dort vu du bist do,*
> *Dortn zaynen mir ale oykh nishto.*

> From the crematory flue
> A Jew aspires to the Holy One.
> And when the smoke of him is gone,
> His wife and children filter through.
>
> Above us, in the height of sky,
> Saintly billows weep and wait.
> God, wherever you may be,
> There all of us are also not.

The bitter irony in that voice thrilled me; the poem gripped me and would not let go until I'd turned it into English. Never having done this thing called translation before, I wasn't at all sure I was doing it right. I sent my version to Glatstein with a letter half-apologizing for the freedoms I had taken. When he wrote back asking me to translate more of his work, I understood his invitation as an assignment. I was longing for what I called real life, the life of tragedy that lay beyond the pale of my uneventful girlhood. I went toward those poems with open arms, happy to be bereaved.

SHON ARIEH-LERER

On Yindjibarndi Poetry

I can see you	strange being	now I can see how long you are
I can see you	wild being	
	your eyes reach everything	

spewing	light	your eyes reach
everything		

From "First Truck" by Pambardu (tr. Shon A-L)

These eyes that reach everything in the opening of this Aboriginal poem are the headlights of the first truck crossing the Pilbara plains of Northwestern Australia into the land of the Yindjibarndi. Tradition has it that the blind poet and singer Toby Wiliguru Pambardu composed this intensely visual *thabi* (a form of poem/song) in a dream. Pambardu lived during the early twentieth century, at a time when his culture faced momentous changes that had made tradition fragile, and his poetry is one of the most vivid records of these changes. Among his subjects are the first trucks, machines, and mills ever seen by the Yindjibarndi people.

For many indigenous Australian cultures, sung poetry is often a vehicle for naming and thereby understanding and owning one's surroundings. In ancient song cycles, such as the Arnhem Land epics *Djanggawul* and *Kunapipi*—which the poet Mudrooroo has called the Aboriginal *Iliad* and *Odyssey*—language and poetry are profoundly linked to the world's creation. The three Djanguwul siblings row in a small canoe from the underworld to a proto-Australia and create the continent's landscape through an intricate ritual of naming. The poet Pambardu, by singing about a truck, a most strange and alien creature, introduces it into Yindjibarndi reality. The truck is understood in Yindjibarndi terms: it is a strange being with "two sorcerers inside of it, making it roar."

According to Yindjibarndi mythology, at the time of creation, *Ngurranyujunggamu* (when the earth was soft), the spirits divided the Pilbara people, who all spoke the ancient Ngaardangarli language, into many separate tribes, giving each its own laws, territory, and language. These languages today are related—some perhaps as closely as Dutch and German, others perhaps as German and English. The old Yindjibarndi poets considered it particularly good style to adorn their poetry with words from many of the neighboring languages such as Kurrama, Ngarluma, and Martuthunira, some of which are no longer spoken. As the Ngarluma poet and storyteller Smallpoxer once said: "The Yindjibarndi do not straighten out their language (*wanggai wayumargu*), nor do they stretch it (*wanarramargu*); they just mix other peoples' words into it." This word borrowing, together with other intriguing properties of Aboriginal languages, makes poetic Yindjibarndi seem like an altogether different language from the commonly spoken Yindjibarndi.

When sung, Pilbara languages often undergo phonetic alterations. If the performer finds a certain combination of words sonically unappealing, he will often modify the pronunciation of a word, sometimes leaving out certain consonants altogether. Although this makes for beautiful cascading verse, it also makes it difficult for younger Yindjibarndi speakers to catch the exact words being sung. Listening to poetry is further complicated by the rapid un-enunciated style of speech which is standard in Pilbara languages. Just as sharp over-enunciation might come across as hostile to an English speaker, what most English speakers call "speaking clearly" comes across as hostile in Pilbara. Consequently words tend to be mumbled.

Aboriginal poets navigate not only the different languages of their region but also different levels of their own language. The same concept might have a word in ordinary speech, a different word in ceremonial language, and yet a different word in the respectful language, Padupadu, which was traditionally used when speaking to one's mother-in-law, one's circumciser, and the circumciser's family.

Padupadu is now no longer used, and many words which contemporaries of Pambardu would have understood are extinct as well. "It's a language that we've never really heard before," says Lorraine Coppin, Archive and Language Manager at the Juluwarlu Aboriginal Corporation of the Yindjibarndi people. She is talking about some of the language found in traditional songs: "And then when we explain to the elders," she says, "the elders say: 'This is this word.' And I'm thinking, 'No, but in our language this is this.' They say, 'But this is a different language for songs altogether.'"

Poetry and the Natural World: Feature

Sandra Alcosser,
Feature Editor

Literary Animals

When the nuns invited me into the convent in the Midwest I went willingly.

Their whispery skirts in the morning darkness on the other side of the bedroom door. Late afternoon whispery laughter in the kitchen among mineral clatter. I was not Catholic but believed I would be initiated into mystery by sleeping within the walls.

Chiyo-ni, an eighteenth-century Buddhist nun wrote of such a retreat.

nuns' temple
feast for the women –
the sound of crickets

Once a sister put her private book of poems in my hands, full of carnal passions for the great other, and I realized that we shared a cloud of unknowing, but our mysteries were our own. I had come to teach poetry to Catholic children.

In my life, if I ever questioned the Master Letters of Emily Dickinson, I need only recall Sister's poems.

But more than one mystery inhales us.

Oh to be like Darwin who gathered wonder toward a great theory.

One lifetime to study the beaks of finches.

Or one lifetime to brush bones on a bare hill to find a nest of baby dinosaurs cowered together under a seventy-million-year-old mudslide. Or one lifetime to collect the nests of insects, then at the end to mail them off to the Field Museum in Chicago for another to sketch the roof of a wasp nest, to catch the small designer as it falls from the nest into a human artist's hand.

Decades later I am invited into another Midwestern cloister—this time to be with scientists instead of nuns—and entrusted again to bring poetry to celebrate the tribes and species of the world and the radiant symmetries that join us.

I speak with a fine poet, a mother who jogs the streets surrounding the zoological park in the company of escaped peacocks. Within the park polar bears live; grizzlies swim and bump chests with her children on the other side of plate glass, and the children leap in rapture.

Hearing the tales from the jogging poet, I invite others to send news of their mysterious connection to the physical world. As unexpected as peacocks on the dawn sidewalks of Illinois, the news arrives.

Kwame Dawes, in his moving essay, "The Chameleon of Suffering," addresses the challenge of *the poet's place as one who must feel and yet be far away enough from feeling to allow him or her to exercise form, the making of art at the same time.*

> I dress in secret, discarding my exile skin.
> I constantly pat my pocket to feel the comfort
> of my utility accent, exotic as a *slenteng* trenody,
> talisman of my alien self, to stand out visible against
> the ghostly horde of native sons, their hands slicing the air
> in spastic language. I too am disappearing in the mist—a dear price
> for feasting on the dead with their thick scent of history.

The chameleon, you see, writes Dawes in his essay, *does not stop being a lizard. It does not alter its internal self, but it still manages to mutate into something quite different by the remarkable act of empathy—that is the capacity to absorb the nuances of the world outside of it and become one with that world. Something changes in the chameleon, something that goes beyond the superficial. The art of becoming is part of its genius, and, as I have said, a function of its capacity to survive.*

And so now for the news that celebrates and interrogates our mysterious connections through the translations and poems of Pura López Colomé, Forrest Gander, Ellen Bass, Molly Peacock, David St. John, Annie Finch, Brenda Hillman, John Smelcer, Steve Kowit, Jane Hirshfield, Frank Stewart, Pattiann Rogers, Mary Jane Nealon, Brian Blanchfield, Peter Sears, Marvin Bell, Saudamini Siegrist, Dorianne Laux, Martha Serpas, Jessica Flynn, Melissa Kwasny, Pablo Neruda, John Felstiner, Rainer Maria Rilke, Joy Manesiotis, Allen Braden, Jan Heller Levi, Joe Millar, Tanya Mendosa, Eamon Grennan, and Kwame Dawes.

Over a century before Mallarmé wrote his poems on the perishable wings of fans, Buddhist nun Chiyo-ni painted and inscribed *haiga* on fan-shaped rice paper. She entered the mystery of the temple as a young woman filled with wonder, and a lifetime later, gracefully released her ties by foregrounding the moon—symbol of enlightenment that her time here had brought her:

I also saw the moon
as for this world—
ah—goodbye.

Sandra Alcosser

PURA LÓPEZ-COLOMÉ

Three Lacustrine Scenes

1. Somniferous

I didn't believe literal
delight
could exist.

Watching the changeable sky,
lying in a boat
rocked in a primeval cradle—
with my tulle marriage veil
and a lace shroud—
by the living hand
of the wind.

Knowing everything to come,
genesis says
this isn't a ferry, just a rowboat,
a ship of idiots, an endless
craziness.
The angel-hair
of the clouds
dissolves and from behind
them, a howl
—quick, hide yourself, here's your home—
seems to echo from,
pertain to,
some neighboring cordillera,
a valley rivered like the nerve system
of leaves when, without shame,
they bare their undersides
or when the undersides shamefully suggest
the schemata of a body
marked by muscles and dendrites,
pertinences, *what pertains to me,*

my own body parts
which begin to go numb,

to go haywire,
dying off even as my pulse
tries to pump them with life,
so many huffs of air.

I was born there.
Benighted.
No thanks to the spellbinding
fisherman who called me to follow,
soundlessly, in his steps,
but thanks instead to the actual dreamer
of that dream stripped of its terrors:
that dream of letting go, of being lulled,
of looking clearly,
steadily into the blue
instead of losing myself to the longing
to walk on water.

2. Coming To, Again

The keel advances, carving out
a hitherto hidden road.
The air has yet
to be opened—
by the scythes of two faces
intent on cutting every
sweetness from the afternoon—
onto a small forested island
where nymphs once played
in the slits between one shadow and another.

On that day, I was ready to taste everything.
And my palette wouldn't deceive me
and I'd know each dish.
With nothing on my mind, I drifted under the low bridge.
A drop of its scent wet me.
I gripped the heavy oars and the pole,
although I couldn't steer or see a thing
that might take the bait.
The instant stretched itself out,
and I kept on expanding
the cruel circle.

3. Merry-go-round

Three horses came down the hill
and sumptuously entered
the river's transparency.
One
waded out next to me.
At times, it paused to drink.
At times, it looked me in the eye.
And between us both,
an ancient murmur passed
on its sojourn.

*

Your three horses, stallions, studs.
With their hooves plunged into the mud
and water at their haunches
laving their bellies.
Drinking and grazing
on the undulation of their silhouettes.
One, that one there,
the sorrel
whose sadness reminds me of a childhood mare
my father swapped
for two dappled grays,
caught me by surprise, dreaming:
in the moistness of our eyes,
manes riffling, weeds trailing in water,
a private space orients
—me, it, us—
in nearness, then lets
me, it, us
fall away.

Translated from the Spanish by Forrest Gander

ELLEN BASS

The Lesser Gods

Jupiter's bruised. Something smacked into it Sunday,
leaving a black eye the size of the Pacific—
its strong gravity like a shield protecting the fragile earth.
As one astronomer explained
"We should thank the giant planet for suffering for us."

I'm not sure Jupiter is a Christ
but as I sit on my front steps, garbage and green waste
lined up curbside, plastic wheels deep in spent rose petals,
sunlight spilling on the blossom-bent spines,

I think how easy to be inspired
by the more theatrical gods: the sun, the moon,
the god of desire, bees throbbing in the throats
of these roses, the roses, how natural to praise them.

But what about all the modest
neglected deities—the overlooked
who've never had a temple built to them?
This morning I raise my cup of fragrant coffee to
the god of mold pulsing in the shower grout, rust
eating the bent lip of the paint can. Bacteria
toiling in the landfill and all the other detritivores,
millipedes and woodlice, burying beetles.

Also the fly god who lands on my hand,
thorax glowing an emerald iridescence.
And the god of maggots whose infinite mouth hooks
scrape the corpses of reindeer and doves,
raking our own humbled flesh after our visit
to this small planet. They graze,
filter, scavenge and browse.

MOLLY PEACOCK

Elle Supine at Her Pool

You've done a lot for American film, he said.
You'll be remembered.
It went into her like rain.
A chorus of doves rose up in her.
She felt slender as a manuscript page
gilded with gold
not yet dry.
She had to look up. She had to see the flatterer.
But his face was hidden beneath his armor and flip-top helmet.
(She had a brief hallucination that if she flipped it, she'd find
a skull covered with maggots.)
Below the helmet, he wore a long fur-and-wool cape,
and he smelled of rosemary.
After a moment of staring, her eyes locked with the eyes
that might be behind the visor.
Then she watched him disappear, literally,
through the striped canvass walls of her poolside cabana.

But at the very end his fur cape snagged on the cabana pole,
and he turned again, stuck out his bare hand without its gauntlet
and reached back to force the cape in with him.
Then the whole of him disappeared.
She was chilled as a lake on a spring morning
after the ice had broken up and melted, just above freezing.
She knew he had been real, because there,
on the chaise next to her,
was his forgotten gauntlet.

She hardly dared to pick it up.
When she approached it, her pale, veiny
hand went right through it.
It was only apparent to her eye.
Slowly, the glove began to vanish, with a slight fizz.
It was a bit like sitting in your hotel room after your lover leaves,
except all he had done was hand her a compliment.

Even though it was quite chilly,
Elle took a swim.
Emerging from her pool
Elle curled around herself in a floppy towel.
The advantage of being older, she mused,
is that you recognize a rare moment when it's happening.
Even if he had been a figment of her mind,
Elle appreciated the figment for what it was:
luminous, if tarnished, gratification.
That afternoon while she was visiting
her fifth husband in the hospital
the embroidered gauntlet materialized in the back of her lingerie drawer.

*

She was a widow, naked in a chaise at her pool,
behind her own high privet hedge.
I've come back for my glove, he said,
as if only sixty seconds had passed, not three times sixty months.
What will it cost me?
He was as flirtatious as he was the first time.
"How do you know I have it?" she asked.
I know. Well, of course he did.
Loose, limber, he was perfectly naked,
except for his helmet, one gauntlet, and his floppy leather boots.
Small, really, the actual size of a man
who could fit into a suit of museum armor.
No erection, she observed,
Well, we aren't spring chickens.

She got up, not quite as pale as he was,
and sauntered casually to her bedroom closet
as if she were on camera, as she had been recently,
and partly in the buff, too, a great old lady returning
to the screen in a daring cameo.

She was living on the compliments she had gotten for that.
You don't need as much food when you're older.
"The price of the return," she said sweetly to him,
holding the long, embroidered glove out toward his grizzled chest,
"is a look at your face."
He bowed his head immediately so that she could reach his helmet.
Elle flipped the hinge.
Nothing was there!
She stood on her toes and craned her face forward
to look down into the helmet
and saw the face of a child with a Buster Brown haircut.

His face! she presumed at first.
But it was also a girl's face. Her own?
Almost.
It was Rosemary, the child actress
from silent films—Rosemary
as a tomboy with thick straight bangs.
Elle sat down by her pool
and watched him don the glove
then disassemble his cells into a vapor
that passed through the privet with a pleasant hiss of champagne bubbles.

Compliments
tell you what you are, what you already knew
but when other people know it, too,
the lake inside you deepens.
You reflect them in your waters,
Elle thought, *and they reflect you in their eyes.*
"That's narcissism!" the precocious Elle once shouted at Rosemary
who reposed in satin at a dressing room mirror.
"No, darling," she said to her daughter,
"narcissism is craving your own reflection.
A compliment is a response to one's effort at being."

All around the pool the privet hedge
enclosed a vast emptiness.
I need you even now, she thought, *even now.*
Into the stillness her ache almost echoed
as if it were a sound.

The Smell of Music

No, No, Never and No More
were the Negativo String Quartet:
the two No's violins,
Never the viola, and No More the cello.

They were negative about EVERYTHING
oops, well, NOTHING.
But they filled the air with music
—that's positive, isn't it?

"No!" First No said, "because you can't *see* music."
"And," said Second No, "you can't *touch* music."
"Or taste it," Never said. "You *can*
sort of smell music, though," said No More.

"That's the smell of the upholstery in the seats
of auditoriums, or the plastic of the CD cases,"
the Violins corrected. But Viola
admitted to a bit of perfume.

The Quartet was not famous. However,
they were *known*. To be recognized, yet not
to suffer the disadvantages of fame is a state
so ideal they could never admit they were in it.

Contrary to the vicissitudes of fame, ease
is the path of the known,
smooth as the satin on a Guarneri finish.
"Oh it was NOTHING," they said to one another

as they did favors for themselves,
producing scores of synchronicities
and the occasional juicy dissonance
that No, No, Never and No More could really

become desolately *no-worst-there-is-none* about
but then they would buoy, as on a midnight Pacific
of calm, rich dark negatives uniting them in
their trademark Negativo effect:

Can't see it, can't touch it,
can't taste it. . . exactly. . .
Or does it have a slight taste of squid ink with a few drops
of lemon? their audiences wondered.

A slight, brief piquancy to the nostrils,
the smell of earthly harmony,
the perfume of agreement in such accord
that, though it is rare as ease, seems like nothing.

DAVID ST. JOHN

The Olympus Theater
for Joe Millar

When I go to the movies
I always hate standing in line
I get real jittery just like
The ghost of Delmore Schwartz
I want to step straight into the darkness
The simple darkness & just sit
All the way against the back wall so
No one can watch me watching those
Liquid shapes crawling along the cave wall

But today at The Olympus Theater
I'm in line to see the new print of my favorite
Film – Antonioni's *L'Eclisse* – & so here I am
Exposed to all of mid-town Manhattan
& I see coming toward me wearing
A gunmetal-&-purple sort of lacy frock
By Vivienne Westwood
Leering like a satyr as he approaches
Looking exactly like a bruised eggplant in a tutu

My old friend Dionysus
& he must be going someplace special
The way his hair is all poufed & fluffed
At the shoulders & his transient's goatee has been
Trimmed & waxed so that he
Resembles both D. H. Lawrence & a garden spade
He walks right up to me & he doesn't say
Hello he just looks up at the marquee & sneers:
That's *so* you – all that second-hand emotion . . .

Come on Dice-Man I say
Feel like joining me at the movies?
No way he says James Brown & Wilson Pickett
Are playing together tonight & I plan
To raise some significant hell – then he says

What about you my thin wild Mercury?
You're looking a little speedy & sick & hollow
Why not *you* come with me – I'm on my way uptown
For the midnight show at The Apollo

ANNIE FINCH

Wolf Song

Act I

As audience enters through tunnel, the song "'Lil Red Riding Hood" (Sam the Sham and the Pharoahs, performed by Bowling for Soup) plays on speakers. LITTLE RED RIDING HOOD *and* RED *lead audience members into the performance space.*

Scene 1

Lights out for several moments, then come up dimly to reveal a forest. THE BOY WHO CRIED WOLF (FENRUS) *is asleep, curled under a tree at stage right. It's fall and leaves are falling and piled around him. Dim slow music of crickets.* DEER CHORUS *emerges gradually from trees and behind banners. Most of* DEER CHORUS *stands together to sing while some of them remain dancing.*

DEER CHORUS:
> Here is a story of the wolf song, story of the wolf song—
> Tails on the trail through the deep forests with us,
> Eyes in the dark and in the dawn with us,
> Story of the wolf song, the wolf song,
> Aaaaaaa——-aaaaaah!

DEER SOLOIST:
> A child is asleep in the forest
> The boy who cried wolf is asleep

DEER CHORUS:
> The boy who cried wolf is asleep
> Ssssh! Sssssh! Sssssssh!
> Let him sleep . . .
> Ssssh! Sssssh! Sssssssh!
> Let him sleep . . .

SILENCE, then the words again in a regular stuttering stop-and-start kind of rhythm that will advance in tension, the periods of silence growing shorter and shorter, until the Boy Who Cried Wolf finally wakes into his dream.

DEER CHORUS:

      Let him sleep . . .
      Until he wakes to a terrible dream

SILENCE, slightly shorter

DEER CHORUS:

      The boy who cried wolf will awake
      Into a terrible dream
      A dream that has haunted the forest
      Of all of our hearts for too long
      The boy who cried wolf will be taken
      Out of the spell of his sleep
      To wake into cruelty and slaughter,
      A landscape his people won't keep;
      He will wake to a terrible dream . . .

FIRST HALF OF DEER CHORUS:

      Ssssh, let him sleep. . . .

SECOND HALF OF DEER CHORUS:

      He will wake to a terrible dream . . .

FIRST HALF OF DEER CHORUS:

      Ssssh, let him sleep. . . .

SECOND HALF OF DEER CHORUS:

      He will wake to a terrible dream . . .

FIRST HALF OF DEER CHORUS:

      Ssssh, let him sleep. . . .

      SILENCE, slightly shorter

DEER CHORUS:

      Around him the trees are as silent as change
      The crickets are keeping him quietly here

      SILENCE, slightly shorter

DEER CHORUS:
> The crickets are keeping him quietly here
> The leaves drift down slowly to cover his forehead

> *SILENCE, slightly shorter*

DEER CHORUS:
> The leaves drift down slowly to cover his forehead
> And he dreams . . .

> *SILENCE, slightly shorter*

DEER CHORUS:
> The story begins with a dream
> The wolf song begins with a dream of a wolf

> **WOLF DANCERS** *fade back into trees as BOY WHO CRIED WOLF wakes, stirs, leans on one arm, and watches what will unfold. But he always remains asleep; periodically throughout Scene 2, he will continue to lie down again and close his eyes, even at moments of great excitement and action.*

Scene 2

Lights dim again and then rise gradually to reveal the exterior of LA LOBA'S *cabin in the woods (perhaps rolled in on wheels, or suggested by the bodies and gestures of dancers). It is still fall and leaves are falling; orange leaves are piled on the ground.*

> WOLF *enters cautiously, approaches cabin, and knocks gently. Silence. Knocks again.*

VOICE OF LA LOBA:
> Little Red Riding Hood, is that you? I was just mixing up some potions. Come in, darling!

> WOLF *enters the cabin. Beat.*

VOICE OF LA LOBA:

>AAAHHHH! Stop, wolf, stop! Don't eat me!
>*Silence. Wind in the trees. Distant wolf howls. Light moves over the house.*
>*Enter* LITTLE RED *at age of eight, with a basket. She runs up to the house,*
>*knocks breathlessly. Silence. Knocks again.*

LITTLE RED:

>Grannie! Grannie!

VOICE OF WOLF:

>Little Red Riding Hood, is that you? I was just mixing up some
>potions. Come in, darling!

LITTLE RED [opening the door]:

>Grannie! You wouldn't believe what happened to me in the woods! I
>met a big wolf! And she talked to me! Just like a person talks!

VOICE OF WOLF:

>Really! Come right in, dear—tell me all about it!

>LITTLE RED *enters the house.*

VOICE OF WOLF:

>Darling! Dear! Don't you look delicious!

VOICE OF LITTLE RED:

>Grannie, What big eyes you have!

VOICE OF WOLF:

>The better to see you with, my dear! Ahhh GRR!

VOICE OF LITTLE RED:

>Grannie, what big ears you have!

VOICE OF WOLF:

>The better to hear you with, my dear! Aha GRRRR!

VOICE OF LITTLE RED:
> Grannie, what a big mouth you have!

VOICE OF WOLF:
> The better to eat you with, my dear!
> Aaaah GRRRRRRRRowl!

VOICE OF LITTLE RED:
> AAAHHHH! Stop, wolf, stop! Don't eat me!

Silence.

A moment too late, HUNTER and BOY WHO CRIED WOLF come rushing in.

HUNTER *(running into house):*
> Stop, everyone! Stand back, everyone! Stand back! Calm down! I have a gun!

VOICE OF WOLF:
> GrowllllLLL!!

Two gun shots. Then silence. HUNTER and BOY WHO CRIED WOLF emerge from the house dragging the dead WOLF (Idea from CJ: papier-mache head on a large stretchy gray-brown shaggy blanket fastened with a long piece of Velcro that can be ripped open).

VOICES OF LA LOBA AND LITTLE RED *(muffled, from inside the wolf):*
> Help! Help!

VOICE OF BOY WHO CRIED WOLF:
> What's that? Papa?! What's that?!

VOICE OF HUNTER:
> What is it, Fenrus? What is it, Boy Who Cried Wolf? Is this like that time you kept crying wolf and there was no wolf at all? Are you doing that again? Look, I don't hear anything. Here, let's get this wolf out of here. Wow, she's really heavy—as heavy as three wolves! Well, we can use her skin. . .

VOICES OF LA LOBA AND LITTLE RED *(muffled, from inside the wolf):*
> Please help us!

VOICE OF BOY WHO CRIED WOLF:
> Papa, really! Papa, I hear something! I'm telling you—I hear something in there! There's somebody inside that wolf! There's somebody inside the wolf!

VOICES OF LA LOBA AND LITTLE RED *(muffled, from inside the wolf):*

> Let us out! Let us out! The wolf ate us! We're in here! Please! Help! Come on! Let us out!

VOICE OF BOY WHO CRIED WOLF:
> There's somebody inside the wolf, Papa! Somebody's calling—sounds like a few people!

VOICE OF HUNTER:
> Oh Fenrus, Fenrus, if you insist on being so silly—Really, ever since you became the Boy Who Cried Wolf, you just can't get enough of everybody listening to you all the time! Ok, Ok, let me see. *(half-hearted)* Is anybody in there?

VOICES OF LA LOBA AND LITTLE RED *(muffled, from inside the wolf):*
> Yes! Yes! *We're* in here! Help! We need to get out! Please, let us out!

VOICE OF BOY WHO CRIED WOLF:
> Papa, see? See, Papa? There was somebody in there!

VOICE OF HUNTER *(grumpily):*
> Oh Fenrus, you and your ideas again. Hold on, hold on! I'll cut the wolf open!

VOICES OF LA LOBA AND LITTLE RED:
> Oh, thank you!

> *Moments later, all four of them come out of the house,* HUNTER *and* FENRUS *carrying the dead wolf.*

DEER CHORUS (*as they all emerge from the house*):
    Poor Little Red, Poor La Loba.

        They went inside the belly of the wolf,
        Deep inside the belly of the wolf . . .
        The big jaws opened and ate them,,
        Deep inside the belly of the wolf
        Where the dark growls begin,
        Where the dark growls begin . . .

LA LOBA (*kneeling by the wolf, staring at her face*):
        It was much gentler than I had thought,
        Your howling. It softened to dusk,
        Dusting with my slow milkweed hairs into night,
        With the silk belly down of an intimate brush

        HUNTER *stands over her for a moment, then turns to leave.*

LA LOBA (*sober and quiet, addressing* HUNTER):
    Thank you. You saved us.

HUNTER (*with gruff respect*):
    Think nothing of it, Red's Grannie.

    LA LOBA (*with dignity*):
My name is not Red's Grannie. Anyway, Hunter, from now on, I have
a new name. From now on, I will call myself is La Loba. Wolf Woman.
In honor of this animal. La Loba.

HUNTER:
    Sure, R—La Loba.

He turns to leave. The sleeping BOY WHO CRIED WOLF finally
wakes up, stretches, looks around, startles, and runs over to his father.

BOY WHO CRIED WOLF:
    Wait, Papa! Wait!

He runs over to HUNTER and takes his hand. Together, they stare at LA LOBA curiously.

BOY WHO CRIED WOLF:

What was it like in there, Ma'am? What was it like inside, inside *(with terror)*—the wolf?

LA LOBA:

Boy Who Cried Wolf, it was—Someday, when you're older, maybe you'll understand . .

She says no more. BOY WHO CRIED WOLF *and* HUNTER *walk off quietly.*

LA LOBA: *(to herself):*

You carried me inside my own sweet life once more,
Then were joined by another, and then the down
carried me inside my own life once more

HUNTER AND BOY WHO CRIED WOLF *(calling from edge of stage):*

Goodbye . . .La Loba.
They turn to LITTLE RED and all say their goodbyes in the background while LA LOBA continues her meditation over the WOLF.

LA LOBA:

Coming out of the forests, gray form emerging
Soft fur emerging like flowers
Here is your pelt
Your tail electric with life
Flying wild in my hand
Brush made of goddess
You're the friend of the wild
Alive in your death
You fill my life still

LA LOBA *gets up and, as if in a private trance, walks towards the woods.* RED *runs after her.*

LITTLE RED RIDING HOOD *(hugging her):*
>
> I don't care what name you have—I'm so glad you're alive, Grannie!

LA LOBA *(seriously, turning away from the woods, still distracted but pulling herself together):*

> I'm glad you're alive too, Little Red . . . Now do run home to your parents! They'll be terribly worried.
>
> *LITTLE RED runs towards the other end of the woods, and LA LOBA stands and looks after her.*

LA LOBA:

> Why do I feel this new loneliness?
> What happened to me in that place?
> What is the hope without hoping,
> the sweet wildness that leaves an old trace?
> The Wolf, dead and empty, soul in her eyes;
> She killed me, yet I live inside her
> earth-rich belly more than in my own eyes.

DEER CHORUS *(interrupting and finally interweaving with her voice):*

> Oh Little Red, oh La Loba,
> deep inside the belly of the wolf . . .
> Big jaws opened and ate them,
> deep inside the belly of the wolf
> Where the dark growls begin.

LA LOBA:

> I came alive where the growls begin!

DEER CHORUS *(some dancing, all singing):*

> She came to life where the growls begin.
> This is the story of the wolf song, story of the wolf song . . .

LA LOBA:

> I came alive where the growls begin!
> And now I begin to sing them alive

I sing in the heart, I sing in the voice,
I sing the bones that have no choice
It's time to move and come alive
The bones will need you to survive
Eye and nose and fur and skin
It's time to make the wolf begin
Eye and nose and fur and skin
It's time to make the wolf begin

DEER CHORUS *(some dancing, all singing):*
This is the story of the wolf song, story of the wolf song . . .

Lights down. DEER CHORUS *dances without singing*

END OF ACT I

BRENDA HILLMAN

Early Sixties Christmas in the West

It takes all the strength of the girl & her mother holding the knife
to slice the holiday bird. Lipton onion soup flakes floating in the pan.
One pinch of irreverent parsley recalls a belief in plants having feelings.
The father reads Camus by the fire. Each book is a Bethlehem. The
crèche has an arch where violence is delayed.

Around the teenage galaxy
      a halo of dark matter

In the nearby desert   iron & silicon

          Between the dimensions
in a disciplined curved sleep
      fat cherubs assert their right to exist
      for they make more sense
         than McNamara about Communists

Patterns float independently on the girl's apron. Mr. Postman
by the Marvelettes. Like Demeter, the mother is great at using
leftovers, and the daughter finds a skill for bringing fragments
from the dead: *My. heart. aches. &. a. drowsy. numbness.* The brothers
play chess: thump-thump, wooden-skirted figures on ovals of
green felt.

Between Semesters, the Fragments Follow Us

As a heron stalks the smart frog,
    time stabs the mini-brenda
(we had a little panic, then it grew—!)
Valved season, approaching Imbolc:
     sounds of the newly dead
eee-^eeyyy tumble like Russian gymnasts,

        thousands of herring purr
       through the eelgrass [*Zostara*] with—at the end
of the middle of the end of empire—plastic
buoys, rope, arabic bronze kelp washed up—
   take me too, present tense, take us,
driftwood, each aperture
     so mongrel-sized…

Across Tomales, children merge with screens,
      & farther in: pre-rectangles on the backs
      of turtles; there is sexual laughter
in the dune grass—
over the shards, stars buckle
    & wheel… Some of the fragments are lost,
      Osiris. Your lover will find them
with her quantum style—

JOHN SMELCER

Song of the Rain

A soft rain begins to fall.

A ground squirrel comes out from the rocks,
his small head cocked—

both of us listening to the raindrops singing.

Translated from the Ahtna Athabaskan language of Alaska

The Box Elder Bug

When Mary asks if the little bug that I've just carried safely out on a stick
        & shaken into the garden was a box elder bug, I put down
the *Union-Trib*, clear my throat, & say in my most authoritative manner,
        "It most certainly was a box elder bug." She nods in that typical
wiseass way of hers & says "I bet you don't even know what a box elder
        bug looks like," to which I reply: "the box elder, commonly referred
to by entomologists as *Leptocoris trivittatus*, is a dark brown coreid with three
        longitudinal red lines on the thorax and red veins in the first pair of
wings. It feeds," I add as an afterthought, "mainly on the leaves of the silver
        maple, that is to say the box elder tree. Hence its name."
Well, actually that's what I would have liked to have said, but couldn't
        because in fact I had no idea whatsoever what a box elder bug looks
like, so I didn't know if the beautiful little creature standing on its elegant
        black legs that I'd just saved from the sharp claws of our cat Bert was
in fact a box elder bug or not. Nor did I know the box elder bug fed on the
        box elder tree, or that the box elder tree was also a silver maple, at
least not until I walked into what I would like to call my study, that shamble
        of books & manuscripts where, at my old Pentium 4, I looked up
"Box Elder bug" on *Britannica Online,* & saw at once from the photo that the
        creature I'd taken outside was not a box elder bug. But more
importantly, just about every box elder bug website Google comes up with
        refers to it as a pest, & there are all kinds of instructions on how to
exterminate it, simply because it tends to winter in human houses, though in
        fact it does no damage whatsoever. The worst it can be accused of is
crapping on draperies creating tiny spots that are hard to remove.
        Well, to hell with the draperies. The poor little things don't even
damage the box elder trees they like to eat from. In short that beautiful little
        box elder bug is utterly harmless. If anyone's a pest for chrissake it's
us, isn't it? *Homo satanicus* our own sanctimonious, genocidal, torture-loving,
        insecticide-happy, maniacally exterminationist species, a species
that—Well, don't get me started. No, the bug I took outside & shook off
        that stick wasn't a box elder, though I have no doubt whatsoever that
exquisite little fellow with his red cap & long handsome legs was every bit as
        benign & seemed, as I carried him out, full of dignity & grace, despite
what must well have been his perfectly understandable fear that he was being

carried to his doom, some wretched Gaza or Auschwitz or Nagasaki
for bugs, though he is in fact far safer outside than in a house with seven
rambunctious cats & he won't freeze this week: it's the evening of the
first full moon of spring—& the weather has turned absolutely luscious &
the mountain lilac is in bloom & the snowy alyssum & African daisies
& every which sort of miraculous tiny vivid wildflower here in the back
country hills. I mean our job is to look after each other, isn't it, &
save whomever we can? I look around me for the first time all day: In the
western sky the darkening reds of dusk. Tecate Peak, sacred Mt.
Kachama looming over the hills of Mexico. Then I step back into our tiny
house in Potrero & sit back down by the fireplace beneath the photo of
that old Palestinian shoemaker that my uncle George took many years ago,
to my left the Cambodian Buddha Patrick gave me, & by my left foot
that little tin armadillo on the chipped brick hearth. In the *Union Trib* I am
taking in the most recent horrors that our human brethren have
unleashed upon one another when Mary looks up from the book she's been
reading & asks me if the bug I just took outside was a box elder, & I
nod, as I've already told you, in my most authoritative manner & fold the
paper & clear my throat & tell her that yes, it most certainly was.

JANE HIRSHFIELD

I Ran Out Naked in the Sun

I ran out naked
in the sun
and who could blame me
who could blame

the day was warm

I ran out naked
in the rain
and who could blame me
who could blame

the storm

I leaned toward sixty
that day almost done
it thundered
then

I wanted more I
shouted *More*
and who could blame me
who could blame

had been before

could blame me
that I wanted more

The Promise

Stay, I said
to the cut flowers.
They bowed
their heads lower.

Stay, I said to the spider,
who fled.

Stay, leaf.
It reddened,
embarrassed for me and itself.

Stay, I said to my body.
It sat as a dog does,
obedient for a moment,
soon starting to tremble.

Stay, to the earth
of riverine valley meadows,
of fossiled escarpments,
of limestone and sandstone.
It looked back
with a changing expression, in silence.

Stay, I said to my loves.
Each answered,
Always.

Love in August

White moths
against the screen
in August darkness.

Some clamor
in envy.

Some spread large
as two hands
of a thief

who wants to put
back in your cupboard
the long-taken silver.

It Must Be Leaves

Too slow for rain,
too large for tears,
and grief
cannot be seen.
It must be leaves.
But broken
ones, and brown,
not green.

FRANK STEWART

On Not Going Out
—from *Coming and Going After Po Chü-I*

Too lazy to get up,
from my window I see snow
on the peaks at the sky's edge.

My old wife brings tea.
Noisy browsers want their grain.

As if I couldn't hear every protest,
the green stubble is sulking

under their unclipped hooves.
Thirty years on my knees at court,

with a room too short for my bed,
now this. Good luck, traveler.

Remember not to stop until
you've reached the Han. Otherwise

put away your sword, learn
to play deaf, and to truly adore,

even on a sunny day,
a radish for breakfast.

PATTIANN ROGERS

A Doxology of Shadows

They float and sweep. They flicker
and unfold, having neither electrons
nor atoms, neither grasp nor escape.
They are nearer than angels, more
reliable than lovers. Like skeletons,
they could be scaffolds; like memory,
they could be skeletons. When
of cattails and limber willows
on a summer pond, they are reverie.

Layering each other in a windy
forest, they can cover and disfigure
a face to a puzzle of shifting pieces.
If straight and unwavering when
crossing grassy lawns and clearings,
they are measures of time, true
of direction. Shadows of minnows
on the creek bed below are either
darting ripples of black sun over
the sand or reverse reflections
of surge as fish, design as soul.

They bring the devices and edicts
of winter, of spring, into the house,
over walls, ceilings, staircases—
the inside motion of a blossom falling
outside, a bird beyond the window
swooping a passage of pure flight
through the room. Shadow-drops
pearl over sofa, table, books,
replicating rain slipping in gold
down leaves and branches at dusk.

I sit on the floor within the shadow
network of a winter elm, its architecture

spread across the rug. The substance
of this structure is less than the bones
of a bumblebee bat, yet it holds me.

Some shadows are much esteemed,
those of canopies, awnings, and parasols.
Many ancient tales record sightings

of ostriches seeking the black relief
of cloud shadows on the savannah,
following them across the treeless plains
like magi pursuing the holy star.

Maybe the metals of meteors, the drifting
remnants of galactic debris, the ices
and gravels of disintegrating comets
in their orbits cast showers of tiny pale
shadows (like spells or blessings or praises
upon us) as they pass between sun and earth.

With no fragrance—neither spicy, sweet,
nor mellow—without sighs or summaries,
without an aim of their own, like wraiths
and ghosts with no heft of any kind—the sole
matter of shadows is lack. Disappearing
in darkness, they depend for their being
on light. Therefore, they cannot be evil.
Some people still do not believe.

A Definition by Narrative: The Jester's Bell

It fell off his cap one day in the middle
of his backward somersault handstand bow
and went bouncing and ringing down
the stony street, rolling into a gutter ditch.

That bell—it was worth no more
than a clay coin, no more than half
an orange, no more than bread
without butter, or a one-night bed.

It could have been buried in the slops
tossed out from the windows next morning
or carted off with the kitchen garbage,
dumped (shining with a dim glow upside down)
into the muck of a pig's sty.

It might have been blown away by a blizzard
the following winter, the sheen of its cold
ringing like an icy star flying with the snow.

Some heard its familiar tinkling hanging
from a string around the neck of a prowling
cat, its sound echoing in the ears of fluttering
wrens and robins. It might have been stowed
away in an underground hovel by a pack rat
or tucked in among the crinkled foil
and glitter of a bower bird's love nest.

Some knew it to be the life-or-death
bell waiting among the medicines
on an invalid's nightstand.

It was remembered in trick and prayer—
in the sexton's soft tolling for vespers,
in the gold bell-bauble worn between

the breasts of a barmaid, recognized as itself
among the bells on the toes of a fine lady
riding a white horse up the steep hill
toward Banbury Cross.

It was claimed by a venerable sage to be
descended from one of the 72 bells edging
the robe of the High Priest Aaron; claimed
by another to be cast of the same metal
as the bell chorus ringing the rim of the Great
Khan's royal rolling canopy.

Maybe it followed a sewer to the sea
in the rain of that first night, dipping
and bobbing like a bird on the waves
and winds, floating all the way to Africa,
where it was spied by a robber merchant,
then sewn to the fringe of his camel's
blanket, jingling through the journey
over desert mountains and dunes.

The fate of the bell is unraveled
and reraveled nightly, accompanied
by guffaws, beseechings, and cheers,
in tavern gossip, in rumors recited
by homeless bards, in songs bargained
by rascally minstrels, in whisperings
over cradles. Vile threats are abroad
everywhere now, against anyone
who should find and claim this bell.

MARY JANE NEALON

Writing Studio

> Sometimes she will say to a young man wearing sunglasses, Will you kindly uncover the windows of your soul?
> —Tennessee Williams, *from* <u>hard candy</u>

The nineteen eighties were consumed by the image of men in their beds,
in their diaphanous gowns, their bodies insubstantial
in the diaphoretic sheets.
I was allowed to see beyond their sunglasses, sometimes I didn't even ask,
   sometimes I didn't want to see: their souls were fabricated by them –
had to be, hated as they were in their small towns, in their church pews.
   Their souls danced before me in black tights.

Together we imagined considerable stairs leading somewhere, durable,
   they had to be, to hold so many, so many young men.
To the left of the stairs, the burning of their suffering licks each step,
but to the right a shimmering pool
out of which a large question mark rises – a snake.
Redemption in the curl and trembling skin, *transcendence* from the pool,
   magnificence for their quivering bodies.

Once during those days I had an out-of-the-body experience, drifted
to the ceiling, but I held on,
the pull was strong to stay with my flesh –
I felt such grief imagining how they left, what each one was feeling.

I hope it was a rush, an ecstatic viola.

A yellow bird pecks at the studio door. Its song is a pink hat.
I am going out into the mountain's early July
where grass smells like a fanciful toy.

BRIAN BLANCHFIELD

Paranoia Places Its Faith in Exposure

Some touch is received and the sensation is entire
at contact, and some touch there is a rising into. Lucky
the lover who is encouraged to fit or press
into the hand presented, lucky to have a hand, gloves off.
The hard jar against eyetooth and black jowl the tom
engineers if a fist presents, the kitten in the brick cinders
beneath the broken road, her dusty body knowledgeable.
Pick me up can also be as frequency and antennae do.

PETER SEARS

Up on to the High Flats

I'm driving a county road, past big tracts
of cattle ranches, down into a sudden canyon
and a grove of Aspen along a dry river bed,

and back up on to the high flats
where snow blows when rain falls hard in town,
when the top of a fence post on the side

of the road erupts and a hawk, no, bigger,
an eagle lifts out over the field. I gawk,
I squeeze the steering wheel and check

each next fence post. All the way to Arlington
and the Columbia River I see again and again
that fence post flash, the eagle veer away.

DAVID GOMPPER

Score from Bestiary: Vulture

The Animals

Marvin Bell

VII. Vulture

David Gompper (2009)

MARVIN BELL

from The Animals

We can judge the heart of a man by his treatment of animals.

—*Immanuel Kant*

Rooster Hubris

My master is the sun. He has appointed
me to tell him you are well.
He has asked me to tell him you are up.
Shall I? Shall I? What if today I wait
to hear you sing? Because I, the rooster,
have risen, now your spirit mounts the day.
I am the hero of warfare
and a true hero of the erotic.
I sing the sounds found in no book.
I am the cock-a-doodle-do.
I am a force of nature, an industrious lover.
I am the song of life.
I am, I am, I am, and I do. Listen for me. Oh,
listen to me. I do not listen to . . .
I do not listen to you.
I do not listen *to you*.

American Buffalo

How many we were, American buffalo.
How large we are, each and all, how many we were.
So very many, too many to count,
stampeded to the buffalo jump.
We were made to be your heavy coats.
We were the meat, we were the leather.
We were the sinew for bows. We were the grease.
We made the dung for your fires.
We were the hooves turned into glue.
We were the last of the marrow in hard times, too.
We wallowed to groom. We huddled in herds.
We thundered, and we frightened the birds.
We fought off the wolves and the grizzlies.
We ran through the chutes, away from men,
thundering to get free. Still,
we gave you clothing, we gave you heat.
We gave our hides to shelter.
We were too good to you.
We gave you what to eat.
In the storybooks, we stood until
we were hollow bodies and brittle bones.
Then we collapsed from within. Look for our kind
at the top of the Medicine Wheel. Once,
we had a future that is not the future we have.
Still, we have a past that will remain our past.
We jumped our heavy bodies over the cliffs.
We have learned not to run.

Stork

We sold the stork a story.
We gave the stork its name.

Its voice, a clattering of bills.
We traced the sweep of its wings.

We could see, in the rookery of the storks,
in colonies of pelican and of crane,
in the short flight of parent after parent
to their chicks, outflying the night,
how these birds, so starkly ungainly on land,
can hold up such beauty in the air,
such beauty in the air.

Charley Horse

I am the dead leg, the granddaddy,
I am the corked thigh. Does it hurt?
Oh horse that excels in warfare, I am not thee.
Oh peaceful beasts of burden, I am not thee, not thee.
I trot inside your quadriceps. I snort. You moan.
I canter up and down. Oh, I prance when you wince.

I am an animal, too, because I am you.
Do you have feelings for me?
You *must* have feelings for me.
Because I am you.
Because I am you, too.
Because I am you.
I am you, too.
I am an animal, too.
Because I am you, too.

I am the horse of the deep purple,
I am the horse sense of your flesh.
Can you feel my unshod hooves?
I can feel your hand calming me.
Oh, hear me whinny and neigh.
Shall I live inside you all day?
Am I not real if I feel what you feel?

You have your plow horses, your thoroughbreds.
Why, then, are there sawhorses?
Why are there gift horses,
if not to enlarge the bestiary?

Confess that you gave birth to me.
I am a tiny piece of your bad luck.
I am alive within you. Call me Chuck.

Polar Bear

Look into the white to see me.
I am the loneliness of a polar bear
as the ice melts beneath me.
I am the far beauty in an aviator's eyes,
but he is not beautiful to me.
Look down here, where I walk
in the vast, vacant air that surrounds me.
I scare the Finnish countryside.
The spirit of your forefathers is in me,
walking alone in the unframed cold,
a bit seen but, in the main, this unseen me.
I have not seen the beauty that you see.
I have not seen your love or care of me.
If ever you truly see me, you will draw
me ever larger. I patrol the very top
of a dying planet. I am not eternal.
I am dying, because I am not you.
Because I am me.

Camel

I am more than a camel. I am a mountain.
Do you see in me, humped,
your stooped parent? Do I not kneel, then rise
to shoulder your burdens, and your dreams?

Vulture

We gave you your first flute.
If you would sing of life,
let it be of life and death.

We gave you a wing bone
that bore five holes for your breath.
Oh, if you would sing of life,
let it be of life and death.

We who eat carrion,
who eat the carcasses of buffalo,
and of stork and peacock,
we who dine on raw leftovers,
we are fit to make music, too.

Oh, sing of it. Celebrate the one
who will be there when you need me.
I'll be there. I'll be there,
who will be there when you need me.
When life is over, I'll be there, I'll be there.

Peacock

While you were listening to the whale,
and while you were teaching the chimpanzee to speak,
and training the parrot to ape you,
and running the horse in a circle, and the rat in a maze,
we cried out, all on our own: peacocks! peacocks! peacocks!
Inside each of us was a person, shrieking.
Inside each of us was the beauty we unfolded in feathers.

Fanned out, the peacock has eyes that do not see.
It tiptoes inside a shimmer. In an iridescence.
Regal dragons who scream, they also squeak and bray.
Their terrible beauty gives them away.
Listen how they muster loudly.
They blare like taxis.
They attack like trombones.
They squawk. They screech. They strut.
They are land lovers but can fly.
They have a sound for whatever they feel.

While you were banding the egrets,
and while you were tracking the shark out to sea,
and training the dolphin to kiss you,
and queuing the lions to act, and the seals to juggle,
we cried out, all on our own: peacocks! peacocks! peacocks!
Inside each of us was a person, shrieking.
Inside each of us was the beauty we unfolded in feathers.

Do you like the queenly apparitions that we are?
Do you like the kingly apparitions that we are?
Do we not make your world more beautiful?
And does our beauty not terrify you?
We have more than one effect on you. We have two.

And while you were listening to the whale,
and while you were teaching the chimpanzee to speak,

and training the parrot to ape you,
and running the horse in a circle, and the rat in a maze,
we cried out, all on our own: peacocks! peacocks! peacocks!

Inside each of us was a person, shrieking.
Inside each of us was the beauty we unfolded in feathers.

Coda

How extra-ordinary,
who walk or swim or fly,
all of us, glorious.
We peacocks do not lie.
Listen at dawn or dusk.
We, too, can speak. We can sing.
Like the whale,
like the chimp and the mynah,
like the rooster, like the buffalo,
like the horse, the stork, the camel,
like the high vultures you fear,
we are near. And we are talking, too.
We are talking, each of us talking, to you, to you.
Yes, we are talking to you.
We are talking, yes, we are talking to you.
To you, we are talking to you.

Bee Lord

Follow me home. I live in a hive,
a honeycomb of rooms. My windows
are the beveled eyes of bees
that measure in a grain of sun
repetitions of the deeds of everyman
and woman. I am beelord of a world
weighed in seeds of pollen,
carried by small beasts of lust that thrive
where they kneel down, on parcels of light
extracted from things. From daffodil,
from dunghill, from honeysuckle,
from the spoil of love, from things dead
or alive, so pure a nectar is drawn,
the earth with its fields of summer
is only a fairground to feed the bees.

DORIANNE LAUX

Accidental

There were days I felt so alone I'd walk into the *7-11*
on the off-chance that trading a few bucks for a pack of smokes
might buy me an accidental touch.

The cashiers seemed reticent, handling my sad purchases,
the worn flags of my dollar bills.

But if I dropped a nickel on the counter and we both

reached for it. Or if I held out a slurry of dimes and pennies
in my open palm. She might swirl a fingertip,

heads and tails overlapping   silver, zinc, copper—

and sluice through the pool,
then pluck one out, exposing an hour-glass shaped patch
of skin between the curved, serrated rims.

At the dentist it shocked me how even the thin latex gloves

were enough, my mouth slung open, the rubber covered thumbs
nudging my forehead back, the pressure of a knuckle

resting on my chin. Touching myself

had become a burden, coaxing the flutter to rise
under my hands. I'd end up cupping myself and crying, bent over,
my fist a lump in my pants.

When you brush against someone on the subway,
say a quick *Sorry*
before turning away

or ride a bus, feigning sleep, letting your head loll,
trespassing a stranger's padded shoulder,
I think it's okay.

I think it's better than the alternative.
Though I'm not sure there's an alternative.

I'm not talking about sex, which we know can't cure it,
but loneliness
for which we know there is no cure.

Discord

The knock-out rose has forced
one recidivist bloom, reverted
to the striated pink and cream
it was born to, retreated to the seed
of its original making.

Into the vast library of possibility
we feel the sudden urge to add
one more poem, cramming
the ruffled pages in among
the 10,000 things. One more color,
one more day of the week.

Moby Dick isn't enough for us.
A million elegies is one too few.
Not just bread and potatoes
but potato bread.

This bookcase was a tree.
That hospital was once
a one-room house, one sign
hung above the door on one
rusty nail, one black leather bag,
one stethoscope, one bottle
of coppery iodine, a rubber
nipple, a glass wand.

If one lilac branch in bloom is beautiful
10 branches is more beautiful.
Give us profusion. Infuse the petals
with more cerulean blue.

The hibiscus fan themselves
in the heat, opening and opening.
When they stick their tongues out
I want to French kiss them.

MARTHA SERPAS

Marsh Refrain

The Gulf hums, its waves
rocking and stroking my hair,
varnished, milky, and heavy with salt.

It would part around me if it could,
winding its dials, erasing time.
I list small against the sparkling beige,

a jellyfish, a shell, a tangled line.
I am any and all in its reaches.
My sibling, the trawler, shrinks

to a small button that slips past
the horizon's silver hole. His distance
scares me, and every time he vanishes

I hate him for leaving, his arms raised
in an empty *V*. Beyond him
a guardrail of rigs I could not hope

to traverse. The waves can never
have me. The map I sent is red
and blue and wrapped in cartilage.

Jessica Flynn

Mallards Mating in the Street at Rush Hour

Oblivious to cars screeching around them,
the iridescent male and the brown female
dodge their necks up and down,
circling with a quacking precision.
They take off in a wet flourish, chasing each other,
narrowly missing the hood ornament on a white Jaguar,
and come around again, landing in the middle
of honking drivers to repeat their delirious dance.
When a man walks out of a bookstore
clapping and waving to scare them off,
they ascend vertically like holy ghosts
then nose dive back into the fray again.
Dying for love, isn't that what we all do
at one time or another? We label it romantic,
as we rub a furry bloom of foxglove
against our lips, recklessly ignoring the poison
that lurks in stem, leaf and stamen.

MELISSA KWASNY

Pictograph: Possible Shield-bearing Figure

To the phrase "I mean you no harm," you have added, "I wish you well." How the day trims the night with blue tradecloth. How the night offers long-distance bells. And the wine-makers appear to mix the waters. Lately, the rivers have begun to talk, in their loudspeaker voice, as if projected. As if they were speaking from a crack that opened deep inside the cliff, placed there like a feather in a book. Yesterday, you had one of the Old Days. As they say, your solitude was extended. An implied but un-depicted ground line. A foothill's abstract tradition. The sound of rivers will lead you back there, to what you are being carried along to find: your life, this one, a kind of drowning. Imagine it is summer. The rock shelter is dry. Scrape of chert. Chirr of insects in the fescue. The earth alive in ways you are not. Dead in ways beyond your reckoning.

Outside the Little Cave Spot

The opening to the world is lop-sided, irregular, dipping down like a lock of hair dips down over someone's eye. Outside the cave: liquid–gold–silver. Inside: as if flesh had been scraped off. Of the many ancient virtues, hope is the one you almost forgot. Limestone so dry and jagged, so pockmarked, you could cut your skin. It stops you. Like a clock stops: you are here. From inside, you see that you are often unkind to others. You shake hands without taking off your gloves. There is a motor of living water outside your ear. Little socket. The earth is frozen, cold and skinny and breaking down. You could lean out and lend your warmth to it. You sit here and the cries are muffled. You worry how, in the matter of a single letter reversed, a bit of food during a fast, a shade too dark for the sky-paint, sacred can turn scared and cause harm. This is how large you are. A thumbprint in a cliff. How much you are asked to keep in mind.

Petroglyph: The Blue Hare

We don't know if it's the wind over its surface or the light, but the snow rings. As if the feet of the flowers were stirring here. We make the sign with our boots. We make the sign and we receive. Light is a feeling. We feel light. Then, there is a memory of how long it's been with us: all those dawns, drift of the lemon scarves. Who were we? All those selves never to be recovered. Behind us, the blue-filled tracks of farewell. The light humanity invents is inelegant, broken or scrambled, not like this morning, which pours forth in strong lines. We should enlarge our bedroom windows. Do away with the deck. The goal: to live the interior into the open. With the exception of the hare, all species dig their own separate entrances from the subterranean world. The place of sensitivity may move from eye to ear. Listen: the slowly altering rock, the cave, the path, the flower, the mountain, the beyond.

Geography Lesson

Where is your community located? *Limping and soiled, without access to art or trees—one can see how the people are dragged down.* Does it have a shape? *Rainstorms, field trips, snow days: what catches like the deer's fur on the barbs. When the need is not so great: decadence.* What does the landscape look like? *But the need for beauty is a real need, berry baskets once made of cedar, tule, beargrass, even corn husks, for contrast.* Does it touch any water? *A swath of darkness amid the street lights, which indicates the river, the cottonwood trees far above it, masonic in feigned light.* What is the weather like? *Immense mandala-like starquilt. White sunflower appliqué.* Who lives there? *And the rain and the wind come from the sea in the west, which they have touched, painting the cottages silver.* What animals and plants live there? *Magpies, ravens. Canadian Geese who smear the sidewalks with their green snot.* Who lives there? *Where the designs come from when we close our eyes.*

Kayak

We glide like swans into their habitat: aeries in the slanted trees. We go further than we have ever gone before, past the lone heron, a storm cloud dissipating after rain, and the lesser guards with their brown mates, their ecstatic trill. It is offensive to the forest to speak too loudly or sing there. The reindeer people do not say goodbye, but slip quietly away, and when they enter someone's tent, they stand in the doorway awhile, waiting for their presence gradually to become known. Like kindling being lit and then catching. Mergansers, one ochre next to the obvious white and black male, the two flying so close that she seems his shadow. What you think is a drowned chassis is, in fact, a nesting crane. It lifts off its straw bale and slowly walks away, stiff legs robotically dismantling. How easily, how unconsciously we could disturb. Not like the herons, whose wide-winged disturbance low over the marsh is a shout we hear only with vision. We have memorized the poem about the vixen, the blackbird, and the moon. Perhaps they sense that in us, and do not startle.

PABLO NERUDA

Floods

The poor live on low ground waiting for the river
to rise one night and sweep them out to sea.
I've seen small cradles floating by, the wrecks
of houses, chairs, and a great rage of ash--
pale water draining terror from the sky:
this is all yours, poor man, for your wife and crop,
your dog and tools, for you to learn to beg.
No water climbs to the homes of gentlemen
whose snowy collars flutter on the line.
It feeds on this rolling mire, these ruins winding
their idle course to the sea with your dead,
among roughcut tables and the luckless trees
that bob and tumble turning up bare root.

Translated from the Spanish by John Felstiner

RAINER MARIA RILKE

Autumn Day

Lord: it is time. The summer was immense.
Stretch out your shadow on the sundial's face,
and on the meadows let the winds go loose.

Command the last fruits to be full in time,
grant them even two more southerly days,
press them toward fulfillment soon, and chase
the last sweetness into the heavy wine.

Whoever has no house now, will build none.
Who is alone now, will stay long alone,
will lie awake, read, get long letters written,
and through the streets that follow up and down
will wander restless, when the leaves are driven.

Translated from the German by John Felstiner

JOY MANESIOTIS

Stay

The action is meant to catch crabs, to eat them.
But that is not why they are here, father and daughter:
they love the dock, its floating,

standing on water, the sun, and the bank of seals, mouth
of the bay churning with waves.

They love the release and reel in,
throwing the net pots into green water, how they
sink—lost—, and then waiting,
watching cormorants slice air, seals worming along the far bank,

then hauling in,
hand-over-hand, rope through many hands,

and the reveal,
round form in all its associations, continuous echoes:
bowl, vessel, womb, earth, moon,

although this is only net, a rope of holes—

still, its ropes
hold death and the way of all matter, a way to see

what will happen to our own bodies, the fish heads
wired to the net, eyes glazed and sunken,
opaque, tinged pink,

the heads as bait
(the eyes eaten first, my daughter says,
a crab delicacy),

and the live crabs, stunned to be in all this light and burning air,
reared back, claws open, one shuffling to the edge of the dock,

three caught in the net, their struggle
to keep living
enacted for us, and we—large, human, superior, biped—

helping them to live? Kicking them or flinging them
so they pinwheel through air

to crash into water, medium that sustains them,

or measuring them
to see if they are large enough, and male enough, to eat.

ALLEN BRADEN

Juxtaposition
for Kevin Miller

Ice in a riverbed: a word
In your mouth: each remembers

The other. Your joy only
One reflection: the way grease

From a boy's palm darkens
A page. Each time perishable

Freight thunders by, he feels
Hopeful: The girl he'll leave

Flexes her calves deliberately
Each rung up a picker's ladder

In Coup's orchard by the river.
How can anyone make a living

Of departures: when crossing
The line can mean nothing

But distance, a vanishing point
Beyond which light won't enter?

I mean when the river's iced over
Horses, a few then hundreds,

Surge across: like one current
Over another: both liquid, both solid.

Come spring, quick thaw spells out
Sacrament: Or is that *sacrifice*?

Jan Heller Levi

asap

the root of *bed* is kin to *fodere*, to dig (a grave)
we dig a grave
our bed in the ground

we dig our bed, our bed in the ground
we taste dirt in our ears
earth in our eyes

    we don't long for words
    words don't long for their freedom

we have written our sad stories in the dive of the narwhal
fluid industrious darkness
rising and descending in one motion

and in the marking of birds
illegible (if you're looking for straight lines)

the grass is drinking

the roses are drinking

the dark begins to unjoin from the light

the grass lies down, the sky gets on top
the roses open their mouths to drink the names of everything

you step forward
forward into one and two

forward into leaf touching leaf

inventory

what do we have
what do we see
what do we see without seeing
what have we gained
what do we have left
who is the mother of all our fathers
how does she accompany us
what are our questions underneath our questions
how will we make our griefs our tools

JOE MILLAR

Bestiary

I'm wide awake in the city park
thinking about white port wine in the cold.
You don't know my name or who I am
with your magnifying glass and your notebook.

My face I've hidden and hidden my arms
shaped like the wings of an owl, the draped
wool sleeves of this second-hand coat,
a barred owl the color of amber and smoke
smelling the night's cypress and burnt fat,
smelling the hotel trash near the beach,
hidden the five black knives of my hand,
my face in its splotched greasy cowl.

I circle over the vacant lot
above the crack house
littered with glass, next to the Mission
where the old sailors sleep,
I'm looking for something to kill and eat,
maybe the misbegotten rock dove
standing on one foot outside the coop
fully asleep in the moonlight.

The stars hide behind me
and the leather-wing bats
swerve and dive out of my way
as I plunge toward the night-vole
rustling the leaves, his fur
soft as cashmere,
his small restless feet.

Urban Coyote

In the green dream of spring
I stretch myself out
letting the gray mist hide me
shoving my nose in the garbage pile
chewing egg shells and cheese rinds.
I swallow cellophane, I swallow cat hair,
butcher paper stained dark with fish blood
and run grinning through the blowsy woods
smelling the riverbank's plasma—
I smell the barns and the city dump,
the quail asleep in the tall grass.

In the morning the doctors send over
my lab results: triglycerides and cholesterol,
glucose and prostate antigen,
diets of cold fruit, nuts and water.
I sign the mortgage papers,
I read the bank statement,
I pay the gas bill, I sweep the floor...
Then in the marshy glycemic night
I lick back the pale fur covering my lips,
I steal whatever can fit in my mouth
under the fat April moon.

Tanya Mendonsa

These Simple Pieties Move Me Most

—Hath the rain a father? Or who hath begotten the drops of dew?
from *Psalms*

As I see my small world change around me,
A sadness falls, like rain.
The voices of the birds, as they flee from new noise
Are like bells ringing the end of contentment.
An ending is coming, like that blue rain flower's leaves
Now moving, to cover its face against the dust.
An end to simplicity,
As I see the simple pieties of life
Begin to waver and dissolve,
Like drops in a larger body of water.
In the field below, the farmer is turning the soil with the hoe he has made.
His daughter, who is three, crouches beside the pool,
Its clear surface speckled with lilies.
She plucks a round leaf from it and, frowning with concentration,
Arranges, in a circle, snails as large as her fingernails.
Rising, she goes to her father and offers it to him.
He thanks her gravely, and pretends to eat,
Smacking his lips as he palms each snail.
On their way to school,
The village children pick flowers in season
To set in the crevices of the rocks
Around every wayside cross.
There are puddles in the road.
One little boy stops at each one, to lift his baby sister over.
She stumbles;
He picks her up and staggers on.
These simple pieties move me most.
The house at the bend of the road has duck's-egg blue windows
Set into cream walls.
Balanced on a bamboo ladder,
Very carefully,
A man is painting all the overhangs a melon colour.
In the courtyard, the sand is swept smooth;
It is the pearly colour of the shells in the window panes.
On it, a woman is laying out, in careful rows,

Lines of fat red chilies to dry.
The morning sun drops, as sweetly as mercy,
Through the acacia trees.
It licks the chilies so they shine like jewels.
This is the life that transcends savagery;
The life that crafts bowls and spoons and everyday utensils;
The life that lives with other human beings,
Skin to skin, in the same straw.
This life seems to me to be touched with the holiness of the useful.
Its simple pieties move me most.
But, of course, it will all go the way of the world.

EAMON GRENNAN

Out and About

Morning, the place all light and shade in a patchwork of greens
as leaves turn to a last incarnate memory of how things were:
gush of air, rush of wings: their passionate grapple with daylight,
or a full moon staining them silver so raccoon, coyote, fox—all
nocturnal steppers and sniffers—would have a small shine
to glide by till night gives way to morning, gives way
to their neat repeated disappearing trick that leaves the place empty
except for these seven o'clock shafts of sunfall you walk through,
hearing first, then seeing—on a maple branch beside the stream
swollen by last night's rain—the madcap kingfisher that stops
long enough for you to take in his black unruly topknot, white throat
and blaze of blues, before he's off shouting into the trees' shadow-swirl,
with nothing but his high hacka-rhapsody a brassy cackle behind him.

Out Walking

A speckled freckle-brown net of young starlings
      cast out and carried on the wind
is a wing-brilliant blazon of what happens—
      passing from nowhere into nowhere
in just the breathing space of a moment, the pure
      communal body of *starlingness*
in accelerating action. That's all there's to it,
      except for your own two eyes
rising from the road you're walking
      and watching till the birds—
their web-net in tatters—have vanished,
      leaving air a pale brown
vibration after them. At a loss,
      your left-behind eyes find
the wren, the rainbow, and the dead hare
      (dustier and bloodier than any in Chardin),
and the tiny-from-this-distance
      white houses at the foot of the hill
that stand out like lightning flashes
      in *the great dark back of beyond.*
Up against such absolute facts
      and happenings, you have to ask
how to place them, how to coax
      some of their myriad attendant lights
(terrestrial, aerial, water-bound, mortal)
      into *shape,* how to hold them
still (as in *still life*) long enough
      so their sense will seep through, set
on the sufficient altar of themselves—
      a small recessed stone alcove
out of Chardin—and seen rightly.

KWAME DAWES

Chameleon Of Suffering

Parasite

I dress in secret, discarding my exile skin.
I constantly pat my pocket to feel the comfort
of my utility accent, exotic as a *slenteng* trenody,
talisman of my alien self, to stand out visible against
the ghostly horde of native sons, their hands slicing the air
in spastic language. I too am disappearing in the mist—a dear price
for feasting on the dead with their thick scent of history.

It is easy in this place to grow comfortable
with the equations that position the land,
the green of tobacco, the scent of magnolia,
the choke-hold, piss-yellow spread of kudzu, so heavy
it bends the chain link fence dividing 277;
the stench of wisteria crawling its pale purple
path through a dying swamp. I hear myself turning
heir to the generation that understood the smell
of burning flesh, the grammar of a stare, the flies
of the dead, undisturbed in an open field. My burden
is far easier, it's true. I have not acquired a taste for chitlins
and grits, but I wear well the livery of ageless anger and quiet
resolve like the chameleon of suffering I am.

The chameleon, we know, carries out a very basic technique for survival. It is an act of camouflage. By some remarkable chemistry, the creature is able to change its color in sympathy with the colors near to it. This way it can hide, it can insinuate itself into another environment that may even be hostile, and by disappearing it survives. There is, of course, a metaphor here. The metaphor may have little to do with the biology or evolutionary impulse of the act, but it works well for a poet seeking a way to understand the complexities of home, place, alienation, belonging, and most relevant to us—appropriation.

The chameleon can be seen as somewhat diabolic—a sneaky creature that allows its body to study the colors around it and then transforms that body so it can become a part of that environment. Since other creatures survive by discovering aliens in their midst, the chameleon could well be said to be a threat—an alien threat, if you will. But the chameleon can work as a metaphor for assimilation and belonging. The chameleon, you see, does not stop being a lizard. It does not alter its internal self, but it still manages to mutate into something quite different by the remarkable act of empathy—that is the capacity to absorb the nuances of the world outside of it and become one with that world. Something changes in the chameleon, something that goes beyond the superficial. The art of becoming is part of its genius, and, as I have said, a function of its capacity to survive.

As one who has traveled to different places, I have long understood the importance of being oneself and yet being a part of the space that has taken you in. Finding that balance may well be the most critical skill that a poet or an artist can have.

The poet, you see, must be able to understand this idea of empathy. Empathy enacts a process of becoming, but that becoming is not complete, it does not (and must not) occur with the total transformation of the person who is feeling or understanding. The act of empathy entails being engaged and yet disengaged. Empathy allows the individual to feel, and yet not *become* the other person to the extent that the value of having another around is lost completely. While, an ancient told us, we must mourn with those who mourn, the ancient, by commanding us, reminded us that our act of empathetic mourning is a choice we make, a decision that allows us to be outside of the situation (so we can *decide* to mourn), and inside the situation (so that we *can* mourn).

The poet must also be there and be outside of there at the same time. The poet must feel and yet be far away enough from feeling to allow him or her to exercise form, the making of art at the same time. Here is how the poet differs from the average human being. The poet must both feel and not feel at the same time. The poet must not be so overwhelmed by what he or she sees that the ability to discover the art in the moment is lost. The poet must be both inside and outside of the world observed at the same time. As you can well imagine, one cannot *always* be a poet or something human could be lost. Which is why I like to speak of the poetic instinct rather than simply declare that the poet must always be the poet.

The poet sees in experience the potential for art. This is both our gift and our craft. It is best to simply exaggerate the sinful nature of this impulse so we can have a crude but helpful understanding of what it is about. The poet will steal your experience and use it to make poems. And while the poet may claim that the act of doing so is altruistic, and represents some kind of homage to the subject, the poet is likely lying or simply working hard to assuage the sense of guilt for being a scavenger of sorts. The poet may say that by engaging the experiences of others, by stealing their stories and using them for art, they are in fact "giving voice to the voiceless" or enacting some kind of social work that will edify society in some profound way. Again, while all of these good things may come out of this act of stealing, the impulse is not really about that.

The poet knows that writing poetry is a quest to delight. This, of course, is Dryden's construction, and it is one that many since have latched onto quite wisely. But we must not forget all of what Dryden proposed. "Delight" he says "is the chief, if not the only end of poetry: instruction can be admitted but in the second place." So Dryden does allow that poetry can instruct at some level, and can do other quite sensible things.

I recently discovered a essay by my father, Neville Dawes, that he wrote when he was in his late twenties. He was reflecting on the value of verse and on Dryden. He proposed that "poetry begins in delight and ends in wisdom." A necessary proposition for him, a Marxist writer who would have worried about being a writer if the business of writing did not allow, even if only "in the second place" some opportunity for wisdom.

Having said this, though, I do think this business of delighting is sometimes misunderstood. There is often a feeling that art must not always delight. But that is because we believe that delight only pertains to loveliness, prettiness, lightness, and laughter. Once we get over this limiting understanding of delight, we can begin to see why the impulse to delight with language is as good a reason to live and to write as any. Delight has to do with the pleasure that we get (some might call it comfort, assurance, joy, awareness) from seeing something created from nothing, from discovering something beautiful in our world. Here beauty is the grace of our shared understanding of what is good and affirming about our world. The beauty is less in the content, the theme, the "meaning" of the work, but in the shape of the work, in the very existence of that shape.

So let's return to the chameleon. The chameleon is a freak. That is what it is. It enacts something quite freakish that, frankly, delights us. We are delighted by this alchemy of color that the chameleon manages to enact. It tells us something about this creature, about this creation. So we are delighted by the act of transformation. Yes, the colors that we witness are pleasurable or disgusting, but it is not this that delights us. Indeed, we may be repulsed by the color we see, but remain delighted by the magical act of transformation achieved by the chameleon.

So yes, the making of poetry is something of a freak show. And what is beautiful about it is that we manage to turn experience into something beautiful, something that has a shape, and something that we can consume and understand, something, therefore, in which we can delight. Which is why when a poet chooses to write about subjects that are weighty, to engage with human experience that is often dealt with by social sciences and political theorists, they do not become social scientists or political theorists, they do not become historians or sociologists, they do not become painters and musicians—no, they remain poets, because what they are doing is taking the subjects of these fields and pouring them into the rituals of poetry making. The poet is transformed, but the poet's transformation serves just one end: the making of something delightful called a poem.

I am seeking to explain something that has had to consume my time a lot lately. One of the presumptions about the work that I do is that I am actually trying to do some kind of sociological, historical, political or grandly ideological work in the poetry I have written of late. I am tempted to take credit for these things because in many ways, it is the way that people understand our value as poets. There is something gratifying for the son of a social worker mother and a politically engaged arts advocate father about being told that my work has changed someone's life or has made a difference for some other person. Heady stuff. And headier because it pushes against the constant refrain that poetry changes nothing. But I have to admit that always, not far from my smiles of appreciation for these words of praise is an awareness that the very paradigm of valuing poetry because of its overly socio-political usefulness misses the point of the art, and in many represents something of a mischaracterization of the impulse that has driven the making of these poems. It is harder for people to understand the more basic value of the poet as someone who brings delight. Here is what Shakespeare makes of delight:

> Be not afeard; the isle is full of noises,
> Sounds and sweet airs, that give delight and hurt not.
> Sometimes a thousand twangling instruments
> Will hum about mine ears, and sometime voices
> That, if I then had waked after long sleep,
> Will make me sleep again: and then, in dreaming,
> The clouds methought would open and show riches
> Ready to drop upon me that, when I waked,
> I cried to dream again.

Caliban is reassuring two drunks about the value of the island. You can hear in him such an appreciation of what Bob Marley called "the beauties". Yet Caliban is a slave; he is a man acutely aware of his enslavement and the need to break out of it. He is talking to two people who he hopes will conspire with him to take over the island. The creature is describing one of the critical motivations for his act of political usurpation. And yet, the "sweet airs" are the poetic space for him—the space that fills him with delight and tears. He cries so he can dream. The delight of poetry rests in the shape of poetry. And the shape of poetry is what allows us to turn experience into something quite beautiful, even as it is moving, compelling, transforming and affective.

Perhaps this essay should be about the value of delight in human experience. And I could go to town about this. But what becomes obvious is that such an effort represents a effort to justify art, and this kind of project can become tiring and disheartening as the terms of what is valuable are drawn from a field that does not have the language to understand art's basic value. But let us say here that humans need to be filled with delight to live.

The writing I have done that has sought to engage experience has had to come with some key rules in place. I have had to first accept that I am not a slave to the facts. The facts represent the material that must consume the journalist and the historian. The facts do not consume the poet. Ours is a somewhat less reliable ideal. We are in search of the truth, which is often different from the facts. And the tyranny of truth is not enacted by the narrative (as is the case in journalism) but in the form itself—the shape of the thing called the poem. The poem has rules. It has structure, it has expectations and those expectations are what make demands on the experience. And truth is part of that shape. The truth is emotional, and it is sentimental. It has to do with tone, mood, and feeling and that is not something we can walk away from or ignore. Truth also has to do with the shape of a thing, its pulse and feel. If what is produced does not delight, it has not achieved what the poem seeks to achieve. And so the poet who writes about experience must always be as doggedly committed to the poem as anyone else.

So that is the challenge. As I think of the way that many of these projects have unfolded, I realize that I am busy trying to experience the world through this act of empathy which allows me to change color. But I remain me. I remain the core of these poems and I remain the manipulator of the experience to find something delightful as a result. Yes, people will be moved, people will be touched, people will feel as if they have learnt something they did not know before. Yes, I may even serve as a historian of sorts and yes, I may give voice to the so-called voiceless. But what I am doing is rendering their voice in poetry. This is different from simply reproducing their voice. What I have at my disposal is more than just voice. I have more than just the limits of their language and their experience. I have at my disposal more than the limits of their consciousness. I have a wider palette. When my poem can show them things they did not even know about themselves, when it can reveal to them what they may have imagined by could not speak with delight, I know then that I have achieved art. I have become the chameleon of suffering.

The poet, I believe, (and here, I remain stuck with simile and metaphor trying to describe that which I can't) is an antennae or some kind of live wire that is constantly catching sounds, feelings, ideas, colors, moods, and keeping them in so that they can become part of that grand alchemy called verse. These are the ingredients. We collect them.

As a young poet I worried about this. I worried that I was using people. I worried that I was exploiting their lives. I worried that they would see themselves in my work and be upset. I worried this way because of my own sense of misguided hubris. I simply imagined that I *was* writing them. I was lost then. I did not know that I was not writing them. I was writing poems. There is a difference, an important one. I had to let go of my self-importance. That was the first task. And then I had to regard carefully how much I had misplaced my sense of love, respect and deference for them, for these people I cared about, treating it as something of a justification for the existence of the poems. I had to stop confusing the act of making poems with the act of showing affection as a process of replicating who are they are. What I have learned is that I am offering a gift to these people, but I have no ability to capture them to reproduce them in art. That is hubris. How could I? Instead, I am taking what they have given me and making poems—poems that give delight. But what has gone into these poems is not just them, not just their experience, but much more than that. I am an ordinary creature who has to turn experience into something that has shape and form. Their lives do not. What a poem is is not what a person is. A poem sings its own song. Somewhere we will discover those we write about, but mostly we will discover them as transformed into art. There is an important difference.

So now, all I know is that I am trying to take the emotion and turn it into something that delights—the poem. You will start to see then that the real test of a poem's effectiveness has less to do with what its content is in that crass and crude sense of "what it is about" but in how it achieves its delight. The poem is about the shape of things, the beauty of the thing.

Put another way (and here one must accept the proposition that a blues song is in many ways as much of a poetic form as anything else) the quality of a great blues poem does not rest on the level of tragedy that it describes but on how well it describes whatever tragedy it tackles. This is so basic an idea that is seems pointless to state it, but in a world in which the sensational appears to be celebrated above the way a story is told, it is worth reiterating this basic idea. Thus the poem does not become more moving because a man has been cheated on ten times by his woman, as against having been cheated on once by her. The conscientious poet will find a way to make something of that single act of betrayal. One need not overstate this analogy to make the point.

I have written several books of poems that have grown out of an engagement with various types of existing narratives and sources that could label my work "projects," and that could even challenge their poetic validity. I have heard a number of editors and senior poets complain that much of poetry is about projects and not about the poetry itself. They look with deep skepticism at the themed book, and they rightfully question whether poets are simply responding to the currency of project books. All of this would bother me greatly were I moved to write or not to write by the things that I hear abroad about what is viewed as valid by the wise heads. I wish I were so driven, but unfortunately I write out of impulses that rarely consider publication first. I also have to face the truth that I am moved by narrative. Finally, I write in intense bursts, and so I find myself vamping on a given theme, idea, image, concept or story until I believe I have exhausted that thing. Knowing my predispositions, I have devised ways to counter the pitfalls of these inclinations. So I do not rely on the impulse for the poems to justify the presence of the poems. Instead, I treat the poem as a piece of art that is obligated to itself and somehow obligated to the internal dynamic that one imagines resides in the poem. I take comfort in the fact that I am not the first, nor will I be the last poet to be driven by large projects. I think that the history of literature has taught me that the test of such work is not whether the impulse to write on a subject is pure enough for poetry, but on the quality of the poetry itself—the genius, so to speak, of the chameleonic gesture of the poet. The idea of empathy works for me. It helps me to understand what I am doing as a poet and that is enough. It gives me a framework for approaching my art that is not unrelated to my approach to life in general. And for this reason I remain comfortable with whatever aesthetic emerges from this concept—the basic idea. I embrace, then, my role as a chameleon of suffering; it too works as a functioning metaphor and way to understand what I am doing as a writer. It won't explain everything, but it is a good start.

MARK IRWIN

The Art of Composition is the Art of Transition

I'm walking from my house in University Circle toward the Cleveland Institute of Music, where Pierre Boulez will conduct the student orchestra in Stravinky's *The Rite of Spring*. Later this weekend he will conduct The Cleveland Orchestra in the same piece, along with two tone poems by Mallarmé that he has set to music. It is 1983.

I enter the rehearsal during Part 2: "The Sacrifice, Glorification of the Chosen One," a brilliant transition in which several loud drumbeats link the slow, rhythmic speech of the violins, imitating a gymnopedic fertility, and foreshadow the finale. Each time the student orchestra rehearses the drumbeats, however, Boulez stops them just before the violin passage. "You are stopping after each drumbeat," he bellows. "In great music there is never a stop, only a long pause. The art of composition is the art of transition." I would never forget that salient remark, and still I remember sitting in that auditorium as Boulez asked them to repeat the movement a dozen times in order to get it right, and perfect it was when The Cleveland Orchestra performed the same piece that weekend.

In poetry, the art of transition seems primarily dependent on form, syntax, rhyme, meter, and enjambment. Transition is most apparent through established forms of repetition—the villanelle, pantoum, sestina, or ghazal—where lines or words are repeated and act as a series of fulcrums upon which the metaphor and perhaps narrative of the poem advances. More interesting, however, are those free verse anomalies that radically create their own form out of content. Here, attention and transition become a source of becoming, almost ephemeral because this attention lies at the source of perception. These poems often seem all of one fabric, especially if their syntax can suspend an artfully meandering sentence. A. R. Ammons' wonderfully unpunctuated "Loss" provides such an example.

> When the sun
> falls behind the sumac
> thicket the
> wild
> yellow daisies
> in diffuse evening shade
> lose their rigorous attention
> and
> half-wild with loss turn

                any way the wind does
                and lift their
                petals up
                to float
                off their stems
                and go   (Ammons, 182)

One marvels at the poem's spontaneity, one that describes how daisies lose their physical attention (a movement toward light) in shade, but paradoxically regain it, as now, "half-wild with loss," they follow the wind, a new attention source, and this occurs precisely at line nine, the poem's center where the flower's physical loss suddenly becomes gain through a complete loss to the wind. Ammons' poem turns effortlessly, just as the daisies' petals give themselves to the wind, and his transit seems as invisible as the reflection of any landscape in water. In a poem of both human and vegetal consciousness, the cosmos is revealed through the perception of minute details, or as Blake said, "To find Heaven in a wild flower, /Earth in a grain of sand." The repetition of "wild / yellow daisies" in "half-wild with loss" signals a transit from sun to wind, and the poet allows the reader to feel the physicality of release, something that is one with the wholeness of nature.

One need only look a bit farther into Ammons' work to find more orchestrated versions of transition, from "Corsons Inlet," for example, where the poet finds new forms, then a syntax mimicking a coast's fractals:

                         … I was released from forms,
            from the perpendiculars,
                    straight lines, blocks, boxes, binds
            of thought
            into the hues, shadings, rises, flowing bends and blends
                    of sight: (Ammons 148)

Here the poet allows himself "eddies of meaning," a sort of freedom in which the poet's perception and thought process follows the cues of the naked world, something sublime in its vagaries and boundlessness, something that seems to confirm our position of ultimately not knowing in the 20th century, something confirmed in physics by Heisenberg's Principle of Uncertainty and here by Ammons' ventriloquy of nature, one of complete openness:

        I have no conclusions, have erected no boundaries,
        shutting out and shutting in, separating inside

from outside: I have
drawn no lines:
as

manifold events of sand
change the dune's shape that will not be the same shape
tomorrow . . .   (Ammons, 149)

This informing principle in Ammons' work, one that becomes a kind of "Ars Poetica," seems the most densely significant in "Guide," a poem in which his ontological perspective is fine tuned: present not only in the moment, but by continually succumbing to its direction, and Ammons accomplishes this in his verse mimetically where colons channel phrases, increasing pressure, then releasing thought, the way rock barriers channel water then release it into the chutes of a river.

you cannot
turn around in
the Absolute: there are no entrances or exits
no precipitations of forms
to use like tongs against the formless:
no freedom to choose:

to be
you have to stop not-being and break
off from *is* to *flowing*...   (Ammons, 79)

And later we learn that the wind seems even a higher form of eternity, free of its stasis.

the wind that is my guide said this: it
should know having
given up everything to eternal being but
direction: (Ammons, 80)

Ammons' philosophies are never pedantic but refreshing, in part because they are so natural in their boundlessness. Knowing seems completely abandoned to perception, and it is through these epherereal observations, often detailed and broken with elisions, that his masterful transitions occur. "Guide" ends on one such philosophical elision resulting in a *tabula rasa* and complete abandonment, for the wind is this poet's guide:

> are these the thoughts you want me to think I said but
> the wind was gone and there was no more knowledge then.
>
> (Ammons, 80)

The work of Robert Creeley certainly comes to mind when one recalls a body of work composed of sophisticated transitions, primarily due to his keen sense of rhythm and enjambment. Having developed a feline adroitness of the line from Williams (the balance of off balance), Creeley knows every finger touch in the physicality of words and pays homage in the first stanza of his "For W. C. W."

> The rhyme is after
> all the repeated
> insistence.   (Creeley, 87)

One recalls Yeats' "The function of rhythm is to suspend the moment of contemplation," but with Creeley there's always a haunting epistemology, a keen desire to find the source of being and knowing through the inflection of words and their arrangement. Here are the opening four stanzas from "Words."

> You are always
> with me,
> there is never
> a separate
>
> place. But if
> in the twisted
> place I
> cannot speak,
>
>
> not indulgence
> or fear only,

> but a tongue
> rotten with what
>
> it tastes—There is
> a memory
> of water, of
> food, when hungry.   (Creeley, 103)

His alteration of trochees with iambs reinforces the comfort we all share with words, of always having them, accentuated by dropping the stress on "place" down to the second stanza, and thus reinforcing it, but the speaker also tells us that when "a tongue" is "rotten with what // it tastes—" there is a kind of sustenance, a memory "of water, of / food, when hungry." The poem ends, however, on an ontological complication, one in which we find a hazard, that of relying on words: for all mortals face nothingness without them:

> Some day
> will not be
> this one, then
> to say
>
> words like a
> clear, fine
> ash sifts,
> like dust,
>
> from nowhere.   (Creeley, 103)

Finally, it seems that many of the most haunting moments in Creeley's poetry occur when the consciousness of being in the world is realized through memory, something often reinforced by a notion that language itself "echoes" being through memory. Two very accomplished poems deal with this and appear as *the singular* of his book title. The later "Echo" appears in *Echoes* as the second part of "Gnomic Verses."

> In the way it was in the street
> it was in the back it was

> in the house it was in the room
> it was in the dark it was   (Creeley, 246)

The poem locates the self spatially through time and moves from street (as though that street were a sentence) to back yard, to house, to room, to consciousness, then to the very grace and hopelessness of the past's totality ("it was"), and of course never will be again. What was once *is* becomes *was*: its haunting *here* in memory is of course the *there* we can never pull back to complete proximity.

Creeley's brilliance of transition through syntax is perhaps best seen in his minimalist "Echo" from *Memory Gardens*.

> Back in time
> for supper
> when the lights

Here consciousness becomes a loop through memory triggered by light, that light in memory triggered once again by the present light as it occurs in the poem. Its syllabics begin to provide a clue: three tri-syllabic lines that scan as

> / u /
> u / u
> / u / .

Stresses occur in the left column in lines one and three, over "Back" and "when," and in the right column over "time" and "light." Lines one and three, primarily accentual, push the poem forward, while line two, substituting unstressed syllables for stressed, drags, and allows the act of supper to endure. The final monosyllabic stress on "lights" allows the poem to shine its way, to return to its beginning, such that the effect is a flickering in eternity, a symphonic loop of sorts where the first and last chords are similarly stressed. The word "supper," the only non-monosyllabic word, is heartbreaking, for it is always a last, yet lasting supper in memory, and because the poem has nine lines, the haunting center falls somewhere between "for" and "sup," a forever sip that can never be completely stilled, but one illumined again and again, lit with the eternity of a Vermeer painting.

Here's a remarkable poem by W.S. Merwin entitled "Anytime," a seamless commentary in heptasyllabic verse, where the ephemeral nature of our lives is glimpsed in the metaphorical guise of one day ending.

Any Time

How long ago the day is
when at last I look at it
with the time it has taken
to be there still in it
now in the transparent light
with the flight in the voices
the beginning in the leaves
everything I remember
and before it before me
present at the speed of light
in the distance that I am
who keep reaching out to it
seeing all the time faster
where it has never stirred from
before there is anything
the darkness thinking the light   (Merwin, 492)

Merwin brilliantly captures a cosmos, a life in a day, as the speaker measures his own self against that day in the flux of all that is moving. Beginnings and ends of lines meld invisibly into the poem's metaphor:

and before it before me
present at the speed of light
in the distance that I am

Each moment is this time and *all time*. "The very beginning of the universe," the poet once said in an interview, "is still present in the moment." There is never a stop, only pauses in the realization of what is going, the light that cycles and recycles, that tells us of mortality in the dark. The seamless quality of Merwin's poems, as though all of one fabric, endows the voice with an uncanny range, moving between the temporal and the eternal.

William Mathews' poem "New" captures the flux of spring by contemplating a prior space now filled with an iris's petals.

last week the space
about to be rumpled

by iris petals was only air
through which a rabbit leapt,
a volley of heartbeats hardly
contained by fur, and then the clay-
colored spaniel in pursuit
and the effortless air
rejoining itself whole.

(Mathews, 89)

Mathews finds continuity in space that would otherwise seem intermittent. His music and images keep opening beyond themselves: " a volley of heartbeats hardly / contained by fur…" Is this not to some extent the role of the artist? — To find the "volley of heartbeats" in subject matter that joins us back with the world, the original whole uninterrupted.

Transitions within a poem, however, are often more dramatically ruled by juxtaposition, one of the salient marks of composition in Stravinsky's *The Rite of Spring*, where the plaintive and germinating sound of the bassoon is answered by the harsh and rhythmic sound of violins. In poetry, just as in music, the immediacy and inevitability of subject matter often suffuses *and fuses* all the component parts. Such is the case with much of Sylvia Plath's late work, especially the poems from *Ariel* written in the last months of her life. Poems such as "Tulips," "Daddy," and "Cut" seem dramatically willed into being with their stark imagery, jolting rhythms, and striking juxtapositions. The imaginative power of these poems seems uncanny, perhaps because it must rise above death. Here is the first stanza from "Poppies in October:"

Even the sun-clouds this morning cannot manage such skirts.
Nor the woman in the ambulance
Whose red heart blooms through her coat so astoundingly—

(Plath, 19)

Plath's imagery is precise: the poppy's outer-edge luminescence resembles that of clouds, skirts, but then through juxtaposition she opens up the sublime: "Nor the woman in the ambulance / Whose red heart blooms through her coat so astoundingly—." The urgency of these late fall poppies resonates in the word "ambulance," from the Latin ambulare, to walk. One imagines poppies spilling over a field, their movement juxtaposed against the stationary woman whose heart "blooms through her coat so astoundingly——." The "ambulance / astoundingly" half rhyme reminds one of Stravinsky's juxtaposition of tone in order to create color, even if it means to destroy harmonies.

Finally, it's the speed in which Plath's images open imaginatively and unroll that provides such exquisite transition. Stanzas 3–5 from "Cut" describe a thumb after the top is cut off.

> Little pilgrim,
> The Indian's axed your scalp.
> Your turkey wattle
> Carpet rolls
>
> Straight from the heart.
> I step on it,
> Clutching my bottle
> Of pink fizz.
>
> A celebration, this is.
> Out of a gap
> A million soldiers run,
> Redcoats every one.   (Plath, 13)

The cut finger as pilgrim (from the Latin *peregrins*/foreigner) morphs from "scalp" to "turkey wattle / carpet," which the speaker steps on, "Clutching my bottle / Of pink fizz." The poem moves from tragedy to celebration until "Out of a gap / A million soldiers run, / Redcoats every one." One prefers to avoid comment and leave the reader reeling at this point.

Jorie Graham is a master of transition, primarily through tension. In earlier poems she accomplishes this through the juxtaposition of words and images, while in the later, more intellectual poems she juxtaposes ideas in such a way that one feels the intense dislocation of her subject matter. In "The Phase After History," from *Region of Unlikeness,* she finds frenzied equivalents in two juncos trapped inside a house ("The house like a head with nothing inside.") and a deranged student named Stuart who tries to cut off his face.

One of her most memorable poems, "San Sepolcro," the home of Piero della Francesca and also a place near the poet's own one time residence, takes as its subject matter the revolutionary painting *Madonna del Parto* (Pregnant Madonna), one of the few paintings in which Mary is seen to be visibly pregnant. She stands on a stage where two angels pull back a curtain to reveal a cerulean–blue dress unbuttoning about her distended abdomen.

The Madonna del Parto, Monterchi, Tuscany

Graham's poem opens in the same tonal register as the painting, though in winter, contrasting the religious ardor of the Renaissance with the more materialistic world of the 20th century.

> In this blue light
>   I can take you there,
> snow having made me
>   a world of bone
> seen through to. This
>   is my house,   (Graham 21)

The narrative continues with a description of the town, then in stanza four, halfway through the poem, introduces the painting. Most remarkable is the continuous juxtaposition of spiritual with material images that begins to function on a higher level between stanzas, creating a *frisson*, thus seamlessly binding the work. Beginning midway through stanza two, here is the rest of the poem.

      ...and just below
    the lower church,
the airplane factory.
    A rooster

crows all day from mist
      outside the walls.
There's milk on the air,
ice on the oily
lemonskins. How clean
    the mind is,

holy grave. It is the girl
      by Piero
della Francesca, unbuttoning
      her blue dress,
her mantel of weather,
      to go into

labor. Come, we can go in.
    It is before
the birth of god. No one
      has risen yet
to the museums, to the assembly
      line—bodies

and wings—to the open air
      market. This is
what the living do: go in.
      It's a long way.
And the dress keeps opening
      from eternity

to privacy, quickening.
      Inside, at the heart,
is tragedy, the present moment
      forever stillborn,
but going in, each breath

is a button
coming undone, something terribly
    nimble-fingered
finding all the stops.   (Graham 22)

The latter part of stanza two completes the poem's overture, then begins to function like a musical fugue as the "church" and "airplane factory" are followed by a "rooster" that crows with the simultaneous presence of God and materialism, awakening the city through the sensual details (lemonskins, milk, ice) of stanza three. This synesthetic quality prepares the reader to enter into the sacrosanct painting, but from the painter's realistic landscape, his town.

Beginning with the end of stanza three and through the end of the poem, the poet is no longer juxtaposing images but ideas: s3/ s/4 (mind/grave); s/4 s/5 (weather/labor); s5/ s6 (bodies/wings); s7 /s8 (button/musical stops). Mary needs her blue spirit-mantle to go into labor, and because it is early morning, few have begun the daily labor, yet we can all enter the painting's imaginary time for it is before the birth of Christ, and thus before the crucifixion, *The Gospels*, and *The Book of Revelations.*

Graham has selected a pivotal moment in the "eternally stalled" fruition of world history, and it is horrifying, beautiful, and hence sublime: Mary is played by God as though she were a musical instrument. The poem's suspended and tragic pause ("forever stillborn") in the penultimate stanza reminds me of Leonard Bernstein's statement about the latter symphonies of Gustav Mahler: "In an age of anxiety he was a prophet and his message was death."

I went on to attend several other performances of Stravinsky's *The Rite of Spring*, but none was as memorable as the Boulez until I heard Salonen conduct it with the LA Philharmonic in 2008. He had dramatically slowed the tempo, especially that of the violins, such that you could feel the crawl of green out of the earth. I remembered that Pachebel originally had written his marvelous *Canon in D* as a jig, then kept slowing it down, twisting phrase over phrase. John Lennon did the same thing with his memorable song "Imagine." In *The Rite of Spring,* some of the held violin chords seemed miniature parts of the haunting bassoon melody. The tone poem is seamlessly wrought in death, resurrection and green. "The art of composition is the art of transition."

WORKS CITED

Ammons, A.R. *Collected Poems 1951-1971*. NY: Norton, 1972.

Creeley, Robert. *Selected Poems 1945-2005*, Benjamin Friedlander, ed. Berkeley: University of California Press, 2008.

Francesca, Piero della. *Madonna del Parto*. Monterchi, Tuscany.

Graham, Jorie. *The Dream of the Unified Field: Selected Poems 1974-1994*. NY: Ecco Press, 1995.

Mathews, William. *Search Party: Collected Poems*. Boston: Houghton Mifflin, 2004.

Merwin, W.S. *Migration: New & Selected Poems*. Port Townsend: Copper Canyon Press, 2005.

Plath, Sylvia. *Ariel*. NY: Harper & Row, 1966.

Stravinsky, Igor. *The Rite of Spring*. Pierre Boulez, conductor. *The Cleveland Orchestra*. NY: Sony, 1995

BOOK REVIEWS

Seven Poets, Four Days, One Book
By Dean Young, Christopher Merrill, Marvin Bell, Tomaz Salamun, Simone Iguanez, Istvan Laszlo Geher, and Ksenia Golubovich. San Antonio, TX: Trinity University Press, 2009.

Bling & Fringe (The L.A. Poems)
By Molly Bendall and Gail Wronsky. Los Angeles, CA: What Books, 2009.
Reviewed by **Elena Karina Byrne**

Collaborations that involve automatic writing, chance operations, surrealism, call/response, and the exquisite corpse have never quite been outdated—these writing techniques are granted new life in two exciting books: *7 Poets 4 Days 1 Book,* by Christopher Merrill, Marvin Bell, Istvan Laszlo Geher, Simone Iguanez, Ksenia Golubovich, Dean Young, and Tomaz Salamun; *Bling & Fringe (The L.A. Poems)* by Molly Bendall and Gail Wronsky. At a time in political history when the confused resurrected terminologies of communism and democracy guess at each other on the invisible stage, so too poetry's history creates a battlefield for all its styles of collective identity and individual freedom. Both books speak to what Octavio Paz once identified as "neither me nor the others...to be nobody and oneself at the same time." Or shall we say, in a provocative state of union, to be everybody and oneself at the same time?

Imagine seven renowned poets "declaring the end of meaning" as they converge in "the unknown arms of the unknown" to write, "borrowing from one another's poems" at the Library of Shambagh House, headquarters of the International Writing Program, in four days, in order to dream up a braided single sequence, marrying dream and reality. Opening the door of the unconscious, seven diverse poets put their trust in each other enough to appropriate the "other" voice, to let the engagement of unhinged language create a new consciousness-in-motion on the page. Brendan Constantine speaks to the power of this surrealist impulse when he says, "The word surrealism may be 90 years old, but the fact of the surreal is exactly as old as consciousness. It is a by-product of perception and may well constitute a fourth dimension, one that qualifies the other three as relative to consciousness." The seven poets say, "There's never one language for that," for the confluence of image and idea dissolving, cascading and converging in a "faith of guesses," in one dynamic gesture. There may not be one language, but there does seem to be one created voice, a felt tone, this choir's self-aware octave hitting its right note:

> Taking longer than your life will be my way to you
> Yet, if I try, if only I try not

To say too much but to rather listen
To the rustling of the leafless trees and be
Obedient. I don't
Believe we could just part.
As if catachresis parts a word.
Take my hand, let ghosts of the river
Enjoy us...
...
And everything reverses...verses...

The book's collective rant unfolds between narrative and lyric, finding its subject matters in both the external and internal worlds of experience. The happenstance of correlating correspondence breeds all over the page of each poem installment. Language, in *7 poets, 4 days, 1 book,* is its own fallout act of discovery, at once self-conscious and unpredictable—an incendiary example that a polyvocal (heptagon-vocal) collaboration works and finds common ground, not in Magritte's defiance of common sense, but rather in capturing the common sense in this inspired process of defiance. Like intuition itself, the end result is indeterminate because, as Christopher Merrill points out, "the line ends and ends and ends." Susan Sontag declared, "language is the most impure, the most contaminated, the most exhausted of all the materials out of which art is made." So with that challenge in mind (in mode), language in these two books has the ever-flexive-flux ability to break down, to build and encumber, to set free, to procreate, and to astonish.

In another fecund kind of collaboration, Molly Bendall and Gail Wronsky dialogue right out of Stevens' "gaiety of language," creating the material forms of *Bling & Fringe*. For all its pop cultural bangles and sparkles, its snip and snap of familiar icons and artifacts, this book's language lounges in literary sites of conflict, and within a marvelous opulence of misunderstanding. With a linguistic tongue-in-cheek humor, the book's perverse sense of semantics works like the gravitational pull of planets in an orbit of irony: the readers are somehow participatory, complicit. *Bling & Fringe* aims to overturn our bad habit of putting our trust in the use (and overuse) of names. From the violation of assumptions comes something altogether gaudy and often gorgeous. Even when the conversation of their side-by-side poems returns non-sequitur progressions, there's a shared delirium of felt understanding. In this excerpt from one of the poem-pairs, Bendall and Wronsky, using sound-associative word play, seduce a delightful anarchy of aphorism:

LEAVES/ NEW YEAR

Me   and   James Dean   are   "sexy"
my dog is   "a good friend"   my
        sister–in–law   "the   tree   of   self–im(posed)
chasity" have some Chinese
    Astrology   tea   *oui?* Bee-
g(odd)ess   forgive   me   Tis the
    y(ear) of   the   poet
(lest   we   be   forgot)
    like: Lalla   jumping   mad
DON'T   MOON   ME   and
    the yew tree   with   its   "insatiable appetite"
"like death"   This   is   "the   end
    of   the   year   as   well   as   of
the   poem"   This
        is   the   new   *langue*   sign:
    I   put   it   on   your   bar tab

       Absurdist Eugene Ionesco might echo what happens here in this lingo play: "the 'surreal' is there, within our reach, in our daily conversation." But the beauty of both books is that they work in their collaborative efforts to show that juxtaposed language disengages and engages the imaginative intellect, creating a lively correlation of real knowledge. In a recent interview, Angie Estes assures us that "the mind tethers itself to any hint of meaning, and clings to it like a shipwrecked sailor does to the splintered remains of a smashed hull." So when two poets converse, seven poets from all over the globe get together to collage and weave what they have written, the menage a trois (*I, we,* and *you)* pays the marvelous price of matrimony: a new translation of the self.

Tryst
By Angie Estes. Oberlin, OH: Oberlin College Press, 2009.

Nomina
By Karen Volkman. Rochester, NY: BOA, 2008.

Odalisque
By Mark Salerno. London, UK: Salt Modern Poets, Salt Publishing Ltd., 2007.
Reviewed by **Stephany Prodromides**

In her latest book, *Tryst*, Angie Estes plumbs the white-hot place where wordplay, sonics and etymology transubstantiate into "a fourth / state of matter, electronically charged." Consonance, assonance, alliteration, and homonyms play heavily in these voluptuous poems, where history, food, art and foreign languages open door after door, expanding and burrowing into the place where "a single jagged path" of meaning is made. "Take Cover" is a perfect example:

Take Cover

and *couvre feu*, cover the fire
because when the bell sounds, it means
curfew, it is mellow-drama, facsimile
of a tryst, trusted
meeting place, waiting
like a shelter or decoy, duck blind
with the perfect vision
of the Venetian blind: a number of thin
horizontal slats that may be raised
or lowered with one cord, all set
to a desired angle. Love too we're told
is blind, but desire,
as Aristotle knew, is all
angle, and so he gave us the math
to keep track of our loves: *Number,*
he said, has two senses: what is counted
or countable, and that by which
we count. Remember
to cover the rosemary in winter, uncover
the basil before the sun comes up, and when you take
cover, cover your head with your hands

and forearms, as we learned in school, once
you have crouched under
your desk. In January, beneath the roof
of the house, a sparrow curves
in the scroll of a corbel, and soon
at Carnevale a mask will be held
at half-mast like the lid
of a casket before it lies under
the grass. How much ground
have you covered today? You always take
all the covers, it's true. But do not
take cover under a tree
during a storm—your body will life
its wick to light, and you will gleam
like Venus just before dawn: a satellite
in the atelier where *true*
and *tree* are related, unable to choose
between heaven and earth, to make *seems*
come true.

Working by ear, layering and un-layering meanings, the poem shapes line by line, much as a connect-the-dots picture: the *couvre feu* was the Medieval curfew bell, rung about eight in the evening, which signaled that it was time to cover, or deaden, the fires until morning. Estes weaves "take cover," "*couvre feu*," and "curfew" into the semblance of a protective huddle in the unlit dark. She nudges this concept with "a tryst, trusted / meeting place" to invite the idea of covert romance, then "shelter or decoy" forwards the idea of a clandestine spot, which leads to "duck blind." Circling back to the idea of darkness, Estes adds "vision" and limbs from "Love too… is blind," into "but desire… is all angle," certainly a an evocative visual, considering the warm, dark, secret place to which she's brought us. Here she twists the skein again, moving Aristotle's "math" of love into "what is … / countable, and that by which / we count," a nod back to curfew hours, and more deeply, to fidelity and love.

The heavy "k-k-k" and "sss" consonance in the repeated "c" words and "s" sounds mimic machine gun fire and the hiss of a lit fuse throughout the poem, a not-so subtle reminder of the title's warning, which is borne out in the final lines, when "…your body will lift / its wick to light." By then, the "k" sounds have quieted, leaving us the gleaming, lightning-raised body "between heaven and earth" to contemplate. "Take Cover," indeed.

More than in previous collections, Estes' *Tryst* surrenders bits of the personal, making us *voyeur* to her *gourmand* when she answers the never-simple question: *What are the impulses of my mind as I appreciate this single moment of beauty?* These are virtuoso poems where, "According to Dante… everything ends with stars,"

> … or those paper
> links that wrap themselves around
>   the Xmas tree: eentsy weentsy spider
>   sidling up to each letter, each word, casting and
> binding in silk as if to ravel and
>   unravel once felt the same.
> ("Script: Folio 43")

Light-footed and disarming, Estes' poems bring sound, sense and sensuality to bear as she ruffles language to tilt. Finding success in calculated excess, and a deliberately sexy incoherence ("Am I dying / or is this my birthday?"), *Tryst* is a seduction that unravels the reader along with the poems.

Karen Volkman's *Nomina* also marries etymology, sonics and wordplay with virtuoso skill, but to very different ends. Where Estes' work expands in the natural world, Volkman's seems to parse the intolerable: a metaphysical place where certainty of truth, even mathematical truth, is fundamentally unknowable. "The common / denominator is zero, where the heart beats," in this "ruptured" place. It is the "reticulation of a premise," and the poems' Petrarchan sonnet form speaks to the desire to order this world, to argue a way out of the "bloodied noon," all the while straining at the equivalent desire to let go, and "heed the calling / for harbor, shore, to stall the listing lee / of always-motion, infant and appalling." This poem exemplifies such unrest:

> Never got, and never thought, and yet
> always potent in the never-been
> the ever-urge to always arc, to spin
> aim's injunction in a raw roulette
>
> ever placing never's bankrupt bet,
> carbon numbers, impossible to win
> at null, at zero, an integral skin:
> cardinal animal in an ordinal net.
>
> What fury frauds the nod, what squalid set?

Base Ire, base Err, base *Bas*, the baseless bane
of never's radical, the swelling square

of pallid possiblities that slip and stare:
unsummed digits, unformulated stain
ever's ardor will never not beget.

"Never," "null," and "zero," as well as numerous mathematical references such as "radical" and "square" appear across poems in this book, linking the poems together. Within this poem, the repetition of the word "never" is like a fist: insistent almost to the point of violence. The words ""got" and "thought" in the first line call to the sound of "naught," reinforcing the "never" sensibility. "The ever-urge" for "never's bankrupt bet," which is "impossible to win," speak to the futility of trying for the unattainable. The heavy use of patterned consonance and assonance, beginning with "n" sounds and the word "never," giving way to "a" sounds with "arc" and "aim," and intensifying in the last two stanzas with heavy use of multiple sounds ("f," "b," "s," and "p,") conveys a wild desperation of sorts, as if thoughts are tried and discarded like articles of clothing, because the end result is always the same: "never's radical"—the square root of zero—is still zero, and the "swelling square" of zero (zero squared) is zero, too.

There is no question that these are athletic poems; they open their fullest flower to those with a strong vocabulary (and, it must be said, those who are willing to use a dictionary). Look closely at the words in the poem. Most of them are abstract. Most have multiple meanings, and share etymological links with other words in the poem. For example, "null" means both "having no set but zeros," and "lacking positive substance or content." "Set" can mean "to mount" "to arrange," and/or to harden into a solid or semi-solid state," as when pudding "sets" into a creamy consistency. "Square" can mean "a product of a number multiplied by itself," "something properly arranged with a level," and/or "to reconcile" (i.e., to "square one's debts").

This abstract web of multiple meanings feels, on first reading, extremely reticent, even rarefied. When the words are illuminated against the sonics, however, the poems literally explode. "Never got, and never thought" can be read as a poem tracking a woman's unchecked frustration over the inability to conceive, if we consider "ever urge," "potent" and "beget" to be references to sex, and "squalid set" and "unformulated stain" as references to menstrual blood's refusal to form the "integral skin" of a child… but it can be read in other ways as well.

Meaning is exponential and multidirectional in this book, primarily because of the heavy repetition across poems. Consider this poem in light of "never got, and never thought:"

One says none is nascent, noon is due
when two's bleak blinded hybrid twins the light.
None says no one numbers less than two,
the one who days, the one who darks all night.

Noon's cold name is cloven, frigid height,
a one-division in the random, fault
split in fusion's faction, no one's bright
eyeless acme arcing—cohesive vault.

That one were none's skulled infant, second sight
of two's twained woes, and tangled toxic root,
nearer to nothing, nameless, sequent blight,

as two's black ruse slits mind a riven fruit.
These sumless parents, two and null, make one
Queen of Quotient, who adds her x to none.

"Always yearning / for plummet's pivot—articulate pause," the surface qualities of the poems shimmer, particularly in company with the other poems: the heavy consonance, end rhymes, internal rhymes, and the repeated "none" and mathematical concepts create a musical meaning over and above the etymological one. We make meaning in and across these tensile sonnets the same way we pluck a constellation out of the night sky: by finding patterns in the sound or sense—most fruitfully, when both combine. Volkman's never-land is so "bluely moving—motion will be mute." It is extremely fine work, and finely wrought.

Also working the sonnet form—but with a twist—Mark Salerno's *Odalisque* is story by accretion, a noir take on "the usual fall from grace" of a "scrivener" ex-cop whose tale "ends in bra logic and failed transitive devices," and his lover, a hooker: his "odalisque." Both are "cashiered," but "staying alive and making it though the u-shape of life," in their "two drink minimum," "rundown big town." Salerno drops rhyme scheme *and* punctuation in favor of sonic-boom phrasing, repetition, and double-spaced lines. The result: a blue-collar, pneumatic pressure that he modulates across the story arc:

Now This

The shorter second half and too much articulation
certain amounts of daylight in colored Dixie cups
you and your bomb squad ethics she said I'm tired of

interrogatives tunnel vision cooped up or simply waiting
for a God damned Orange Crush and to be near her
couple-y she said another burning coal down all my life
never heard of Buck-Buck never heard of Acey-Five
because all of the parts left out overnight in TJ
only mention the word moon and you're finished
dream time and clinic noise where M. equals the hero
in fact he is a dream man a blind preoccupation
to enjoy movie star prerogatives from the waist up
or be seen pointing his finger like a teacher
up and down the Strip between Gazzarri's and the Whiskey.

Three-quarters of the way through, when enjambment and pantoum-like re-use reach their peak, it's a "right light moment," and the poems find wings.

Poem after poem, Salerno's stylistic act is striking, and honors the tragedy he presents in a very human way. By pitting low and high culture against formal and informal elements—Roscoe's Chicken and Waffles and The Pottery Barn Rule collide with the likes of Thisbe (Ovid's tragic precursor to Juliet, played to comic effect in Shakespeare's *A Midsummer Night's Dream*), and Ingres (that painter of odalisques)—he lends his characters depth, earthiness, and "... a way to be significant without recourse to the alphabet."

In *Tryst*, Estes tells us we're "completely under the earth but for the writing." These three books find their own brand of light, in very different ways.

Lip
By Kathy Fagan. Spokane, WA: Eastern Washington University Press, 2009.

Hilarity
By Patty Seyburn. Kalamazoo, MI: New Issues Press, 2009.
Reviewed by **Meredith Davies Hadaway**

All the world's a stage in Kathy Fagan's new collection, *Lip*. The curtain rises and falls on players snatched from history, legend, myth, and literature and given voice in an assemblage of arias, soliloquies, monologues, imitations, and interviews. Fagan orchestrates this cheeky chorus in an operatic masterpiece that makes an elliptical transit from comic to tragic and back again in poems that are playful, smart, impertinent and—as the work's title suggests—edgy.

This is *opera buffa*, the poet tells us, a "Neapolitan jaunt from the hilltop to the vernacular." The voices don't come from on high but emanate from the periphery—places where genius and artistry mingle with insanity and cruelty. Joan of Arc, Penelope, and Medea are among those "on the lam from the historical hoosegow" who take center stage in "so many solos."

Not surprisingly, many of these disenfranchised speakers are women. Dancers, "warped thin and pale," describe the extremes by which they prop up the artifice: "When a girl was ill / We suckered up our / Spit for her onto a / Scrap of crimson / Ribbon, rouged her cheeks, / Stained / Her lips, imparted / Expression where none was before. / It was then I saw it best: / Doll. Whore. Clown. Corpse." Fagan's women challenge us to re-imagine those roles from our backstage vantage point.

Like the dancers, Fagan reclaims her stories from scraps and snippets, re-animating those who have expired with a little spit and plenty of crimson. In another poem, Joan of Arc recalls her execution, explaining, "Some say at the end my heart didn't burn. / People like their stories whole. / The truth I am not given leave to know." Fagan doesn't give us the whole story, nor the unknowable truth, but lets us hear what some say, with an occasional glimpse of the heart.

We hear a more playful voice in a poem entitled "Postmodern Penelope at her Loom Pantoum." Our modern-day Penelope puzzles over silly strings of alliteration ("A gull with a goiter gobbling up the _____.") and rhyme ("the womb at the loom"), fabricating poetry that eludes form and "(sub)stance" and cannot escape the inevitable raveling and unraveling in the end:

This is not a pantoum.
It may only be a shroud.
A Stein is a Stein is a
It may only be a shroud.
A Stein is a Stein is a
white space around the box.

Try as she might, this Penelope reminds us, her art cannot forestall death—she has "never weaved a day in her life."

Fagan doesn't let us forget that poetry is basically "lip." Her poems have plenty of attitude. She pokes fun at her own poetic pursuits with titles like: "Go to Your Room Pantoum," "Saloon Pantoum," "Womb to Tomb Pantoum," and "Pontoon Pantoum #505" (an homage to Dickinson). Fagan's poems have plenty of swagger, too, but always mediated with humility and an awareness of the temporal. In a long prose poem, she describes a "constant craving" and its short-lived gratification:

There's always something we almost always want. When we see ourselves in each other's eyes the craving stops but only to be shrouded in smog again, for a promise to be made or broken, for the cursor to strut from left to right, before it struts away.

Whether it's the strutting cursor, the weaving lines, or the elaborate ruse of the dance, Fagan shows us art is ultimately a courageous act. Even when it is ludicrous—or especially because it is so—"lip" has value. In the final poem, Fagan takes us curbside to a "Road Memorial" where a bent crucifix and plastic cherubs mark "the spot where Jesus called our Jim- / bo home." Her rhymed and carefully metered stanzas commemorate the place where "Junior jumped / the overpass" with a reverence that speaks to us, "a people dying for a sign," despite the clownishness of the attempt.

> This crap from Wal-Mart could outlast us all,
> which in our grief is no small com-
> fort, since death lasts so much longer, and has no form.

It's a small stage, Fagan tells us in these songs from its "lip" that mark the spot and hit the mark. The show must go on because—well, Fagan's dancers say it best—"The stage lights caused / Our paste / To shine at times as if / Real moons / Shone in the true jewels of / Breathing / Princesses. I have it / In a book."

★

If you think of Dante's circles of Hell when you eat taco salad—or think of taco salad when you read Dante—you're ready for Patty Seyburn's *Hilarity*. It's about layers, it's about food ("There is No Escaping the Inedible"), it's about redemption. Seyburn puts the "divine" back in "comedy" in what appears to be a thoroughly post-modern journey through myth and disorder, desire and despair, insomnia, dream, and nightmare to arrive at—*wait a minute, salvation?* Yep, of a sort. *You must be joking!* Yes, exactly.

Groucho Marx, whose epigrammatic wisecracks book-end the collection, presides over our journey, which begins in a dime store selling "all forms of prophylactic against despair" in what the poet describes as "a crisis of origin":

> My history, too, has amnesia
> and my cabinet members—or cabal, depending—
> pressure me for my provenance.

Later, I say, we are later.
And: I have never been to Provence.

Seyburn offsets images of despair and disorder with one-liners, puns, and wordplay as she searches through fairy tale, the Bible, conventional wisdom, and the "holy donut shops" of her childhood, for "something prophetic" or at least "something narcotic." In her exploration of the past, she finds that it cannot be reclaimed, even in "the fashioned // facts of memory." The only consolation she offers on the drive "To Hope Street" is: "If it will // make you feel better, you can cry / on the shoulder of the road."

In the second section of the book, Seyburn takes us right to the source, with the warning: *"Duck! God!"* In a series of poems that investigate creation and responsibility, we learn that He (or She) is not behind the "gradual pulverizing" that is our demise. In futile acts of translation we're the makers of our own world. Language, with its expectation of meaning, has also created the notion of extinction:

> I did not invent intent.
> You did.
> And the way indented footprints disappear
> on the ocean's arrival?
> That was yours, too.
> How eloquent.

In "Break, Break, Break," another evocation of oceanic indifference, Seyburn revisits Tennyson's lament for the Sea's unwillingness to stop to mourn the "vanished hand" of the dead. Seyburn's elegy is for the living in lines that are lighter on one level, but even more ominous on another. As she watches her daughter play in the surf, she senses her "fleeing / into the blur" and registers her complaint to the waves:

> I warn them: *do her*
> *no harm*.
>
> A set conveys my empty threat
> out to the powers that be.
> They ripple.
>
> If waves can laugh, this is a funny day.
> *Say what you will,*
> they say.

The third section of the book documents insomnia and nightmares in a kind of dark night of the soul Seyburn-style or, as she describes it, "the Kalamazoo of consciousness." These poems feature the relentless voice of the subconscious in the literal dark, relieved by moments of—you guessed it!—enlightenment: "The more you say halo, / the more you think halo, / the more you feel like someone else— // hey! Is this transcendence?" Seyburn documents this insomnia in titles that watch the clock the way a sleepless person would, hour by hour, nearly minute by minute. But the time seems ultimately to be well-spent: "The room persuades me of / the logic of inanimacy. / The mirror's mereness in the body / of so much evidence. / How is it that so much comes clear at this time?"

The final section of the book is a prose poem sequence that brings us full circle, to re-visit the notion of origins. "The Emergence of Hilarity" gives us the provenance (so elusive in the opening poems) of the belly laugh. It is through laughter that our poetic progenitor discovers an experience worthy of "praise and repetition." Around this discovery he constructs a place of worship:

> He would return many times to the clearing he believed the source of his mirth (he had taken the wrong turn at the forked tree) and established an altar there, of sorts, where he tested another practice... [text continues in next poem] and began to think, to speak, to praise Whatever gave him the impulse to look beyond his loss and brought him back from the hard blows lovingly dealt.

Hey, is this salvation? Well, it's as close as "the Divine Comedian" and Patty Seyburn are going to bring us this time around. "And it pleases all who hear."

Kurosawa's Dog
By Dennis Hinrichsen. Oberlin, OH: Oberlin College Press, 2009.

Letters to Guns
By Brendan Constantine. Los Angeles, CA: Red Hen Press, 2009.

The Endarkenment
By Jeffrey McDaniel. Pittsburgh, PA: University of Pittsburgh Press, 2008.
Reviewed by **Reed Wilson**

"Trickster," "jester," "comic consciousness"—back cover blurbs for these three books describe their poets' voices in this way. All three are terms for what, historically, challenges stentorious seriousness or chest-thumping punditry. The "trickster" of course is a sacred figure in many cultures; indeed Biblical scholars have argued that Satan was originally just such a figure, sent out to beguile and test us, to help us prove ourselves against adversity. Of course, he often has his own agenda too, but that's what makes him interesting. That's what makes him necessary.

★

"Trickster" Dennis Hinrichsen's *Kurosawa's Dog* lopes along at first in staccato, heavily stressed and staggered lines. The poet's narrative minimalism here seeks elemental ground, from the Iowa farmlands of his family, to the desert southwest of his wanderings. Animals appear often: the title poem, for example, is just one of three (the other two are "Bresson's Donkey" and "Tarkovsky's Horse") that remind us how creatures in three different films—Bresson's *Au Hasard, Balthazar*, Tarkovsky's *Andrei Rublev*, and Kurosawa's *Yojimbo*—both ground us in a kind of elemental reality (in a medium made of light and shadow) and evoke, for better and worse, all the possibilities of human imagination: "I dream I am Kurosawa's dog. / I trot with a severed hand in my mouth." And in "Cruel All Moons and Bitter the Suns," the poet conjures an image of his father as a boy, swimming in the Wapsipinicon river, and makes of him "An animal / presence—/ a herd of cattle—companion field— / lies down in his lungs." Beast and field both center and figure the poet's imagination and memory: "There is a wing / in the shadow of / evening," as "Daylight fading" becomes "a colony of doves."

Animal avatars, soul emblems, and totems all image that space between where "human" ends and "animal" begins. And in the heart of this book, literally and figuratively, the verse opens that space into longer, more fluid lines as the poet comes to terms with his father's death. In "Lion and Gin," for example, he "pets" his father "like some big cat a hunter has set on the ground, / though I am in Iowa now and not the Great Rift Valley. . . ." He speaks to his dead father, "a lion on a gurney," in order "to make sure he's dead," as though such profound realization of our animal nature demands language. Later, recalling his father's cremation, he remembers that a further transformation took place. At the moment of immolation, his father was no longer animal and no longer even that "density we might gather round—an aquifer, or gushing spring." He was "mere vapor," only "Fragments of tooth and bone."

How do we face without despair the loss of both human and animal presence, our existential grounds? The volume's final poems answer this by reflecting, directly and indirectly, on the poet's sustaining art. Throughout the book, a mash-up of voices and forms—Zen texts, Dante, Roman verse, native American art and lore, histories of arcana—find unprepossessing place, like knickknacks in a curio cabinet. In "Kiva Burning," Hinrichsen reminds us that, though all cultural products ultimately fail to provide "sustenance enough," they do give enough voice to experience that we can, at least, articulate our *being* in the world. As he passes through a Diné market, all that survives now of a lost native American culture, the poet knows at least that he "could walk and become / one small thing inside / the ordinary. . . ./ Where could I go then that would / not have me?"

In the volume's final poem, "Coyote Bliss," he discovers his totem when he spots the body of "one of God's dogs, / at the road's side, contradictory and ambiguous." Even in death, Trickster "held its carriage, /. . . so much a part of the landscape." Flying home from the desert places he's visited, he knows he too must continue to "eat well (eat anything) sing planet on fire."

★

"Jester" Brendan Constantine's *Letters to Guns* piques our curiosity with its title. Does it allude to the ways our culture seems unwilling or unable to "beat swords to plowshares"? Is this an aural echo of the economic catchphrase "guns and butter," reminding us that, just as economies swing between those two products, so too must a culture choose between articulation and murder? Or does it describe the way Constantine's own poems, his "letters," are concealed weapons with awesome firepower?

The answer is "yes" to all, though more immediately the title describes just one of the book's many invented "realities," a series of epistles addressed to firearms—"*To an 1830 Henry Yellowboy 45 from a standard issue army boot—Sharpsbert, Maryland, 1862*"; "*To a Coggswell and Harrison double barrel elephant gun from a grove of flame trees—Kenya, 1954*," and so on. Constantine's epigraph, from Stephen Hawking, reminds us that "the greatest enemy of knowledge is not ignorance, it is the illusion of knowledge," and these poems become just one of the ways he mocks that illusion. In "Letter I," for example, "*To a pot of huo yao (the original formula for gunpowder) from a pot of ink—China, Han Dynasty, 206 BC - 219 AD*," the pot of ink notes how "The ground shakes, the sky delights / at your first cries." But it also reminds its more volatile "cousin" that though it may "know many glories," and its strength may "last many centuries," ink "will go where you go. I will write you / a thousand names. You will speak only one. / Twins but not brothers, cousins but not clan, / we will die on the same day."

Throughout the book, Constantine hits us with clown antics, these "guns" that spring flags saying "Bang." The poem "Meddling" best presents the poet's self-assessment of his art: "Before I wrote poems," he tells us, "I meddled. . . . I would dress the dog in my clothes and get my parents / to fight over who I resembled," or "I told my brothers there was / no gravity and watched them flail." What stopped him from this, or as he puts it, "What turned me around was a night / . . . watching old movies," when, "tuning / our black & white" he "touched / the glass and found it soft and wet." As he did so, the film's characters "stopped talking and looked around, startled. / I got ready for them to be angry / but instead they just stood there . . . / unable to face me, my terrible colors." This is how Constantine works on us, beginning in absurdist comedy, but ending in equally absurd, and yet deeply poignant, drama. The younger poet learned that "meddling" in others' realities can hurt, and so "turned" to an art that, though it may remind us of the suffering beneath our "illusions of knowledge," also reveals to us, in its "foolishness" (think Lear on the heath here), our redemption.

In "Meeting the authors," the poet is "talking to children about strangers. / *They're people your parent's haven't met,* / I say, they're everywhere." The grown-up meddler-author lures us by what we know (or think we know) into the strangeness of the unknown: "If you go with him, he will keep you," and yet, "You draw him out / by being alone . . . / by making up / what you haven't been told." Constantine's poems, like the jester's motley and *marotte*, the clown's props, are the stranger's "candy and broken glass. . . / toys which he makes himself, or inherits / from the children who speak to him."

Like a gun in hand after it fires, these poems both fire at human suffering and recoil from that firing. In "The Need to Stay," Constantine finds in the "funambulist" (tightrope—or slackrope—walker) another figure for the poet and his craft. This performer, in apparent defiance of the "ground," reminds us how easy it is merely to surrender to gravity. There are days, the funambulist tells the speaker, "when the ground calls to him. / *What's it say?* // Stay."

★

Jeffrey McDaniel's "comic consciousness" in *The Endarkenment* is indeed a dark one, a mind whose matter of fact sarcasm and pointed imagery dagger us when we least expect it. This volume too begins with an epigraph, a mock dictionary definition of the title word: "1. the act or means of endarkening, 2. the state of being endarkened, 3. *capitalized*: an American anti-intellectual movement of the 21st century (known as the Age of Endarkenment)" and finally "4. a cursed state in which the individual is handcuffed to desire and henceforth suffering and attains transcendental misery."

These painfully illuminating poems often provide us with figures for that "misery." In "Confessions of a Flawed Deity" the title character regards the poet as though he were "looking at a crime scene": "It still feels like I am the razor, and you // are the wrist, like I'm the window, / and you're the person about to jump out." And yet, this is the volume's most flattering vision of "god." In another poem, "The Soul Farmer," we're told that "In the beginning, with only a few acres / of humans to care for, god planted / each soul by hand." Now though, "removed from the day-to-day / of his enterprise," he "reclines / in a celestial hammock, nibbling meteors / like intergalactic hors d'oeuvres." As his angels harvest humanity, he savors "the rich taste / of a tormented soul properly marinated / in experience."

This is a "post" poetry then, after the bombs have gone off and we're left in the ruins of truth. In the title poem, the poet tells us he hates "false words / like sunset. The sun does not set. It doesn't / rise either. It just stays there in one place." Though we may get "all romantic," the sun would, if it could, "never come back" and "look for some better planet to nourish." The poet too longs for such a planet where "witnesses must place their hands / on a dictionary when they swear," or "where people only eat animals they wish to emulate." Though he may "some nights . . . like to lie in bed and watch / the God Channel with the volume turned down," all he can see are bits and pieces of a broken world.

Nevertheless, though there may be no such thing as "transcendental misery," the poet does record his own transcendence *from* misery, and this transcendence—a *choice*—tips existential crisis toward life. In a climactic series of subway poems—McDaniel's visit to an epic "underground"—the poet meets, among others, Walt Whitman, whose histrionic generosity to a panhandler offends another rider, one "Walter Whitman, the human being," who asks the poet, "can you imagine /sharing a soul / with that beast?" McDaniel, of course, can, and does. In "Air Empathy" he recounts a trip on "the red-eye from Seattle" when a crying toddler sets everyone on board to wailing, even the pilots, and the aircraft becomes "an arrow of grief quivering in the sky."

How long though might such a craft stay up? Not long, probably, and so ultimately the poet settles instead for what we might call "earth empathy," earned and learned through suffering. "Day 3405," for example, recounts in harrowing detail scenes from the poet's days of insobriety when the "drunkard" in him "could care less. . . that our penis / had shriveled into a limp parachute cord, something / we tugged each night, when the drugs wore off /and we plummeted back to earth. . . ." In a liquor store, trying "to buy a pack of chewing gum for a friend," he imagines, as answer to the clerk's question, "*Anything Else?*" "a swimming pool overflowing with vodka." More importantly though, he also imagines, "I am the miracle. I am the hand reaching / out of the wreck. I don't care if it's true. It's what I need / to tell myself to make it out the door alive."

If Birds Gather Your Hair for Nesting

By Anna Journey. Athens, GA and London, UK: The University of Georgia Press, 2009.
Reviewed by **Sarah Maclay**

To read even the table of contents of this audacious first book is to fall,
I'm afraid, hopelessly in love: "Autobiography as Endless Calico," "Apparition
with Toenail Music," "Lucifer's Panties at the Garden Center," "My Great-
Grandparents Return to the World as Closed Magnolia Buds," "The Nude Model,
Scary Mary, Shifts on Her Satin Pillow" are just a handful of the mercilessly
imaginative titles that hold out their exploding bonbons of eros and cemeteries,
or eros in cemeteries, desire with death, or with "birdskull" or "artificial limb"
and, through it all, a great foxtail's length of recurrent and flaming red hair. By
the end of the first poem—a tightrope walk of extravagant risk, each line so
arresting that it's literally nearly impossible to get to the other side of the page
without taking great pauses to look at the view as your suddenly widening lens
of a mind catches up with its new (and joysmacked) size—Anna Journey will
have re-arranged the furniture in your brain, right down to the last, needless
antimacassar:

Adorable Siren, Do You Love the Damned?

> —BAUDELAIRE

> The devil pries open my red hibiscus like skirts. On the crack
>   corner those transvestite hookers won't quit
> competing with my garden's

> barbed and carnal tongues. The bitch
>   scent of the silver-

> and-pink-clawed possum in heat—all rhubarb-breath and unbelievable
>   udder—is sharp as fuschia

> spokes of my oleander. I could put
>   my eye out looking. I could run with knives. Outside the brine

> of b.o. tangles with perfume—bodies that snag
>   men like my singing

can't. This song won't dress up, won't wear black
        patent leather, won't even shave

its five o'clock shadow—lazy sliver
        slumming the telltale animal. What song, devil, is best
sung from my balcony

in my birthday suit, by my heartleaf nightshade's
        liquory patina? I'm drunk,
though I won't wear heels, honey, or I'd fall

for anyone. I'd fall devil
        over heels over edge over oleander
over open mouth

over birthmark over forked
        tongue over forked tongue
that turns on mine.

Let's revise the metaphor. "Walk" is not quite right. If this is a tightrope act, she's doing cartwheels across that rope. How? With a combination of both wild and bridled sonics; with shocks of kaleidoscopic, gothic image. A penchant for amphibrachs strung one after another, easy as Christmas tree lights, and sometimes an iamb or anapest, manage a sort of roll across long sentences—right into her open *gabinetto* of curios: images that, before even their birth, it seems, are figurative, as well—metaphor-minted (as in julep, as in coined).

It takes me, every time, at least five minutes to read just this poem, so dumbstruck am I, so keeled over and satisfied with each successive line that I just have to stop and stare. If this were a street in LA, I'd already be run over. Multiple times.

The Spaniard poet Mariano Zaro tells his students that a poem needs to get a little dizzy. Well, a volta is one thing. OK. But this is more the kind of thing, I think, he has in mind: look at how the dizziness happens (especially in the last few lines) as this poem unfolds and winds around (and around) its over-and-overs. And the brio of "brine" and "b.o." and "perfume" all "tangle[d]" with "devil" and "crack" and "hibiscus" and "heels" is a signature piece of the way she shuffles her parole.

But it's no card trick—rather, I think, it's a mode of perception made manifest, like "black ballets in the spear grass." The book, the sensibility, is rooted (pun intended, or not) in loamy jobs, assisting customers at the garden center and guiding tours at the cemetery, spots that may, at first, seem opposites, but this is where the soil is: the dead go into the ground or life springs up, or both, piercing as the way "Stravinsky wanted the E-flat // clarinet solo in *Rite of Spring* to sound / like asparagus shoots growing"; death, the dead, are a presence—and a source of curiosity, as much as all the obvious, vibrant life inscribed in this book, even when the speaker longs to "understand / the selfishness of portraits— // their shut door splintering the past's / exact coffin-space."

It's not possible for this book, though, finally, to be grave. The thrust of what's happening here is so deeply rooted in eros—that is, in a mad desire to join—that even the most (seemingly) dislocated, disconnected things— attributes, monikers, dictions, peculiarities, experiences—are bound, finally, to bloom together, in one poem, in one plant:

> . . . Now you are uncertain
> about the scent of the corpse flower, whether it reeks
>
> from standing water, a dark bird dunked in its fetid basket,
> or its own body, its own body that, when it opens
> lets everything in.

There's an erotic section: the third. Ultimately, though, that impulse cannot be sequestered. It's everywhere, like the trace of red hair that binds, oh happy thread, this amazing book together.

The Art of Exile
By William Archila. Tempe, AZ: Bilingual Review Press, 2009.
Reviewed by **Robert Arroyo**

I've always wondered what it means to be a *whole* person. The term certainly hints at a sense of completeness and peacefulness, but if we accept that at every moment we are the sum of our previous experiences, then, at best, we can only be a work in progress. In his first book, *The Art Of Exile*, William Archila holds the past close, not only for remembrance, but also in acknowledgement of how it has the power to constantly reshape. Archila emigrated from El Salvador because of war. His poetry is filled with images of a home that is both beautiful and tragic, that attracts and repels, that holds one back, and pushes one forward.

Not surprisingly, art is the vehicle to and from; the deliverer of pain and surcease, but it also keeps one on the outside; it exiles. The collection begins with a quote from Czeslaw Milosz: *Language is the only homeland.* Language is a safe harbor from which to view what is too hot to feel and too cold to touch. It is not an escape, but a coping mechanism that allows one to look at past experiences, and to be able to begin to build them into the ever-evolving psychic identity.

Even though language offers a way into the past, what's there can't always be completely brought forward. The first poem, "Radio," begins with words from Neruda in Spanish:

> "Puedo escribir los versos mas tristes esta noche.
> Escribir, por ejemplo, 'La noche esta estrellada...'"

I think it's telling that Archila doesn't translate. Either some things are untranslatable, or the poet is unwilling to. Either way, there is incompleteness— the important part is that the poet knows it. Whatever he brings forward, it is woven into what he has become, and because of the incomplete nature of what has been brought forward, it will be revisited, revised—and once again subsumed.

Artists loom large in Archila's work. Not only do Neruda and Milosz appear, but so do Duke Ellington, Coltrane, Monk, Mingus and Whitman. Art begets art. Art, particularly (in Archila's case) music, is a mnemonic which slingshots the artist into memory:

> into this note, blessed and obsessed, perfect
>
> in the palm of my hand, touched by the earth,
> wet and small, dust and bones, the heavy weight of corn,
>
> the wind that comes wrapped in fish and salt,
> the cry of the crow high above the road
>
> where he stands spindly as a tree...
> > ("On first listening to Coltrane")

Music makes the world sensuous, makes the past beautiful, makes memory bearable.

> After the burial, everyone slept with the light on.
> No sounds in the street, but the whistle of a blue cricket.
> I thought of him barefoot, darkening the ground,
> the wings of black birds covering his body.
> > ("This Earth")

But no matter how beautiful the past can be made, the dead there can't be hidden. Death occurs with astonishing frequency in Archila's poetry: Lico, Memo, Henry, a host of unknowns—friends, who should have been the living embodiment of the past, become the heralds of the lost world. Whatever joy there is in remembering them is tempered by the knowledge that they are gone forever. Because memory is memory, it's reoccurring. No matter how often the dead are laid to rest, they rise again, not empty-handed, but with something more to offer. "This is for Henry" begins with *It always starts here, / over the chain-linked fence / with crooked fingers...* and ends with

> On the street corner, a boy
> flashes a hand sign
>
> and it all starts again,
> climbing over the fence, running through east L.A.

No matter how unchangeable the past is, how we see it often changes. First there is just the fence, then—next—the boy. Every visitation comes closer to the bone of what is dear, what is necessary. Each visitation forces a reevaluation of what is believed to be true, and whenever the past changes, the present does, too.

Art is a representation, nothing more. It is the spirit of the truth, not the truth itself, the words never right. As Archila says in "Immigration Blues, 1980,"

> I'm a man with black hair, raw accent,
> Spanish syllables caught in my throat,
> words in English locked in a dictionary,
> a foreigner everywhere I go.

We are who we are, looking for a way to find out who we were: our only home the shoes on our feet, the clothes on our back, what we keep in our head—no matter how broken.

Self-Portrait with Crayon
By Allison Benis White. Cleveland, OH: Cleveland State University Poetry Center, 2009.
Reviewed by **Louise Mathias**

Allison Benis White's first collection, *Self Portrait with Crayon,* maps the resurrection of the self after what is arguably the most painful of childhood traumas—maternal abandonment.

The poems form a loose conversation with the work of Edgar Degas, a smart choice, far beyond the biographical parallels (Degas also lost his mother at a young age—she died when he was 13). This strategy provides White with a direction and container for emotions that are almost uncontainable in their velocity and threat. The prose poem form acts as a second container. These are poems that threaten to burst their seams, and in order to evoke that quality, seams are necessary: "Obscene as the taste of blood and the closeness of her tongue behind her teeth," as she asserts in "The Ironer." Just as the mouth holds the blood from spilling, the prose poem form allows the exploration of flammable content.

The frequent appearance of Degas' dancers seems appropriate as well; the work has a choreography that is stunning to witness, as White moves through these poems with the precision, control, and delicate movements reminiscent of a ballerina: "Her hands held above her head briefly in the air crown the shape of what is no longer there" ("Seated Women Donning Her Hat").

But what I'm most fascinated and amazed by in this work is the tone, equal parts fierce intimacy and strange distancing. This gives the poems their otherworldly quality, even as they swell in domestic situation. "People lose their minds and leave while cooking salmon," she says. Notably, she doesn't name the person who has lost her mind, but she does depict the exact domestic situation that creates a vivid picture in the *reader's* mind. Hovering between oblique aphorism ("People exist for as long as possible until it is too difficult to matter") and intentional holes in the narrative ("This is an external narrative: when I was small"; "We said things, amazed at the amount"), White skillfully brings to light the experience of dislocation that characterizes the way a child's psyche processes deep trauma. Take, for example, the poem "Self Portrait—Red Chalk on Laid Paper," quoted here in its entirety.

> Blood on my forehead before I knew it was blood. It was a low branch and I walked with my head down, listening to a woman. We crossed the parking lot. A few trees planted in rows between cars, and a low branch, a small offshoot trimmed back, almost a fingernail, scraped the top of my head. Of course there was warmth and the strange look on her face, conflated with the color of fingertips. I sat down or crouched and then a white towel she had retrieved from her car, pressed to my forehead. We said things, amazed at the amount. The skin of the scalp is thin. Other people slowed to glance. Periodically pressed to the cut and pulled back to check, the blood on the towel widened, like paper folded in half over paint and opened, as if to say the rest is fascination.

Here, and elsewhere, I'm reminded of Gregory Orr's book of essays, *Poetry as Survival*, in which he describes those scenarios of "extreme desolation, in which all connections between self and outer world are snapped, along with those connecting the self to its inner life, and the very integrity and coherence of the self is profoundly shaken." The speaker is left without a choice but to piece together experience, identity, in order to reclaim the self. "Because it was worse than the truth. Than anything anyone could ever do to me. Which means I was mine. Like exhaustion from desire, the embrace was white blond" ("Absinthe").

White has devised an arresting and sophisticated language for grief that is both utterly personal and entirely universal, while avoiding any trappings of the "confessional" or the linear (predictable) narrative. The book has a quality I find largely lacking in contemporary poetry, a quality of inevitability and emotional urgency—simply put, these feel like poems that *had* to be written, combined with an original, provocative style. *Self Portrait with Crayon* is an act of fierce beauty, innovation and hope.

Slamming Open the Door

By Kathleen Sheeder Bonanno. Farmington, MN: Alice James Books, 2009.

By All Lights

By B. H. Boston. Huntington Beach, CA: Tebot Bach, 2009.
Reviewed by **Fred Moramarco**

Samuel Johnson famously commented on Milton's great elegy, Lycidas, "Where there is leisure for fiction there is little grief." Johnson was complaining about Milton's use of the conventions of the pastoral elegy in framing a poem about a classmate at Cambridge who drowned off the coast of Wales. If you're really grieving the death of someone, Dr. Johnson implies, you don't give him a Greek name, turn him into a shepherd poet who died before his prime in a "watery bed."

I thought of Johnson's remarks while reading *Slamming Open The Door*, a suite of elegiac poems by Kathleen Sheeder Bonanno about the murder of her daughter. There is little fiction here—her daughter is her daughter, Leidy Sheeder Bonnano, pictured smiling and very much alive on the page before the Table of Contents. There are no bucolic sentiments in the book, only the hard and painful contours of a mother's grief.

It's not easy writing poems about major traumatic elements in one's life. There's always a risk that the subject matter itself overwhelms the artifice and craft required to write any poem. Who wants to pay attention to alliteration, metaphor, near rhymes, and other poetic devices, when you're reading (or writing) about something as terrible as the murder of a young woman, and especially when you're reading about that murder and its consequences as described by her mother.

The sheer authenticity of the emotion that drives these poems rises above the potential pitfalls, although not completely. Bonnano is at her best when she hones in on her own physical and emotional sensations and weakest when she slips into a prosy retelling of what actually occurred.

From the first poem in the collection, "Death Barged In," Bonnano captures how fully this kind of death occurring in one's life utterly changes everything. The entire landscape of the rest of her life is altered irrevocably the moment Death enters. The zen-like title of the book, "slamming open the door," (it reminds me of the "sound of one hand clapping") refers to this unwanted but almost majestically urgent entrance:

> In his Russian greatcoat,
> slamming open the door with an unpardonable bang,
> and he has been here ever since.

From that moment forward, he is everywhere, on the phone, at dinner, and even climbing into the marriage bed, snuggling "mute" between husband and wife. And, of course, we find him hovering behind the poet at her writing desk, clamping his two huge hands on her shoulders and whispering:

> *From now on,*
> *you write about me.*

The writer at this moment has found her imperative subject. To write about anything else would seem trivial and wasteful.

The book has a novelistic narrative drive, which is both a strength and a weakness. Some of the poems seem included merely to fill narrative gaps, as when a few horrific sentences from a newspaper article are rearranged as "poetry":

> Leidy S. Bonanno, 21,
> was found dead
> late Tuesday
> inside her first floor apartment....
> the killer used
> Bonanno's telephone cord

To choke her
then left the body on her bed.
[He] covered her face
with a bed pillow,
and locked the apartment
doors [before he] left,
police said.

Bonnano takes us through the various stages of discovery in the process—
from the time she first hears about her daughter's death right through the trial,
conviction, and sentencing of her murderer, and then past it to the inevitable
"getting on with life" that must follow. After not hearing from her daughter for
several days after leaving many messages, she and her husband drive to Reading,
Pennsylvania, where her daughter works as a nurse, from Philadelphia where they
live, and on the way there they get a cell phone call from someone who tells her
she's been spotted working her nursing shift. The relief is palpable. They head
back home and when they get there she calls the hospital "just to make sure."
When she is told her daughter has not been to work for two days, we seem to
enter the body of her reaction:

This is the time
for your throat to thicken,
for your fingers to get rubbery,
for you to call the police . . .

Bonanno allows the reader to inhabit her grief and feel her rage. You can't help
but admire the straightforward honesty of a poem called "Communion," which
I quote here in its entirety:

When your minister
Proposes *forgiveness*—
Because, after all, he must—
He lifts the word
Like a wafer
Into air.

You counter
by hoisting the cup of wine.
Here's to hate, you say,
slugging it back,
eyeing the dregs.

She is also very good when she manages to find, in the midst of all this woe, some actual humor. In a poem called "Swooping" she describes her sister's crush on one of the detectives who testified in the case. Her sister fantasizes that the accused killer attempts to run from the courtroom, and the detective shoots him, then swoops her into his arms.

> There will be no swooping,
> I say, unamused,
> *think of your husband.*
> But I am thinking of mine,
>
> Who says that I can
> Have anything, anything,
> I want that might please me.
> And I say, *Okay, I want*
> *to have an affair,*
> *or I want a teacup Chihuahua.*
>
> And my husband says,
> *Yes, alright,*
> *maybe the affair,*
> *because dogs are a lot of work.*

Although many of the poems seem indebted to the style of Sharon Olds, whose book, *The Father*, also chronicles the events leading up to and away from the death of a person central in her life, *Slamming Open the Door* is an intensely individual book that takes a steadfast look at what is probably one of the most traumatic events a parent can experience—not only the death of a child, but her violent murder. Like *The Father* and also like Tess Gallagher's *Moon Crossing Bridge* (written after the death of Raymond Carver) and Donald Hall's *Without: Poems, 1998* (about the death of his wife, Jane Kenyon), this is a book written out of necessity, not choice, and necessary books are almost always a welcome addition to our poetry shelves. *Slamming Open the Door* is no exception.

★

Full disclosure: Bruce Boston was Managing Editor of *Poetry International* for most of my ten-year tenure as Editor. Together we shaped the identity of the journal and I gained enormous respect for his unfailing eye and ear for the precision of poetic imagery and speech. These are of course essential qualities for an editor, and though we worked quite closely, in all that time I never really got to know his poetry. They are also essential qualities for a poet, and though I knew he wrote poetry, and occasionally, at some event sponsored by the magazine, he read a few poems, I had no idea of either the extent or the depth of his work. So despite my many interactions with him over the years, I come to these poems as a first-time reader, and it's as if I now know him in a much fuller and deeper way.

In *Claims for Poetry*, Donald Hall famously defined poetry as "human inside talking to human inside." *By All Lights* gives heft to that definition. This is a book that shines a light on the darkness within, not in any kind of confessional or self-indulgent way, but in a manner that underscores the ongoing intersections of our private lives with the physical and social worlds that surround us. Like his mentors, Philip Levine and Larry Levis, Boston gives riveting attention to those intersections to discover the moments of illumination within them.

He is very much a California poet, in touch with the flora, fauna, and geological contours of the California landscape. In "The Bicyclist," for example, he sounds like what a park ranger might sound like if he or she had Boston's poetic gifts:

> Somewhere the dwarf geranium's brittle
> copper leaves, the gray rosemary,
>
> the prickly lilac, root-bound
> in terra cotta, carry us wholly
>
> through October, while the still
> fruited boughs of the fig ring in alarm
>
> and the nights grow shrill.
> Today, the rider's stripped back
>
> glints against the blood-flecked
> shoulders of the canyon, his pedals grazing
>
> the perfect sprouted gasps of wild mustard.
> Beyond the strand of mindful willows,
>
> He skids between two burning pepper trees,
> Where even the murder of crows
>
> Calls *gone, gone, gone.*

Throughout this book, Boston is deeply in touch with the seasons (unusual for a Californian) and nature is nearly always animated and personified. Here, in the deepening Fall, the willows are "mindful," the wild mustard "gasps," the canyon itself has "blood-flecked shoulders," and the "still fruited boughs of the fig ring in alarm," because they seem to know and understand their days are numbered. The bicyclist, appropriately looking like both a prisoner and referee with his "stripped back," seems an emblem of humanity itself, bringing its mechanical presence into a world it is both imprisoned by and tries to control. But of course transience cannot be controlled, as the quiet and echoing Buddhist conclusion of the poem underscores.

To really convey the flavor of this book, poems need to be quoted in their entirety (as above) but since my space is (very) limited, let me offer just a few lines to whet your poetic appetite:

> there is no place
> to go and not be
> in hiding.
>
> ("The Savage, Our Fathers")

> And I lie here
> This flesh the suit of a diver
> Hung on my bones
> Afraid that somewhere
> Nothing is wrong
>
> ("Seasonal")

> How often the moon evades
> the acacia, powders the trembling purple
> of its leaves and leaves—a wafer balanced
> on the tongue of its own light, dissolving
> in the perfect morning mirrors of the sea.
>
> ("Vista")

Enough. You get the idea. These are the poems of a keen observer who finds nature's metaphors in "the palm at the end of the mind," as Wallace Stevens put it. They convey a lingering sense of the brevity, fragility, sacredness, mutability, and ultimate mystery of life. Reading it, I feel as if I've made a new friend, though I've known Bruce for many, many years.

The Looking House

By Fred Marchant. St. Paul, MN: Graywolf Press, 2009.
Reviewed by **George Kalogeris**

What has always distinguished Fred Marchant's verse, to my mind, is his willingness to take a hard look at human suffering while maintaining his tender, yet unflinching tone. It's the kind of keen aural sensitivity that I think Chekhov was getting at when he spoke of "the delicacy which is necessary when dealing with another person's soul."

As in his previous collections, there are typically three types of Marchant poem: political meditations (which often spring from his experience as a CO in the Vietnam war), lyric poems of large-spirited tenderness and sometimes even visionary beauty, and starkly engaging elegies. In order to show what I admire so much about Fred Marchant's poetry, I'd like to concentrate on two elegies—not because I think they are more convincing than some of the other poems in the book, but because I feel they mark a new stage of development in the poet's work, as well as the deepening maturity of middle age. However intently Marchant peers into the looking house of the human condition, and voices what he sees, there's a natural tendency towards resurgent lift and buoyant lambency at the lyric heart of his gift. The elegies provide the necessary counterweight to these generous energies; like loaded scale-pans, they plumb the downward pull of grief in gravid lines that are no less tremulously irrepressible, and equally humane.

In "Balpeen Hammer," a breathtakingly vivid poem about a coma-stricken father's dying breaths, the lines are remarkable for the way that the force of Marchant's empathy is in direct relation to the poem's intense concern for unemphatic rendering as a way of staying true to the way things happened in the gravest of circumstances. The poem starts as follows:

> He lay sideways on the bed,
> the flimsy curtains on their runners
> stirring when the nurses rushed by.

Though we do not yet know that the father is hovering between life and death, the placement of the word "sideways," suspended between "he" and "bed," is already leading us in the direction of *deathbed*. The hurried, harried, yet orderly pace of the Emergency Room, as well as the muffled rush of panic in the son's chest, is an evocation made palpable by the repetitions of "u" and "r" sounds: *curtains, runners, stirring, nurses, rushed.* Each time the curtains rustle along the line what ripples through the verse as we read it—and holds us in its almost giddy, horrifyingly gratuitous sway—is the flimsiness of the flesh curtain, and the awful realization, like an insistent whisper, that the mortality of a loved one hinges upon the frailest of runners, the panting breath.

Later on in the poem one of the nurses gives Marchant a "grape popsicle" to hold against his father's parched lips, and instructs him to "keep an eye on it."

> I rested the ice on his tongue,
> but held the weight off,
> balanced it in my hand.
> I remembered a balpeen hammer,
> a miniature, the size of a popsicle,
> my favorite among all his tools.
>
> There was no claw at the back,
> but round steel, for *peening,*
> the shaping and smoothing of metal.
>
> That's how I wanted his minutes
> to pass, no thrash or heave,
> Just a steady tapping away until done.

It's one thing to stay vigilant to the limitations of the sympathetic imagination, especially in a poem concerning the gravely ill, another to allow a plain-spoken register to keep its own vigil by remaining attentive to quotidian detail, vibrant as the mundane can be with the latent potency of contingency and circumstance. There's lyric solace here, but it's too eye-level with what it's describing to offer any consolatory lift once the reader's eyes have lifted from the page. Nevertheless, the ring of such even-toned courage endures in the ear. Lovely, too, the way "rested" is more than half-in-love with easeful death, but refuses to melt (like the grape popsicle) into pathos, or worse, into self-congratulation. The poem is not oblivious to the fact that it's being forged, for the sake of a son's art, on the dying father's tongue, but there's no preening here. Just the gentle tapping away of a father's fading hammer-blows becoming the son's heart-felt meter, his measure of sorrow. Like perfect pitch testing its sound on a tuning fork, the poem's *peening* is one with its *keening.*

In "Democratic Vistas," Marchant's very beautiful elegy for his mentor and friend, Saul Bellow, the sonorous undertones of plain statement and their indelible trace of simple honest gesture are fused together with the force of moral instruction.

Third Day

since you died.
You would attach nothing to the number.
You would lean your head back and laugh if anyone did.

So I will count it up this way:
this be the day after the day after the day.

Neither earth nor sky has begun to notice,
as you would have predicted.

You once said that if words would pay
close enough attention to the body,
then the soul would follow.

Here lyeth the body.

Marchant occasionally uses rhyme, but nowhere more effectively than here, as the tautness of the monosyllabic terms for transience (way/pay/day) are held in check, momentarily, by the more opulent, unspoken rhyme for "follow": as if the open-voweled ring of the great novelist's name, and the expanse of American speech that *Bellow* now stands for, were a new democratic vista of the vernacular, horizon-wide as the language of the nation, and worthy of Whitman. And there for us to follow, with the surety of a homing instinct.

Though a full discussion of them is well beyond the scope of this review, I would like to note that perhaps the two major poems in this book are the longest ones, "Ard na Mara" and "The Custody of the Eyes." In their imaginative depth and historical range, as well as their capacity for sustained verse-narrative, they are high-water marks in the poet's oeuvre.

In the harrowing "Words for Faraj," an exiled Iranian writer recounts having been subjected to a mock hanging: "When they wake you what hurts the most is // that the afterlife should seem so ugly and familiar." At the other end of the tonal spectrum is the exquisitely affirmative flicker of momentary beauty in "Pinckney Street," a lustrous lyric that quivers like an early spring branch against the horizon. In this poem a friend with an eye for the transience of blossoming flowers explains: "for three weeks each year / and beginning tomorrow / this will be the most / beautiful place in the city." And then, in the midst of the tall brick buildings, and as if what's imminent in nature were already happening in language, the "star magnolias" are "like the shook foil that Hopkins wrote about."

What the very different registers of these poems have in common is an act of bearing witness that is borne out by a language of intense listening. And what Fred Marchant has said in eloquent homage to the work of William Stafford applies to his own work in equal measure: "Hearing has a somewhat passive connotation; deep listening, as Stafford presents it, is a profoundly active turning toward. It is a 'listing,' that listening, that cocking of the ear, that pause in which one allows for authentic consideration of the other."

The Looking House is also a listening house, a dwelling place of the American demotic. It contains torture chambers, though the cries coming from them are muted. And yet those agonies from deep in some labyrinthine cellblock are never so distant that we don't instinctively recoil—as if from an echoing that was atavistically calibrated to the acoustics of the inner ear. On the other hand, in poems like "Pinckney Street," Marchant has built a lyric temple inside the hearing, a small Rilkean hut of pure song.

Then, Something
By Patricia Fargnoli. North Adams, MA: Tupelo Press, 2009.
Reviewed by **Tim Mayo**

"Remove Your Shoes, Place Your Pulse on the Table"

"Remove your shoes, place your pulse on the table," a quote from the first poem in Patricia Fargnoli's sixth collection, tells us that we are about to embark on a very special journey. However, it is the book's title, *Then, Something,* which indicates what this collection is about. The title comes from Robert Frost's poem "For Once, Then, Something," part of which Fargnoli uses as the epigraph to this book. In the Frost poem, as the speaker is looking down a well, he thinks he sees something beyond his own reflection and below the surface of the water, but then loses sight it of as the water is disturbed. Fargnoli is now in her seventies and the exploration of what else might exist, waiting to be perceived, beyond the physical world, becomes the unifying concern of her book.

In the collection's introductory poem, "Wherever you are going," the speaker dispenses advice to an unidentified (who could easily be us) interlocutor about to leave for an unknown destination that we later surmise is the afterlife:

You will want to take with you the mud-rich scent breaking through March frost and lemons sliced on a blue plate, their pinwheels of light.

This is the first couplet in the poem, and, to my mind, it is as close to an elegiac distich as one will ever get in twenty-first century American free verse: a long, loose, six foot line followed by a shorter one of five feet. Although not all of Fargnoli's poems have such lengthy lines, there are enough which require a wider than normal page that in order to retain the integrity of these lines the publisher has graciously made the book large enough to accommodate their meaningful and graceful lengths.

This particular poem also enumerates a varied number of both worldly/physical and spiritual items which the "you" of the poem will want to take or have to give up. It is important to note, here, that this first couplet introduces a motif which is carried on throughout the collection, i.e., a motif of pairing something larger and/or abstract, "the mud-rich scent breaking through March frost," with something smaller and/or concrete and specific: the "pinwheels of light" that the lemon slices seem to make on a blue plate. In this case you have them all together, but more often than not the pairings are large/small and abstract/specific.

Fargnoli is a free verse poet, and the couplets only suggest this elegiac meter, but do not adhere to it. The resemblance here to this meter sets a certain expectation of gravitas without having to invoke the somber, and since most of the collection is composed of poems with shorter lines, the long lines, themselves, when they occur, become a sort of leitmotif throughout the collection.

The poems in *Then, Something* are not just meditations on death. The collection also circles around Fargnoli's agnosticism and ironic meditations about afterlife. Such poems as "On the Question of the Soul," "The Phenomenology of Garbage," and "Prepositions Toward a Definition of God," all proceed with an intellectual playfulness. Nonetheless, beneath their playfulness they are each serious meditations on the questions posed by their titles, just as the poem "Alternate Worlds" also seriously entertains that central question of what else might exist, waiting to be perceived just beyond our physical limitations. Lastly, there are also poems which deal with regret, loss, and there are even angry memories.

It is interesting to note how this collection ends, how it narrows down to a final, very small poem: "Coda." This is Fargnoli's last and most important pairing of large and small. It is the other bookend to the collection and meant to contrast and compliment the expansive lines of the first poem, "Wherever you go." The very size of this poem becomes the speck of dust we must all turn into at death. The woman has turned back into parts of nature, "[become] sand," and the Frost epigraph seems echoed in the intangibility of the ocean and sky the woman has also turned into. "Coda" seems to physically emphasize on the page how small we are in the universe. This fact, whether you believe in a god or not, is a humbling thought—and that is, then, something we can know, just as we know the satisfying strength and beauty of this collection. We can put our shoes back on.

Blue Shadow Behind Everything Dazzling
By Gail Wronsky. Venice, CA: Hollyridge Press, 2009.
Reviewed by **Karen Kevorkian**

Gail Wronsky's poems in *Blue Shadow Behind Everything Dazzling* are concerned with the nature of existence, highly estheticized meditations under whose deceptively pleasing surfaces lie an intellect as tough and specific as a street fighter's. Wronsky lobs resonant and gorgeous rocks at our pretty certainties about ambition, the ardor of just causes, the folly of constructing notions of reality and time. Teasing out liminal and elusive moments of understanding through dances of language, she uses India as the setting for the poems, where she takes notice of the ordinary that arrests the western eye, rendered explicitly and resonantly, as "on a rainy day in Sarnath a neem tree / might bleed pure mercury / out of its leaves, and flood us with / insight almost as if we recognized that particular dance of alacrity and silver as / something we once did." Our condition, she suggests, is one of perpetual longing for what we can't name, but only perceive at-the-edges-of the known, out of the corner of the eye, and in the interstices of language meeting perception.

The result is the "rough opacity" of things, a quality that sends us on private inward journeys, the undertaking of which leads in these poems to where Hindu mythology and theological concerns meet contemporary theory's preoccupations with the slipperiness of identity, and phenomena's fractal instability. The success of these poems suggests that the free verse poem in contemporary voice is the ideal vehicle for such an exploration. Language both lush and exact is nuanced by the uncertainties acknowledged in her lines' suggestive hesitations. "Edges pretend that / one thing ends. / But nothing does end -- / not here / beneath the Ganges / where it is dark" says the eponymous poem. Another poem, "Go, Sure, Why Not?" lays out in a brilliant integration of voice, image, language, craft, and cultural reference the effort to apprehend the flow of nothing and small event that accumulates under the rubric *living,* and the ultimate effrontery of our self-assertive acts. "*One wants / to be singled out,*" the poem concludes, the "one" in these poems not just she who is vulnerable to beauty and history but also to her western heritage of language. And unsurprisingly Wronsky's language retains echoes of some of its master craftsmen, Shakespeare and Keats, but also the honed honesty of the thing-focused gaze of early modernist William Carlos Williams, and the snappy attitude of that voracious consumer of urban edge Frank O'Hara, to bring to life "the bright world [that] / sometimes lets itself be seen."

Love and Strange Horses

By Nathalie Handal. Pittsburg, PA: University of Pittsburgh Press, 2010.
Review by **Erica Wright**

For a collection that embraces Norse mythology as readily as Christianity or, for that matter, Arabic as readily as English, it is a surprise that *Love and Strange Horses* transcends multiculturalism. Akin to how a symphony resonates in Naples the same way it does in Nashville, Nathalie Handal's poetry pushes against the restraints of culture and even (at times) language. In "Javier," for example, it is unnecessary to understand the lover's words, "Caballero, dos palomas y un vino rojo," to understand his intent: seduction. The ambition of this collection is perhaps the purest that lyric poetry claims, that of music's immediacy. As the poet asks in "The Songmaker—19 *Arabics*," "Who said we need to be strangers, / when we listen to the same music?" It is appropriate that *Love and Strange Horses* is structured around movements: Intima ("belonging" in Arabic), Elegía Erótica ("erotic elegy" in Spanish), and Terre Música ("earth music" in French and Spanish). There are also a number of poems explicitly about music, including "The Hawk Quartet" and "The Bulgarian Orchestra." This approach allows Handal to tackle the common ground between peoples rather than their differences, and there is joy in that space. Even with the big subjects—love, death, religion—there is an embrace of what is unknowable. In terms of poetry, this embrace is negative capability; in terms of life, it is faith: "In a midnight abandoned by the moon, / we tell ourselves we aren't meant to know everything." And yet it is the poet's job to try. In the end, this may be the key difference between music and poetry. Handal poses unanswerable questions and then struggles with them. The struggle is more important than the correct answer. In "Entrances and Other Endings," the speaker questions and explains, "I saw a deer or was it a dragon? Saw a fern or was it an icon? I subtracted the hums from the song." While the difference between a plant and a sacred image may seem significant, it is the music that matters, the poetry above all else.

Ledger of Crossroads

By James Brasfield. Baton Rouge, LA: Louisiana State University Press, 2009.
Reviewed by **Marion Brown**

James Brasfield, a poet and translator, writes poems that hallow ordinary places. *Ledger of Crossroads,* his first full-length collection, travels the globe street by street. Brasfield takes us from "the puddled street" in Kyiv to "MacDougal Street" in New York, Broad Street in the "Heart of Dixie," and back to Ukraine, Tolstoy Street, and N. Pryboya Boulevard, an itinerary that honors poets Celan, Brodsky and Leopold Staff, and painters Van Gogh, Matisse and Motherwell.

Along his way, Brasfield commemorates his father, giving him, as a soldier in "Letter from Germany," desolate voice, ("the rain feels like / Someone slapping you with a wet towel") and youthful appetite, as in the hyperbole of "Alabama / Better have a big sweet potato crop / The year I come home." The speaker dwells in Celan's Chernivtsi, visits Brodsky's chosen café in New York, and stops in Moscow to view:

> Matisse, *Goldfish*
> …in the master's cylindrical bowl
> flanked by arrangements
> of flowers and plants
> that just might paper the wall.

This description in "Identities" introduces us to a keen observer who travels, in part, as pilgrim.

The pilgrim haunts crossroads, places of change, one constant of the road. In "MacDougal Street" he traces different sorts of lines, broken concrete near an intersection where he talked shop with Joseph Brodsky: "the draftsman's / conversation—your lines drawn from the ground." In an essay on lyric poetry, Brodsky speaks of "the timbre of pity" that expresses "the love of the permanent for the transitory."[1] A note of elegy pervades the title poem, "From the Ledger of Crossroads," which takes place under a veiled sky, snow like smoke. The poem begins, "The dead, the disappeared, the desperate," and brings back the triumvirate later, insisting they be "remembered." From a litany of killers over the ages, its speaker derives a truth: "there is no end to history." Moving from the humble, "Each potato is held and peeled," he turns to singular, uprooted figures, rekindlers of light, "like the oil lamp hung above a table."

> Then shadows
> stand at junctures of connection. Stars
> ferry the weight on extended shoulders.

Brasfield's curious use of "ferry" arrests the reader at a critical instant. Reminiscent of Blake's astral personages, the stars are an ecstatic image of immortality.

Transcendence is not the mood of every day. Brasfield constructs cityscapes out of history and the grimy streets where history is committed. The phrases "the static of centuries, / each year its ledger of decrees" in the title

---

[1] Joseph Brodsky, "Altra Ego," in *On Grief and Reason: Essays*, (New York: Farrar Straus Giroux, 1994), p. 91.

poem identify the ages of history with the business of its minute figures. A ledger records their acts, often brutal. Brasfield exercises restraint, restraint that feels painful, in naming sights and smells of Celan's birth city. In "Chernivtsi," "People who return /say the streets are clean in Deutschland," which emphasizes those who do not return. The question "who spread the path / of ashes on the walk?" inverting the later image of "stars scattered / across the blackest night," obliges the reader to wonder about the unidentified ashes a new tenant "found far back in the wardrobe." Honoring lasts only as long as memory, or as long as a poem.

In the depopulated city of Chernivtsi, streets obliterated by ice, "crosswinds" are thoroughfares. Here, Brasfield's irony is of the desolate variety, Deutschland's smoke and ashes and, as Celan has it in "Todesfuge," "a grave in the air." Brasfield locates atrocities underfoot or, in "The Relief," overhead. A sequence of fourteen elegiac unrhymed sonnets makes up "The Relief," the final section of *Ledger of Crossroads*. The relief of the title is a sculpted face from the Hapsburg era on a façade in Chernivtsi. As one might invoke a goddess, Brasfield enlists her to help mourn Antchel, who became Celan, and all the victims of ages of heavy "black boots of Pole, Hussar, Romanian, / the Third Reich, *Homo Sovieticus…*" (4.) Brasfield pairs the "dry-eyed" relief of the fifth sonnet with a Soviet-era woman who remarries at the Palace of Solemn Events. Emotionless, she has seen it all.

In the sixth, the speaker gazes down from his kitchen window, mirroring the plaster face that looks in, and imagines:

> the boy Antchel running with hoop
> and stick down the strasse , who, years later,
> holding the hand of a girl, turned and kissed her.

Antchel cannot be found; yet the kiss is recovered through Brasfield's imaginative sifting. When the speaker addresses the relief, he also speaks to Celan, a reason to give some words in German, which was his mother tongue. The opening of "The Relief"—"Lines of light are always: in them / you wait, anonymous part of what is seen"—apply to Celan as well as the face. Though his presence is felt, the speaker offers testimony, not relief.

This speaker is represented by his Westclox, his steaming cup of coffee and a "cotton curtain" that hangs on his window. The relief stares over it. A similar curtain has appeared in "Chernivtsi," a metaphor for threadbare sky, "a pale, cotton curtain / about to fall from its string." Not only his décor but his persona is unassuming. He lets himself be observed in his kitchen. The sculpture looks in but looks past him.

In "Tracks," the poet addresses himself:

the trolley returns you
to Kontraktova Square, close
to the place called your room—
not your home.

"Perigee" juxtaposes images of homelessness with discomfort at home, "Wind shakes this hilltop / corner house." Home becomes the opposite of refuge, "The inward night is fire is sea is home," which may explain why the traveler favors foreign addresses.

In the second section of *Ledger of Crossroads,* Brasfield draws on family story and roots in the American South, writing in the first person. He insinuates the price of oppression there, in "Heart of Dixie," by shifting the repeated "eyes lowered" from black servants to white employers. The longest poem, "The Illness, 1960," presents the poet as a boy consumed by "The Rime of the Ancient Mariner" in Dore's illustrations. Heat is inside and out, the weather of "July in Alabama," and fever: "I am hot as if standing at a fire." The speaker's diction is eerily calm as he introduces family members, his grandparents, Flo, their cook, and his mother at home pleading with God that she might join her dead husband. Brasfield lets a reader intuit the adults' anxiety while the sick boy sails on his bed "Like a stowaway." Attended by the doctor, Grandmother and Flo, the boy navigates by his own understanding. He apprehends that Grandfather lingers "near the edge of earth" and trusts "in my father's duration as long as I live, / believing he sees what remains." Brasfield's details are convincing as narrative and powerful as metaphor, making a bildungsroman of a three-page poem.

The word history does not pop up every day in lyric poetry but shows itself in *Ledger of Crossroads,* whose poet examines cities and streets where the past lives. Exploring these sites in lucid, heart-breaking language, James Brasfield reanimates the creators to whom he renders homage. He examines himself along with those artists, accomplishing what Joseph Brodsky characterizes as a poet's work, "winnowing [his soul] from the chaff of existence."[2]

---

[2] Brodsky, p. 87

War Bird

By David Gewanter. Chicago, IL: University Of Chicago Press, 2009.
Reviewed by **Peter Blair**

David Gewanter's recent book of poems, *War Bird*, deftly explores the history and politics of America with a personal, intelligent, and incisive play of language. The poems' subject matter spans previous centuries as well as decades from the 1970's to the present, while Gewanter's ingenious use of poetic forms reveals the double and triple meanings that words can have.

The first poem of section one, "In again Out again," opens: "Put words on the move, / on the make, make / your body move in hard play." This poem brings together images of basketball, sex, and marriage, and we feel Gewanter's words darting with a point guard's quickness. He's a poet who knows how to put language moves on us, and to be on the "make" for our attention. He highlights a marriage "that goes / up and down, that dives / for the loose ball, lightfooted comedy / . . . / *In again Out again / Finnegan.*" We move effortlessly from sports to sex to the literary forbear of such word play, James Joyce. Gewanter's quick and deft "language moves" seem to dunk on us describing with an expert eye the cultural garb of the players the speaker remembers from his school playing days, "one styling / a Mao hat, one / Detroit porkpie & fedayeen scarf / and, sitting next to me / one Fruit of Islam soldier cap." He references America's not-so-melted pot of races while describing a comic book by Elijah Muhammad where the white people get "zapped" by flying saucers. His fellow basketball player on the bus points out "'now that's you right here, / that's the jews,' little / black-ink white / men plummeting from a bank." America is a social experiment that might fail, and Gewanter's poem reads the cultural fault lines.

Similarly, "Body Text" reads the body's "text," its failings over a bloody political history: "Now we pay for our figures: / when the dictator proclaims / 'the future is in your hands,' / rebels chop off a thousand arms, / asking the victims, 'short sleeve or long sleeve.'" This violence is also mirrored in the "body" of language: "every fault, a body's true instruction: / the botched colon and missing period, / the 'terminally disorganized / Appendix.'" The poem references Hobbes, Rousseau, and the speaker's classmates pictured in his high school yearbook, asking, "Can our bodies turn innocent again?"

In "Hamlet of Merano: The Lotus Eaters," Gewanter describes a village with "frilled, puritanical / collars of snow, melting in the sun of Italy— / heroes drift here: they kill for high ground, / grow lazy and forgetful, then give the land away . . . ." Somehow the kings, queens, and tourists who have visited create a backwards *Hamlet*: "the one act play with no revenge." History is forgotten or passes on without us. Gewanter asks "Who . . . would not name himself king here, / and forget who is king?" The price for eating the lotus blossoms is stasis, not "tragical-comical-historical" but the absent-mindedness of Polonius. Politics goes on repeating itself because "The eye sees what it remembers, the imagination dreams its rut / is fresh." What to do in the face of such grand vanity that besets us all, "even Kafka" and Ezra Pound (both of whom visited Merano), is to expose ourselves to the exposé of poetry, which traces connections, contradictions and maps the forgetfulness by going to the roots and double ironies of words themselves, as Gewanter's poems relentlessly do.

The political/social implications of language exist even in a café we casually enter every day. In "Break-Up Café," Gewanter recreates a café in words on the page as William Carlos Williams creates a language equivalent of a sycamore tree. Like a language hologram, the sections are titled "*Table by window*," "*Couch*," "*Last booth*," and so on. We can walk through it and hear the people discuss sex, or an arrogant, greedy man in the armchair who loves his house more than his father because, in his words, it makes him money the easy way: "time for another re-fi / Why not live off the house? It makes more / dough than I do. I call it my dad." Gewanter includes a news story on the rack, people at the counter, and even a poem in a notebook lying in the lost and found, a poem of angry retribution on the nameless poet's mother. Everyone is breaking up, or is about to, and Gewanter presents this broken world as vividly as if one walked into the actual brick and mortar café where, if one is alert, one hears, as Ezra Pound says, "the news that stays news."

These first four poems of *War Bird* set the stage for many of the poems that follow which take on the global, complex news of politics and war. The title sequence, "War Bird," is a poetic journal about the Poets' Anti-War Rally in 2003 when Laura Bush requested poems and then canceled an event because so many poems were against the war in Iraq. In the first stanza of the poem, we see Gewanter's words "on the move" again:

> The massed and pillared wings of
> the White House never fly—
> > whitewashed yearly, they stand
> impervious
> to metaphor,
> to hawk and dove, and red armies
> of ants.

Once again the resonance and connotative richness of the language create the harsh sense of power moving its own way regardless of attempts to question it or call it to truth. Referring at times to past presidents Nixon, Reagan, George W. Bush and the imagery of falconry, the poem shows the human machinery of the state is as impervious to the poets as the White House wings. As poets read against the war, "[t]he falange of Secret Service men ... chat like critics into their black / lapels," a "proconsul Chevy Suburban noses" the poets aside, and like Nixon, who watched football during Vietnam War protests, Bush "goes for the burn, / racing the / cut tongue / of his treadmill to a dead heat."

An earlier poem, "1972: The Battery," describes equally futile protests against that previous war, Vietnam. The speaker's student council, "to fight the CIA, / burns its records, then disbands." After the Cambodia bombing news, another "battle" begins when students vote to keep the flag down: "cheerleaders cry, and loyalist / football types rebel: they hoist it up, ring the flagpole." When "grainfed hippies" storm the phalanx, they are easily repulsed. Yet somehow that power is impotent without the moral compass of poetry. "War Bird" ends on a stark image of that American power:

> Flapping wildly, the falcon claws
> the head shape, squawking,
> gyrating to
> hold on,
> imperial lunge and lunge,
> biting at the skull it fed, as
> semen slowly drips into a
> rubber dam.

Contextualized within an exposé of American imperialism, this image of a Washington, DC zoo-keeper trying to breed falcons has ironic overtones of unnatural physical force.

In another poem that takes on the sordid state of international politics, Gewanter notes the terrible toll the wars in Iraq and Afghanistan have taken on the soldiers who fight them like a "break-up café" of human history. In "American Incognito," a poem with sections whose themes merge and diverge like a jazz musician improvising, Gewanter contrasts our broken army vets with Thomas Jefferson's fascination with mammoths, and a dinosaur spine dug up by a sewer worker in Washington, DC. In some of the most moving passages in the collection, Gewanter documents the suffering of war vets, from the grimy conditions of Walter Reed hospital with cracked walls and mice infestations to the irony of a soldier "wounded when burning poppies, now afloat / on morphine. 'As a state,' he once emailed, / 'Afghanistan is next to Mars.'" Another soldier, an army colonel, stands in an Iraq sand / thunder storm where, "What falls from the sky is not water / but mud, raindrops pulling clouds of sand / into large wet globs." The man simply says, "'You've got to embrace the suck.'" Part of "the suck" we must embrace is about the President who put our soldiers there. Gewanter contrasts this sandstorm scene with Bush's DUI and Laura Bush's "yellowcake Chevy mow[ing] down her boyfriend: / *vehicular homicide*: the car found guilty."

In another section of "American Incognito," he writes of Washington, DC's history: "Beneath the marble, beneath the paper laws; / the paved boglands and legs-up taverns, / the slave-built steps of the Capitol." Here Gewanter notes, like all of *War Bird*, the essential contradictions not just at the heart of our personal experience and our empire, but of the American experiment itself. The poem reflects in its cogent and concrete lyricism that America itself is a terrifying performance of contradictions that splits the country and almost kills it, but somehow we survive. Think of President Obama, our first African-American President, walking up those "slave-built steps of the capital" to address congress about health care while others are spit on and harassed.

It reminds me of what Jurgen Habermas, the philosopher and social critic, wrote about the founders of our republic. They somehow "performed" the democracy despite the massive contradictions in what they were attempting to do. In other words, their statements, such as "All men are created equal," didn't include all men and certainly not women. Those statements, however, and the voicing and performance of them in what Habermas calls "the public sphere," had the power to go beyond their historical moment. They accessed what Habermas believes is a "universal core of moral intuition in all times and places" (206). By "embracing the suck" of those contradictions, the poems of David Gewanter, in *War Bird,* have that same power. He performs in his language, in personal and social ways, with all of its contradictions and ironies, the democracy that we have not yet achieved, but that we are still trying to become. This is a moving and worthwhile collection.

Works Cited
Habermas, Jurgen. *Autonomy and Solidarity: Interviews.* Peter Dewes, ed. London: Verso, 1986.

Determination of Place
By Per Wästberg. Translated by Hildred Crill. Stockholm, Sweden: Ars Interpres, 2008.
Reviewed by **Elizabeth Clark**

Per Wästberg, the Swedish poet, essayist, novelist, reporter, editor, and activist, is famous in his own country for his incredible productivity. He's the author of over 30 books, and in his recent collection of poems, *Determination of Place*, translated into English by Hildred Crill and into Russian by Regina Derieva and Alexei Prokopiev, he writes eloquently about both the drive to write and the difficulty, even impossibility, of representing reality with words. This frustration is clearly illustrated in *Double Exposure*, a short poem that appears early in the collection, in which the pressure exerted on a pen results in the splitting of its nib: "…and the writing became blurred and double: / two versions, one of which is / the other's shadow and pursuer." In trying to describe reality a split occurs, and the words become the pursuer of that which they attempt to create or describe. Interestingly, the speaker in *Double Exposure* is both the reader and writer of the text, and still has difficulty interpreting the text he is writing. "Words don't let themselves be speared." The gap widens, and it is too late to have a light touch; the nib is irrevocably broken.

The English translator, Hildred Crill, has recreated the confidence of the original and the deceptive simplicity of the lyric voice. The poems address the reader with a directness that invites a shared contemplation with their speaker. As in "Double Exposure," many of the poems use the relationship of the speaker to the prosaic details of daily life to explore philosophical questions. As Wästberg writes in the book's title poem, "Small answers for big questions: / It doesn't get worse, it doesn't get / better than this." Like the pen and its nib, the objects and actions named in these poems are common ones (boiling, chopping onions) and Wästberg uses them as signposts to try to map his location. As he burrows into reality "like deathwatch beetles in old woodwork…reality, grateful for the attention, / arrange(s) itself to a landscape and a home."

Wästberg finds his most powerful and overarching metaphors in the task of the cartographer. For Wästberg, making maps, the reduction of three dimensions to two, is an urgent and powerful act, but he is very aware of the erasure of these maps: "We are movable stones on a map the wind erases." Not only are the maps erased, they are also inadequate. He writes in "Water of Darkness, Clear"

> The power of those who describe is great.
> They mark out sunken islands,
>   indicate a forgotten shipwreck,
>   a feldspar mine with the sign
> "work of men which later on closed down."
> The maps, spread out, are numerous enough
> to suffocate the world.
> But they do not cover it.

Closely related to this fascination with maps is a parallel obsession with the figure of the traveler or explorer. The collection's final poem, "Anders Sparrman – Circumnavigator, Stranded," is written in the voice of an 18th century Swedish naturalist who sailed with Captain Cook. (Wästberg also recently released a historical novel based on Sparrman's life.) In the poem's imagined monologue, Sparrman recounts the things he's seen on his travels—the orangutan, the lion, the Antarctic icebergs, the death of his fellow travelers—and claims they have turned him into "a semaphore telegraph at humanity's fringes." Sparrman's travels lead to questions about reality itself: "I stumbled over the boundary / to myself and found myself on a village street in the universe."

The figure of Sparrman is interesting as a stand-in for Wästberg himself. Both are men who have travelled widely and brought news home to Sweden (as Wästberg writes of his native country "...A captain's cabin. The storerooms still large. / We rock in the swells from a delayed future..."), and both fought passionately for the international civil rights causes of their day (Sparrman was an early abolitionist, and Wästberg is the founder of Swedish Amnesty and tireless anti-apartheid activist). And as Wästberg considers the end of Sparrman's travels, it's clear that he is foreseeing his own as well. If the mind at work here ever finds a place to rest before the ultimate end of its journey, it is in the tender long poem "On Love," a meditation on a successful love affair late in life. In it Wästberg writes, "Our hands move toward each other / assured of rest. / Nothing to write about. / Much to live in."

Water the Moon
By Fiona Sze-Lorrain. Grosse Pointe Farms, MI: Marick Press, 2009.
Reviewed by **William La Ganza**

The cover photograph of Fiona Sze-Lorrain's *Water the Moon* is of a large and dusty old clock on a public building. Its hands, extending beyond the centre, form a cross, recalling the four Chinese constellations corresponding to the points of the compass. The author has left Asia for Europe, breaking from family and tradition to start a new life in Paris. The collection is in three parts: 1. "Biography of Hunger" is about a step toward the unknown, a longing for familiar tastes left behind and a struggle with ambivalence about the past; 2. "Dear Paris" explores the vicissitudes of her life in Paris and being with her husband, much older than she; 3. "The Key Always Opens" explores the existential challenge of disorientation.

The erotic opening lines of "Biography of Hunger," "At the tip of every tongue, / the wind, a chasm – / desire enters the forest. . . ," are juxtaposed on the next page with the image of her grandmother in the kitchen. Her cooking is highly appealing to the senses, with "every seed warm to her touch," "crimson bean paste" that "foams." The food seems alive: "Grains of red beans churn in her palm," "Jump, of course they jump!" The moons she is making with "white dough" are "pert," each like a "chalked face" that she "water[s]" with "green tea." This fertile image of Chinese culture in the East is mitigated by disillusionment at the hypocrisy of Mao, who embraced books even as he "poison[ed]" the "spirits and minds" of the people. Survivors of Tibet carried the dead inside them: "Those who perished / before arriving / built their tombs in those / who escaped." The author feels that she and her father are "two cultures apart," he being "afraid to write feelings," she a "palpitating heart" longing for "more / than a paper response." Ancestral links seem tenuous: holding a map from her grandfather, she realizes that she can "no longer / remember" him—"I am merely a tourist."

At the beginning of "Dear Paris," the author, "barely twenty-one / ... starving and shoeless" is in a new city beneath a column topped with a statue of the flying Spirit of Freedom: "Wings of fear and anxiety capture / my feet when they reach la Bastille." She is on the cusp of a new direction in her life, with new possibilities. On her palm is written the address of a man who has been "waiting / five years": five years that "can free me from the past." The moon is often present; it is also frightening: it "symbolizes fear in my culture / a dark force that hunts / until you cower." On this first night, the moon "was nowhere."

Even as the frequent references to the moon suggest a self-conscious chronology, the author "disregarded age / as a formula for life" when she married a man "[t]hirty-one winters" older than she, his "skin ravaged, wrinkles / resembling silvery gills." Seemingly blessed by the moon, and the harmony of their union, recalled by the repeated "o" sounds in the lines, she is there with him "where windows open wide to the river, / silk curtains in an abating wind, / reach out to their nakedness, / Two bodies curled in a roomful of moonlight, / lying perpendicular / to each other, a destiny parallel."

"The Key Always Opens" touches the subject of crying and what it might mean, or conceal. "Think twice about sadness. / Her eyes tell a story / different from their tears," the author warns. Elsewhere, "Tears / dismantle sleep and fall as autumn leaves." In the poem "A Lot had Happened: A Five Act Play," the author explores a series of human moments and the agony of ambiguity integral to the symbolizing of thought through language. "That is a cry that cries and cries a cry. / ... A tear in a cry and a cry in a tear. A tear with a cry and a cry with / a tear. / A cry tears. It is tearing." A tear can blur sight; emotions can make moonlight seem "austere." This seems to be the key: the wonder we feel before the moon is not engendered by its luminosity, but by our perception of it: "Yet the light is no mystery – the mystery / is how something moves to filter light through." Both geographical and psychological movement are necessary to having a hand in one's destiny, to existential well-being and enlightenment: "Open your eyes. Feel the earth? / Leave your roots. Leave your ancestors. / … with a bleeding heart, you flee / all your life along a shadowed curve."

Stone Lyre: Poems of René Char
By René Char, Translated by Nancy Naomi Carlson. North Adams, MA: Tupelo Press, 2010.
Reviewed by **Susan Wilde**

Nancy Naomi Carlson's collection offers a fine sampling from René Char's fifty years of poetry. In *Stone Lyre,* Char creates his own mythology of life, love, and nature—he uses creatures and bestiaries, both meditative and intensely lyrical—making this a volume of poetry worth re-reading. Carlson opens the book with "Invitation," which not only brings the reader into the book but also shows some of the lyric and language one can expect to see throughout. The poem starts by "summon[ing] the loves," where "love" is described as "pursued and tortured by summer's scythe—whose white torpor embalms the night air." Love is fleeting, but not helpless because "love" fills the night with "white torpor," taking slow seductive action in opposition to night. Char's work often explores binaries, the yin and yang of things, but not in a predictable way. He takes leaps that make the reader want to see where he will go next.

Desire is everywhere in this collection. It can be disastrous. In a short ekphrastic prose poem about a Georges de La Tour painting, "Magdalene with Smoking Flame," the speaker wonders what would happen if someone could interact with the painted figure: "One capricious day, others, though less avid then I, will remove your canvas blouse, will invade your alcove. But leaving, they will forget to smother the light, and a drop of oil from the dagger of flame will fuel the imagined solution." Violent language is used without describing the violent act, creating an ominous tone that works more effectively than describing the act of rape, which is implied by the tearing of the blouse. The imagined consequence fits the imagined crime, burning the painting from within.

Not only does Char's work burn from within, it sometimes burned the author with the strain of producing such intense work. "Magdalene Keeping Watch" describes Char's encounter with a mysterious woman on the metro; the poem acts as "A prayer without submission." The young woman's presence reminds him of his youth: "Memories flood my mind: my quest for enigmas that dates from the time I discovered life and poetry." When he discovers her name, it gives him the answer that he already knew. "In truth, I am not surprised at her name. That very day, I had just completed *Magdalene with Smoking Flame,* inspired by the painting by Georges de La Tour, still on my mind. That poem really took its toll." Here in bodily form is his muse to affirm that the cost of the poem was worth it. Once he realizes that she is Magdalene, Char's poem about writing poetry doesn't use the regular tropes of an ars poetica. He embodies the creation of a poem in a woman, possibly a muse, but one in physical form, not the mystical form of myth.

Carlson's choice of selected works gives a sampling of poems about love, loss, myth, and nature. In the end, it is Carlson's native gift with the English language—her lyrical undertones, musical variations, and her wonderful play with syntax and alliteration—that make this collection worth reading and re-reading aloud just to hear the musical effects of the lines.

Carpathia
By Cecilia Woloch. Rochester, NY: BOA, 2009.
Reviewed by **Sarah Maclay**

The primary risk in *Carpathia*, Cecilia Woloch's autumnal, dusky new collection, is what Natasha Trethewey calls a "willingness to feel deeply," and in fact it's as though the poet has taken a vow against coldness, a vow to be unprotected by irony. Even the book's second poem, "Anniversary," which could be taken as mainly or simply ironic—as the speaker, by implication, is alone with her memories, rather than in the presence of her beloved—is fueled, instead, by the shock of disbelief, as marriage turns to divorce: how could this have happened? Or even, *did* this happen? But the sensation of deep unsettling goes far beyond one relationship, as it opens along the edges of what is conscious, into territory that begins to overturn archetypes. For this reason, it's best to read the book as a whole. Whatever the pleasures of the individual poems—and there are many—what is ultimately most compelling emerges as a kind of after-image that haunts the whole journey.

I have written before about the way Woloch's poetic landscape issues from a terrain of "beauty and reckoning," how it teeters in that balance. Here, too. Except now there's an even greater sense of inner "raggedness" in these poems that mostly dwell, in the literal realm, in Paris, Kentucky and Carpathia—and in the aesthetic realm of clarity and closure, but in the context of a life passage in which both clarity and resolution are refused—repeatedly, and in more than one context—except as endings. Against the backdrop of early memory—father and mother in bathroom, steam, "dark hair slipping / out of its pins"— the sanctum providing the greatest adult comfort is not the culturally sanctioned nest of union with a man. Nor is it any other "home," exactly, when, as in the dream-begotten prose poem "Postcard to Ilya Kaminsky from a Dream at the Edge of the Sea," "Houses had fallen, face-first, into the mud" or, by the end of the poem "Ground," there is even a linguistic confusion between *home* and *bone*—by implication, the grave being the more welcoming. Rather, it is found, almost by accident, in the midst of relentless travel, in " . . . le Jardin d'Isabelle," where the speaker is once again the beloved of both man and woman—not parents, this time, but an adored Parisian couple. Otherwise, beyond that enchanted garden, love is mostly a falling apart (repeatedly, jaggedly), and the languid safety of "my mother / soaping my father's back" is replaced by mother and daughter, working with wet towels in the father's last hours, but unable to cool his raging "last fever" until finally, around 4:00 a.m., "surrendering him."

Yet beyond the highly conscious renderings of early memory and the surge of adult loss are even more haunting moments that linger in a backdrop of snow-blue light, moments that call up an unresolved, underlying tenderness that creates a hazy halo around what might otherwise feel like the *certainty* of an ardent internal reckoning with demons, internal or external, by list or admission. This is where the truest wildness of the book lies, and also one of the most curious turnabouts of our expectations of gender. It hinges on three images that, taken together as clues, illuminate what starts to feel thematic: the dying father's simple, yet mysterious gesture—a raised hand in the dark; a chance encounter on the Metro with a neatly dressed stranger who suddenly, dramatically collapses and gashes his head as people do little but watch or "clip their nails" while the speaker rushes frantically for help; and the image of a geographically distant lover, or perhaps former lover, as pale and ghostly as a snow cloud.

It is almost as though the poetry of certainty—let's call it that: the poetics of a delicate and painterly clarity leading to aesthetic closure—*allows* this more mysterious, threatening story to emerge beneath the level of narrative. In a reversal of role expectations, it's the female force here—in this case, so active, less Florence Nightingale than Prince Charming—who is unable to "save" the men she loves, whatever the relationship, from their particular human frailties—death, collapse, despair masking as self-hatred. The "Girl in a Truck . . . ," with or without her "lacy bra," is not quite yet able to kiss the beloved awake from a sleep or despair that precludes (or occludes) intimacy. The father, the subway stranger, the snow-like lover—these are only three of many images of men who disappoint or can no longer protect (even themselves), from lovers to "leaders" of nations, including the "brute" in "Brasov, 1989" and, by implication, those whose "shining lies" have led to war in the Middle East ("Shine"). Thus, the book's large presence of elegies for the speaker's father is not an intrusion into the somehow-not-working middle-aged love story in the foreground, but rather a necessary counterweight and reference and frame.

In these haunting depictions, it's not the female but the male—in death, collapsing, pale, asleep—who is revealed as vulnerable. And it's this inability to *resuscitate* the (often beloved) male—from death, from despair, from disappointment—that is finally unbearable. The father's hand moves spectrally up towards heaven. The distant, ghostly lover, suspended, pale, like snow that won't or cannot fall, cannot come down to earth. Curiously, when the whiteness of skin (eerie, as well as luminous, in the dark) is attributed to these male figures, it takes on an entirely different connotation than it might if, as in European fairy tale tradition, the *woman* were Snow White. Rather than the conventional purity or (inert?) virginity often attributed to this symbolism, there's a sense, in these portrayals of the male, of radiant vulnerability and possible error. Meanwhile, in the speaker, real grief; an inner conflict between moments of anger and moments of longing and memory that preserve a once luminous and true connection, now pierced—even the possibility of loving anew now punctured by distance. Because the figure collapsing in the subway is a stranger rather than a beloved, we're allowed, by proxy, to get the full shock and measure of the impact, not only of the range of frustration and impotence of the female speaker/protagonist, but of its actual *strangeness*—thus, the poem's dreamlike quality as it tracks her failing attempt to help. And so the speaker remains suspended in a world where she is allowed to taste—deeply, palpably—the love of the male, both paternal and erotic—but having tasted it, is unable to bring it back to life when it vanishes.

Even the cover of the book colludes in giving us this sense of eerie suspension, of luminous blue falling—what looks, from afar, like a lacy princess dress, or even wedding dress, more blue than white—is suspended above an ancient bridge, below which is water but also a blood-red marshland. But what looks, from afar, like lace, turns out to be the filigree of maps—is it the dress of a bride, or a traveler, falling through a sky too darkly blue to be day?

Behind the dress is a "carte postale," true to one of the main motifs of the book—and it's not just the idea of intimacy brought up by postcards and letters that lets us in to the very craw of feeling, but the actual diction. Call it a kind of letterspeech—unmediated, transparent—that risks (gasp!) actual sentimentality, as well as sentiment. As in letters dashed off to good friends, terms of endearment and the occasional gush are preserved here, rather than banished: "dear heart; Oh, lamb." This seems to me a conscious choice, a further method for refusing coldness—that is, a refusal to hide behind the cold, or even the refracted, which is maybe surprising only because it brings on a sudden awareness of how cool, how edited, we have gotten, we poets. This approach stands in stark contrast, almost as a defiance of any intellectual or aesthetic strategy that might come between a reader and the world of this poet as one who *feels*, even more—and in spite of the strength of both memory and image—than as one who *sees*. We can think of it as one more strategy for banishing chill and distance, the author leaning toward us as if to rub warmth into our hands, to kiss us awake.

The Homelessness of Self
By Susan Terris. Sausalito, CA: Arctos Press, 2011.
Reviewed by **Jim Natal**

"Is her biography fiction...or her fiction biography?" Susan Terris poses this question in "Homelessness of Self," the title poem of her seventh full-length collection. She may ostensibly be asking this about someone else, but as Terris' superbly paced book develops, it becomes clear she is the subject of her inquiry.

The "homelessness" of the title refers not to a person without shelter, but more to a shrewd intelligence adrift in memory, questing through the whitecapped "shook foil" that is both the surface of a summer resort lake and the shimmer of existence. And like the house on that lake, the poet understands and accepts that life is a "summer's lease" and frames her musings with that comprehension. The poet inhabits a "first name only universe where time means / not stopping, a continuous river / going somewhere hot or cool or inexplicable." She appraises the arc of her life with "no fear of / the never again. Only fear of what-if and ever."

The poet's girlhood is an otherness that she owns yet scrutinizes, particularly in the poems that form the lovely opening section. A reflection of the natural world she immersed herself in as a child, she sees herself as a "brown fawn of a girl," a girl who "ran through / fields, a sheep dog at my heels, / or cantered bareback / through blistered furrows." In the stunning poem "Tasseling," she also metaphorically casts herself as a field of young corn: "She's tall and still green with corn-tassel hair / and feet rooted in earth." The corn "may be tasseling but it's not yet ripe." Her surge into womanhood confuses her and, at topsy-turvy odds with her mother, she observes that she's "a girl without context." In a later poem, now a mother herself, she delves further: "The daytime moon is a clouded mirror and in it I see the puzzled girls, myself..."

There is a close association with the natural world—of being not *in* nature but *of* nature—that blows like a steady onshore breeze. In Terris' poems, the world and its creatures are in constant motion—"flags and tulips shift in April wind," millions of eels and garfish fan "wildly in all direction," "bright bits of matter spin like fireflies in a jar," a jack pine's branches are "brave with egrets," and falling birds are as "white scraps of paper." Bees, in particular, provide a background swirl and hum at key moments; they "waver in sunlight" and are notable for their "honey and sting—life enhancers." She recalls a "bee-loud glade, where her counselor / kissed her on the lips, a beginner's secret as she / practiced for a lifetime of them."

The concept of secrets—whether the beginner's secret above or the "secrets of the hive"—comes up repeatedly. "A secret," Terris writes, "is like a potato hot from the campfire: you want it even if it will burn you." Or: "Sometimes you can see a thing without seeing. / That's the worst and best secret, a way of / being kept. Even an elephant camouflages in shade." Or: "In the moment is the secret. Learning to keep one…is how we grow up." However, despite any promises of discretion, "what I've lost must be spoken." And in the revealing she provokes more questions: "How did I get here? Can I ever go home? Once upon a time. Once upon….Once…."

Fairy tale figures of speech occasionally pop up like a jack-in-the-box, perhaps an echo of Terris' past career as a prolific and successful writer of children's books. There is no childishness, though, in the uses to which she puts the images and language of childhood stories. For example: "As you sleep, legions of orb spiders web your torso, / weave a delicate garment into the hairs / on your chest and back, over shoulders and arms." And "On a three-legged stool by a three-legged desk, / she sits in the laundry room—her hair / a place for nesting birds, her hand-rinsed scanties ticking drops onto tablet and floor." This is no girl with a curl in the middle of her forehead but "some other too-tall nursery girl // grown beyond haystack and piper." In Terris' poetry, mortality becomes a "Knock-knock" joke and her parents sleep in a "dollhouse bed in the room with a missing wall." Extending the dollhouse image, she observes, "The dollhouse was such a safe haven. Miniatures / may give the illusion of control, yet control has / vanished with the walls."

The wisdom of an intensely examined life is sprinkled throughout the work the way that "swallows pepper the sky," each nugget demanding, in a good way, a stop to consider. Yet it's conditional wisdom, not always hard and fast: "Sometimes safety is unbearable…"; "Sometimes all direction is misdirection."; and "The ageing body is a kind of cardboard jigsaw / where more and more pieces go missing." Terris reserves her wisest (and often wryest) comments for matters of love, sex, and the minefield of marriage: "all broken hearts mend with a scar" and "A scar is, after all, a joint of sorts, evidence of a life / lived, even if the joint has begun to crack." The book's final poem, "Marriage License," begins: "Marriage is a cave with an underground river / and an unreliable torch" and goes on from there in marvelous musings. The allusion to a life / lived, even if the joint has begun to crack." The book's final poem, "Marriage License," begins: "Marriage is a cave with an underground river / and an unreliable torch" and goes on from there in marvelous musings. The allusion to the breakup of the marriage of close friends after the husband's dalliance with a much younger woman shows Terris at her sharpest:

> Check this: *hen-pecked* by its gender is something
> a married woman does to a husband. No one discusses
> the rooster who will peck at a hen's eyes and heart.

There are magic circles, runes, and incantatory verse, too, all in the service of coming to grips with the inevitable end of the lease and all that has transpired since its signing. "The sky," she writes in "Temporary Dislocation," "has / jagged gray holes; but we won't care, / but there may yet be a blue beyond blue." Smart and funny, arresting and totally engaging, *The Homelessness of Self* is a summation as well as a promise of more brilliant poetry to come.

The Gingko Light

By Arthur Sze. Port Townsend, WA: Copper Canyon, 2009.
Reviewed by **John Tritica**

Arthur Sze's poetry reflects Philip Whalen's assertion that "poetry is a graph of the mind moving." Sze's poetry adds the corollary: poetic perception is deepened by a mind in rapid motion, drawing attention to the faculties that order experience with a skill that is astonishing. In the opening poem of *The Ginkgo Light*, "Chrysalis," he tells us:

> Corpses push up through thawing permafrost
>
> as I scrape salmon skin off a pan at the sink;
> on the porch, motes in slanting yellow light
>
> undulating air. Is Venus at dusk as luminous
> as Venus at dawn? (5)

Rather than narrate his poetry in a neatly consumable package, Sze captures the mind in swift associative motion, positioning poetic images so that they act to defamiliarize perception at large. In "Chrysalis," for example, he juxtaposes the visceral intensity of the first line against the quotidian experience of washing a pan, which is further placed beside the differing qualities of Venus's light during the crepuscular. Sze exercises a kind of semantic torque that cracks open possibilities, involving the reader in rapid shifts between the immediate & the remote, the palpable & the abstract. He often introduces an open-ended question to propel the mind & poem forward, as would a Zen koan. This is poetry of the eye & the hand, reflecting how carefully placed images move through vertigo to clarity in a poet's vision.

Sze structures the book around a temple ginkgo tree that survived the nuclear bomb dropped on Hiroshima. The book unfolds in meditative serial poems, such as "Chrysalis," "The Ginkgo Light," "Spectral Line." In "Chrysalis," Sze brings to life the double-lobed, unusually reticulated leaves with the precision of the objectivists: "fan-shaped, slightly // thickened, slightly wavy on broad edge…" (7), following this directly with the image of falling golden ginkgo leaves' "mindless beauty of the quotidian" (7), in order to draw aesthetic attention to the everyday *extraordinaire* that surrounds us. The collection's title poem similarly combines precision & wonder: "August 6, 1945: a temple in Hiroshima 1130 meters / from the hypocenter disintegrates, while its ginkgo // buds after the blast" (24), which allows the poet to address the enormity of the devastation later in the poem: "to recoil from darkness is to feed the darkness" (26). One of Sze's essential poetic procedures throughout is to engage opposing poetic energies in order to shed light on experience, resulting in a work of dramatic tension, haunting and poignant ("A ginkgo / flames into yellow-gold, while, elsewhere, red tulips flare on a slope. The mind weighs, / balances antinomies…," 39).

Occasional short lyric poems, such as "The Gift," "Tesserae," "Fractal," "Qualia," "Equator," & "Virga," provide space between the longer pieces, modulating a structural rhythm. Sze's intense attention to the existential now is informed by Zen contemplation; his focus on the nuances of the ecological world is informed by such Chinese poets as Wang Wei & Tu Fu (whom he has translated). There is a joy in naming the plants & animals of the world, & an investigation of specifics of the local landscapes of New Mexico (Sze's home state) & Japan. Combining Asian spiritual & poetic practices with an innovative form of defamiliarization, he presents a writing of high value that issues from clarity of vision, & enriches the practice of & discourse about contemporary poetry.

THE LOS ANGELES REVIEW

divergent,
west coast
literature

http://losangelesreview.org

ellipsis
literature & art

● ● ●

Ellipsis is the student-run
national literary magazine at
Westmisnter College
of Salt Lake City.
We have published both
established and
up-and-coming authors
and artists since 1967.

● ● ●

We are now accepting fiction,
nonfiction, poetry, and
visual art submissions for our
2012 issue. Our deadline is
October 31, 2011

● ● ●

Sample Issues: $7.50

Westminster College • 1840 S 1300 E • Salt Lake City, UT 84105
www.westminstercollege.edu/ellipsis
ellipsis@westminstercollege.edu